Studies in Public Choice

For further volumes:
http://www.springer.com/series/6550

Dwight R. Lee
Editor

Public Choice, Past and Present

The Legacy of James M. Buchanan and Gordon Tullock

Springer

Editor
Dwight R. Lee
Southern Methodist University
Dallas, TX, USA

ISSN 0924-4700
ISBN 978-1-4614-5908-8 ISBN 978-1-4614-5909-5 (eBook)
DOI 10.1007/978-1-4614-5909-5
Springer New York Heidelberg Dordrecht London

Library of Congress Control Number: 2012953268

Printed on acid-free paper

Springer is part of Springer Science+Business Media (www.springer.com)

Preface

This volume was conceived when Larry Kenny asked me if I would be willing to participate in a plenary session honoring Jim and Gordon on the fiftieth anniversary of the publication of *The Calculus of Consent* at the March 2012 International Public Choice Meeting in Miami. There was to be three separate discussions: the first on the impact of *The Calculus of Consent*, the second on the work of Buchanan, and the third on the work of Tullock. I asked for a few days to think about what I might say during which my wife insisted that I owed it to Jim and Gordon to say yes. But almost immediately upon deciding to accept Larry's invitation, I received an invitation to attend a Liberty Fund conference in San Diego the same weekend as the Public Choice Meeting. I was very much tempted to turn Larry down and accept the Liberty Fund invitation, telling my wife how much I enjoyed Liberty Fund conferences. Her response was, "Yes I know, but if hadn't been for Jim you would have never been invited to a Liberty Fund Conference." I e-mailed Larry the next day letting him know I would be happy to participate and chose to make my comments on the impact of *The Calculus of Consent*.

The plenary session went well with interesting comments by Geoffrey Brennan, Hartmut Kliemt, and Randy Holcombe on the work of Buchanan; Roger Congleton, Heinrich Ursprung, and Arye Hillman on the work of Tullock; with me leading off on the impact of *The Calculus of Consent* since I was the only one who chose that topic. After the session, Larry Kenny and Nicholas Philipson, Editorial Director for Business, Economics and Statistics for Springer Academic Publishers, asked me if I would be willing to edit a volume including papers from the session participants and others who would have interesting things to say on the intellectual legacy of Buchanan and Tullock. I said yes.

Springer imposed a rather tight deadline on receipt of the chapters, and three of those who participated in the session were unable to commit to the project. There were, however, plenty of students (which in the broad sense includes us all) and former colleagues who were willing and able to meet the deadline.

This volume begins with an overview discussion of the impact of *The Calculus of Consent* in particular, and of public choice more generally, by J. R. Clark and myself which expands rather significantly on my presentation in Miami. We argue that though Buchanan and Tullock, through both *The Calculus of Consent* and other contributions, have had a significant impact on scholarship in economics and political science, there are some notable disappointments in their impact on economic education, some areas of economic research and in political reform. We end, however, with a cautiously optimistic assessment of the long-run influence of public choice on political reform.

The remaining chapters are ordered roughly in accordance with a continuum beginning with discussions focusing on the theoretical work of either Buchanan, Tullock, or both, moving to discussions of the impact of public choice in general on particular issues with some autobiographical emphasis, and finally to those discussions that approach the contributions of Buchanan and Tullock primarily from an autobiographical, or personal, perspective. This continuum is too loosely defined to determine a precise ordering of the chapters, and it should not be assumed that the ordering reflects any judgment on the relative importance of the chapters. I want this volume to be both informative and interesting, and I believe every chapter contributes to satisfying that goal. Let me now turn to providing brief summaries of Chaps. 2, 3, 4, 5, 6, 7, 8, 9, 10, 11, 12, 13, 14, 15, and 16.

Randall Holcombe focuses on the work of Buchanan in Chap. 2. Holcombe argues that Buchanan's work on institutions as a means of facilitating exchange in the development of public choice is broader than its application to political processes because his interests and writings extend to differences in political and market exchange resulting from the institutional differences in the two arenas. On the other hand, because of his concern in the importance of institutions, Buchanan's work in public choice has been narrower than the broad body of work within the public choice literature.

Chapter 3 by Roger Congleton makes what initially seems like an implausible argument – that much of Tullock's work is more profound than commonly thought because he did not appreciate fully how important his work was. The plausibility of the argument is based on the claim that Tullock has been very good at pursuing his comparative social advantage. He was doing exactly what we would want a tirelessly creative economist to do – throw out as many interesting ideas with the potential to push out the frontier of knowledge as rapidly as possible and let others "plumb its depths."

Geoffrey Brennan and Michael Brooks consider in Chap. 4 Buchanan's conception of liberty and its connections to and tensions with a broad body of his work. For example, Buchanan's conception of a libertarian affinity with anarchy and his constitutional contractarianism raise some interesting philosophical concerns.

In Chap. 5, Richard Wagner considers two different ways of assessing the legacy of Buchanan and Tullock as it relates to establishing public choice as a field of scholarly inquiry. Wagner argues that examining the effect of an analytical approach aimed at understanding the political process is similar to making a choice between the Laspeyres and Paasche approaches when constructing index numbers. This follows from Wagner's view that the political process is more like a piazza than a parade, with the order observed in a piazza based not on everyone accepting and rehearsing a predetermined plan, but on people with different plans following rules of courtesy and collision avoidance in achieving them. This important difference makes an approach more in line with the construction of Paasche index numbers the preferred way of evaluating the scholarly contribution of Buchanan and Tullock.

Donald Boudreaux considers Buchanan's work on constitutional design in Chap. 6. Boudreaux emphasizes what he sees as a tension between Buchanan's more constructivist approach to constitutional reform and Hayek's view that constitutional improvements emerge through a more evolutionary and spontaneous process. While Boudreaux agrees with Buchanan's concern that "Evolution may produce social dilemma as readily as social paradise," he gives the nod to Hayek once he considers the problems inherent in voting (in particular, the problems of expressive voting) that would be required in direct constitutional reform.

In Chap. 7, Janet Landa reexamines her earlier work that applied public choice theory to an interesting feature in the swarming behavior of honeybees. In her earlier work, she explained an empirical finding that scout bees use unanimous voting to make collective choices on the location of a new nest site with Buchanan and Tullock's discussion of the advantage of unanimous voting. In response to recent empirical findings that scout bees in fact choose new nests with a less than unanimous vote, Landa makes use of the analysis leading to Fig. 5 in Chap. 6 of *The Calculus of Consent* to make her analysis consistent with the new finding. Landa also puts forth an interesting explanation for the ability of scout bees to sense when a decision has been reached despite their inability to count.

In Chap. 8, William Shughart discusses the important contributions Buchanan and Tullock have made independently in such scholarly areas as public finance, law and economics, and bio-economics, and, of course, their most noted joint work, *The Calculus of Consent*. Shughart also summarizes, in an idiosyncratic way, three areas of Buchanan and Tullock's work that have influenced his thinking and writing – the cost of collective decision-making, rent seeking, and the analysis of public budget deficits and debt.

In Chap. 9, John Goodman credits the work of Buchanan and Tullock for insights that are essential to his understanding of the politics of medicine. He makes use of basic public choice analysis to explain the incentives to politicize medical care and then to explain why the promises made to justify that politicization (lower cost, more equal distribution, etc.) have not been kept. The examples are primarily from the British National Health Service, but the American healthcare policy, though different in many details, is following a path that can also be explained by public choice.

Nicolous Tideman pays tribute in Chap. 10 to an important contribution Tullock made to public choice with a bold decision to publish a paper containing a complicated argument by an unknown (at least to Tullock) graduate student which made a startling claim before he (Tullock) fully understood it. The paper claimed to prove that it was possible to motivate people to report their preferences for public goods truthfully, and Tullock quickly published it in *Public Choice* because he knew it would be important if true. Tideman reports on the events by which the paper came to be understood and expanded upon by himself, Tullock, and others.

Chapter 11 by David Henderson begins by expressing his appreciation for the encouragement and help Buchanan and Tullock gave him as a 20-year-old thinking about an academic career in economics. He then argues that foreign policy is one area in which public choice analysis could be productively extended more than it has been and supports his position with the results of such an analysis.

John Baden is a key scholar in the development of the New Resource Economics (NRE), which promotes free-market approaches for addressing many environmental and natural resource problems. An important component of NRE research involves realistically comparing the effectiveness of market and political approaches at aligning private incentives with socially productive activities, comparisons to which public choice contributes. In Chap. 12, John discusses the development of NRE and points out how both Buchanan and Tullock (as well as the Ostroms and others) and public choice insights were helpful at key junctures during that development. He also draws interesting parallels between the problems Jim and Gordon encountered because of destructive incentives within the University of Virginia during the mid-1960s and the same problems during the development of NRE at Montana State University a little over a decade and half later. As Baden points out, the parallel is not an aberration.

In Chap. 13, James Gwartney discusses how Buchanan, Tullock, and the public choice literature had a major impact on his career and approach to economics. Over Gwartney's career he has written many scholarly articles, but he focuses his chapter on his economic principles text, *Economics: Private and Public Choice*, (which was first published in 1976 and is now in its 14th edition with coauthors added) and economic education. The motto of his textbook writing could be that without a knowledge of both the market and political processes, one cannot understand how alternative institutions and policies will affect outcomes. His big disappointment is that public choice has not had more impact on economics principles courses, which still assume government is an effective means of correcting market failures, but devote little time, if any, to acknowledging, much less discussing, government failure.

Instead of focusing on the contributions Buchanan and Tullock have made directly to economic thought, in Chap. 14 Richard McKenzie discusses their indirect contributions with a personal tribute to their largely unheralded dedication to assisting the academic efforts of their students and colleagues. By giving examples of how both Buchanan and Tullock, in their different ways, provided much needed guidance to him during his career, McKenzie suggests that neither of them could be mistaken for the "economic man" in economists' models. And as McKenzie found out when expressing his amazement to Betty Tillman at Buchanan's promptness in providing detailed comments on papers sent to him, he (McKenzie) was not being favored a bit by Buchanan over many others.

Bruce Yandle's tribute to Buchanan and Tullock in Chap. 15 reinforces that of McKenzie's. His story includes personal encounters with Buchanan and Tullock as a graduate student, faculty member, and government economist, and tells how they contributed to his professional growth. He also discusses the power of Buchanan's and Tullock's insights in terms of how disruptive they were to the intellectual status quo.

Randy Simmon's concluding chapter tells how the work of Buchanan and Tullock affected both his academic and public life and how it provides a useful framework for understanding his experiences during 6 years on the city council and 4 years as the mayor of a small Utah town. Given his academic background in public choice, he was not surprised to experience people acting badly when competing for political favor while showing compassion and concern for each other when acting in small voluntary groups.

Let me conclude by thanking all the contributors for meeting the deadlines with informative chapters that convey the enormous respect and gratitude we all have for Jim and Gordon. I would also like to thank Larry Kenny for his academic entrepreneurship in organizing the Miami session to honor Jim and Gordon on the fiftieth anniversary of the publication of *The Calculus of Consent*, and which initiated the work that culminated in this volume. I would be remiss not to thank Nicholas Philipson of Springer for his enthusiasm for the project and encouragement along the way. But my biggest thanks go to my wife, Cindy Crain-Lee, whose organizational skills, attention to details, and meticulous editing of the manuscripts as they came in kept the project on schedule.

Dallas, TX, USA Dwight R. Lee

About the Authors

John Baden

John Baden earned his Ph.D. at Indiana University in 1969 with a dissertation focused on economic anthropology. He applied public choice theory to explain the organization and success of the Hutterite communes. He worked with Vincent and Eleanor (Lin) Ostrom at Indiana University, and they introduced him to Gordon Tullock and James Buchanan. In 1969, just prior to the first Earth Day, Baden received a NSF postdoctoral fellowship in environmental policy. He applied public choice to environmental and natural resource issues and with his colleagues at Montana State University developed the New Resource Economics aka "free-market environmentalism." He has taught anthropology, economics, forestry, and political science at Indiana University, Montana State University, Utah State University, and the University of Washington (UW). At UW, he founded the Environmental Management MBA Program. In addition to his academic work, including ten plus books, Baden is an intellectual and social entrepreneur. He has founded three think tanks (PERC, FREE, and Gallatin Writers) and two university institutes. He and his wife, Professor Ramona Marotz-Baden, own and operate Enterprise Ranch near Bozeman, Montana. In addition to producing grain, hay, and livestock, they developed a fly-fishing program for wounded warriors and others with special needs.

Donald J. Boudreaux

Donald J. Boudreaux is professor of economics at George Mason University in Fairfax, Virginia. He is the author of *Globalization* (2008) and *Hypocrites & Half-Wits* (2012). He blogs with Russell Roberts at www.cafehayek.com.

Geoffrey Brennan

Geoffrey Brennan currently splits his time roughly equally between the Australian National University and North Carolina, spending each spring semester jointly at Duke and UNC-Chapel Hill. He is the author (with Jim Buchanan) of *The Power to Tax* (1980) and *The Reason of Rules* (1985), (with Loren Lomasky) of *Democracy and Decision* (1993), (with Alan Hamlin) of *Democratic Devices and Desires* (2000), and (with Philip Pettit) of *The Economy of Esteem* (2004) – plus over 200 papers in refereed journals (some dozen of them with Buchanan and only one, though a special personal favorite, with Gordon Tullock). He is currently working on two book projects – one on philosophy and economics for Princeton University Press and one with Alan Hamlin on "analytic conservatism."

Michael Brooks

Michael Brooks is an associate professor at the University of Tasmania. Michael completed training to be a high school teacher but was drawn back to economics, completing a Masters of Economics at Monash University and a Ph.D. at Virginia Polytechnic Institute and State University. He has tutored at Monash University, lectured at Central Michigan University and the University of Tasmania, and published on rent seeking and pollution taxation. In recent years, he has written on taxation, expressive voting, and the economics of esteem with his friend and former supervisor Geoffrey Brennan. A keen electric guitarist – though the years are now taking their toll on the hands – and an avid dog obedience handler.

J.R. Clark

J.R. Clark earned his Ph.D. under Buchanan and Tullock at Virginia Polytechnic Institute (VPI) and currently holds the Probasco Chair at The University of Tennessee at Chattanooga (UTC). He has published eight books and 75 academic articles in the United States and abroad in several languages. Prior to UTC, he held the Hendrix Chair at UT Martin, and a research fellowship at Princeton University. He is a past president of The Association of Private Enterprise Education (APEE) and currently serves as vice president of The Mont Pelerin Society and secretary/treasurer of both The Southern Economic Association and APEE. His popular media work has appeared in The Wall Street Journal, Investor's business Daily, The New York Times, Atlanta Constitution Journal, Newark Star Ledger, and The Tennessean. His most recent publications include "The Impact of Economic Growth, Tax Policy and Economic Freedom on Income Inequality," in Economic Freedom: Causes and Consequences, 2011. New York: Nova Science Publishers, Inc. pp. 121–127. Joshua Hall and Robert Lawson Eds., and "Shrinking Leviathan: Can the Interaction

Between Interests and Ideology Slice Both Ways?" The Independent Review, Vol. 16, No. 2, Fall 2011, pp. 221–236, with Lee, Dwight R. Clark holds an Airline Transport Pilot's rating and currently flies light jet aircraft.

Roger D. Congleton

Roger Congleton is the BB&T Chair in Economics at West Virginia University and coeditor of Constitutional Political Economy (beginning in 2013). He was a student of Buchanan and Tullock during their Blacksburg days and their colleague for more than a decade during their Fairfax days. He is the author of more than a hundred papers on public choice and constitutional political economy. His most recent books include *Perfecting Parliament* (Cambridge), *40 Years of Research on Rent Seeking* (2 volumes, edited with A. Hillman and K. Konrad, Springer), and *Democratic Constitutional Design and Public Policy* (edited with B. Swedenborg, MIT Press).

John C. Goodman

John C. Goodman is president and CEO of the National Center for Policy Analysis, where he is also the Kellye Wright Fellow in healthcare. Goodman received his Ph.D. in economics from Columbia University, and he has taught and completed research at Columbia University, Stanford University, Dartmouth College, Southern Methodist University, and the University of Dallas. He is widely known as the "Father of Health Savings Accounts," and modern healthcare named him one of four people who have most influenced the modern healthcare system. Goodman is the author of more than 50 studies, including "A Note on Existence and Uniqueness of Equilibrium Points for Concave N-Person Games" (Econometrica), "A Theory of Competitive Regulatory Equilibrium" (Public Choice), and "Political Equilibrium and the Provision of Public Goods" (Public Choice). He has written or coauthored ten books, including *Patient Power: Solving America's Healthcare Crisis* (which introduced the idea of Health Savings Accounts) and *Priceless: Curing the Healthcare Crisis* (which argues for real prices for both medical care and health insurance). John Goodman's Health Policy Blog is one of the most frequently trafficked health policy blogs on the Internet.

James D. Gwartney

James D. Gwartney holds the Gus A. Stavros Eminent Scholar Chair at Florida State University, where he directs the Stavros Center for the Advancement of Free Enterprise and Economic Education. He is the coauthor of *Economics: Private and Public Choice* (South-Western Press, 2010), a widely used principles of economics text that is now in its 14th edition. He is also the coauthor of *Common Sense Economics: What Everyone Should Know About Wealth and Prosperity* (St. Martin's Press, 2010), a primer on economics and personal finance designed for the interested layperson. His publications have appeared in both professional journals and popular media such as *The Wall Street Journal* and *The New York Times*. He received his Ph.D. in economics from the University of Washington. His current research focuses on the measurement and determination of factors that influence cross-country differences in income levels and growth rates. In this regard, he is the senior researcher responsible for the preparation of the annual report, *Economic Freedom of the World*, which provides information on the institutions and policies of 140 countries. This data set, published by a worldwide network of institutes in 70 countries, is widely used by scholars investigating topics ranging from economic growth to peaceful relations among nations. During 1999–2000, he served as Chief Economist of the Joint Economic Committee of the U.S. Congress. He was invited by the incoming Putin Administration in March 2000 to make presentations and have discussions with leading Russian economists concerning the future of the Russian economy. In 2004 he was the recipient of the Adam Smith Award of the Association of Private Enterprise Education for his contribution to the advancement of free market ideals. He is the former President of the Southern Economic Association.

David R. Henderson

David R. Henderson is an associate professor of economics at the Graduate School of Business and Public Policy, Naval Postgraduate School in Monterey, California, and a research fellow at the Hoover Institution at Stanford University. From 1982 to 1984, he was the senior economist for health policy and, from 1983 to 1984, the senior economist for energy policy, with President Reagan's Council of Economic Advisers. He blogs regularly at Econlog, http://econlog.econlib.org/. Henderson is the editor of *The Concise Encyclopedia of Economics* (Liberty Fund, 2008). It is now on the Web at http://www.econlib.org/library/CEE.html. It has been translated into Russian and Arabic. His book *The Joy of Freedom: An Economist's Odyssey* was published by Financial Times Prentice Hall in the fall of 2001 and has been translated into Chinese. He also wrote, with his former student, Charles L. Hooper, *Making Great Decisions in Business and Life* (Chicago Park Press, 2006). It has been translated into Japanese and Korean. He also writes a regular column, "The Wartime Economist," for www.antiwar.com. He has written about 200 articles for such popular publications as The Wall Street Journal, New York Times, Barron's, Fortune, Los Angeles Times, Chicago Tribune, Public Interest, National Review, Red Herring, and Reason. He has also written scholarly articles for such journals as Journal of Policy Analysis and Management, Defense & Security Analysis, Independent Review, Cato Journal, Contemporary Policy Issues, Econ Journal Watch, and Energy Journal. He has testified before the House Ways and Means Committee, the Senate Armed Services Committee, and the Senate Committee on

Labor and Human Resources. He also appeared on C-SPAN, CNN, the Jim Lehrer Newshour, the O'Reilly Factor, MSNBC, and the Stossel show and has done radio interviews with NPR, CBC, BBC, KQED-FM, and many regional radio stations. Born and raised in Canada, he moved to the United States in 1972, where he earned a Ph.D. in economics at the University of California, Los Angeles (UCLA).

Randall G. Holcombe

Randall G. Holcombe is DeVoe Moore Professor of Economics at Florida State University. He received his Ph.D. in economics from Virginia Tech, where he wrote his doctoral dissertation under the direction of James Buchanan. He taught at Texas A&M University and at Auburn University prior to coming to Florida state in 1988. Dr. Holcombe is also senior fellow at the James Madison Institute, a Tallahassee-based think tank that specializes in issues facing state governments. He served on Florida Governor Jeb Bush's Council of Economic Advisors from 2000 to 2006, was president of the Public Choice Society from 2006 to 2008, and was president of the Society for the Development of Austrian Economics in 2007. Dr. Holcombe is the author of 12 books and more than 150 articles published in academic and professional journals.

Janet T. Landa

Janet Tai Landa is professor of economics at Canada's York University, and a founding editor in chief, Journal of Bioeconomics (1999–2009). Since Oct. 2010, she is a guest professor of the International School of Financial Law, East China University of Political Science and Law in Shanghai, China. She was a student in both Buchanan's and Tullock's classes; her 1978 Ph.D. dissertation was written under the direction of Buchanan, with Tullock and Tollison serving in her five-member dissertation committee. She held a number of fellowships, including a National Fellowship, Hoover Institution, Stanford University; a research fellowship, Workshop in Political Theory and Policy Analysis, Indiana University; and Peter Klockner Foundation Fellowship, Department of Economics, Gerhard-Mercator University, Duisburg, Germany. Using Buchanan and Tullock's public choice approach, together with Coasean law-and-economics approach, Landa has published many empirically based theoretical papers on some social phenomena discussed by legal scholars, anthropologists, sociologists, and biologists. She is the author of *Trust, Ethnicity, and Identity: Beyond the New Institutional Economics of Ethnic Trading Networks, Contract Law, and Gift-Exchange* (University of Michigan Press, 1994). Currently, she is completing a second book to be published by Springer: *Success of Chinese Merchants and their Trading Networks: Ethnic Cooperation, Competition, and Conflict*. Landa is fluent in spoken Mandarin.

Dwight R. Lee

Professor Lee received his Ph.D. from the University of California, San Diego, in 1972. Since that time, he has had full time tenured faculty appointments at the University of Colorado, Virginia Tech University, George Mason University, and the University of Georgia where he was the Ramsey Professor of Economics and Private Enterprise from 1985 to 2008. He is currently the William J. O'Neil Professor of Global Markets and Freedom at Southern Methodist University in Dallas. Professor Lee's research has covered a variety of areas including the economics of the environment and natural resources, the economics of political decision-making, public finance, law and economics, and labor economics. During his career, Professor Lee has published 150 articles in refereed journals, 277 articles and commentaries in magazines and newspapers, 50 chapters in books, 35 book reviews, 9 monographs, and coauthored 14 books and been the contributing editor of 5 more. He has lectured at universities and conferences throughout the United States as well as in Europe, Central America, South America, Asia, and Africa. He was president of the Association of Private Enterprise Education from 1994 to 1995 and president of the Southern Economic Association from 1997 to 1998.

Richard B. McKenzie

Richard McKenzie was a graduate student at Virginia Tech from 1969 to 1972, with both Buchanan and Tullock on his dissertation committee. He recently retired from a chaired position in the business school at the University of California, Irvine, after having written a large number of journal articles, general audience commentaries, and books on economic policy and methodology. He coauthored with Gordon Tullock *The New World of Economics*, which was, in its first five editions released in the late 1970s and 1980s, groundbreaking and widely adopted in colleges and universities throughout the world. In 2012, *The New World* was released in a substantially reworked sixth edition for new generations of economics students.

William F. Shughart II

William F. Shughart II is the J. Fish Smith Professor in Public Choice at Utah State University, editor in chief of Public Choice, a senior fellow of The Independent Institute, and past president of the Southern Economic Association. A former economist at the Federal Trade Commission, Professor Shughart received his Ph.D. in economics from Texas A&M University and has taught at George Mason University, Clemson University, the University of Mississippi, and the University of Arizona. Professor Shughart's books include *Taxing Choice: The Predatory Politics of Fiscal Discrimination* and *The Elgar Companion to Public Choice* (edited with L. Razzolini);

The Organization of Industry, *Antitrust Policy and Interest-Group Politics*, and *Modern Managerial Economics* (with W. Chappell and R. Cottle); *Policy Challenges and Political Responses: Public Choice Perspectives on the Post-9/11 World* (edited with R. Tollison); *The Political Economy of the New Deal* (with J. Couch); *The Causes and Consequences of Antitrust* (edited with F. McChesney); and *The Economics of Budget Deficits* (edited with C. Rowley and R. Tollison). His forthcoming books are the second edition of *The Elgar Companion to Public Choice*, coedited with M. Reksulak and L. Razzolini and *The Oxford Handbook of Managerial Economics*, coedited with C. Thomas. Professor Shughart is the author of more than 200 peer-reviewed articles, book chapters, and book reviews; his popular articles have appeared in The Wall Street Journal, Los Angeles Times, Oklahoman, San Francisco Chronicle, Investor's Business Daily, San Jose Mercury News, Philadelphia Inquirer, San Francisco Examiner, Kansas City Star, Pittsburgh Post-Gazette, Washington Times, Detroit Free Press, Clarion-Ledger, Vision Hispana, National Post, Providence Journal, and many other publications.

Randy T. Simmons

Randy T. Simmons earned his Ph.D. in political science at the University of Oregon where the planned direction of his graduate studies was completely redirected by reading Buchanan on freedom and Tullock on social dilemmas. Aside from 2 years in the Office of Policy Analysis in the Department of Interior, he has spent his career at Utah State University, most of it in the political science department and is now the Charles G. Koch Professor of Political Economy in the Department of Economics and Finance and director of the Institute of Political Economy. He is a senior fellow at the Property and Environment Research Center (PERC) and the Independent Institute. His recent books include a new version of his 1994 book with William C. Mitchell *Beyond Politics: The Roots of Government Failure*, *Aquanomics: Water Markets and the Environment* (edited with B. Delworth Gardner), and *Green vs. Green: Conflicts in Environmental Priorities* (with Brian Steed and Ryan Yonk). His forthcoming books are *Political Ecology: The Politics of Environmental Science* and *Green Energy Policy as the New Industrial Policy*. His recent journal articles are on entrepreneurship in the bootleggers and Baptist model and the effects of different voting systems on democratic outcomes.

Nicolaus Tideman

Nicolaus Tideman is a professor of economics at Virginia Polytechnic Institute and State University, in Blacksburg, Virginia. He received his bachelor's degree from Reed College in 1965 and his Ph.D. from the University of Chicago in 1969. From 1969 to 1973, he was an assistant professor of economics at Harvard University. In 1970–1971, he served as senior staff economist for the President's Council of

Economic Advisors, with special responsibility for urban issues. He has been at Virginia Tech since 1973, as a postdoctoral fellow, associate professor, and professor since 1985. He has published numerous professional articles, primarily in the areas of urban economics, public finance, and efficient public decision-making.

Richard E. Wagner

Richard E. Wagner is the Hobart Harris Professor of Economics at George Mason University. The integrated treatment of economics and politics in *The Calculus of Consent*, which he encountered in his final year as an undergraduate, was instrumental in leading him to study economics at the University of Virginia. Since leaving Virginia in 1966, he held faculty positions at the University of California at Irvine, Tulane University, Virginia Tech, Auburn University, and Florida State University before arriving at George Mason in 1988. During these years, he has published a variety of books and articles on a wide variety of substantive topics, nearly all related in one fashion or another to one of the themes of Virginia Political Economy that were alive and nurtured during his 3 years as a graduate student.

Bruce Yandle

Bruce Yandle is professor of economics emeritus and dean emeritus at the College of Business & Behavioral Science, Clemson University. He is also distinguished adjunct professor of economics with the Mercatus Center at George Mason University. Yandle was employed as a senior economist on the regulatory review staff of the President's Council on Wage and Price Stability during the Ford Administration and as executive director of the Federal Trade Commission during the Reagan Administration. Author/editor of 16 books, he is an editorial board member of the European Journal of Law and Economics. He was a member and chairman of South Carolina's State Board of Economic Advisors.

Contents

Contributors

John Baden Foundation for Research on Economics and the Environment, Bozeman, MT, USA

Donald J. Boudreaux Department of Economics, George Mason University, Fairfax, VA, USA

Geoffrey Brennan Philosophy Program, Research School of Social Sciences, Australian National University, Canberra, ACT, Australia

Political Science Department, Duke University, Durham, NC, USA

Philosophy Department, University of North Carolina-Chapel Hill, Chapel Hill, NC, USA

Michael Brooks School of Economics and Finance, University of Tasmania, Hobart, TAS, Australia

J.R. Clark The University of Tennessee, Chattanooga, TN, USA

Roger D. Congleton BB&T Professor of Economics, West Virginia University, Morgantown, WV, USA

John C. Goodman National Center for Policy Analysis, Dallas, TX, USA

James Gwartney Gus A. Stavros Center for Economic Education, Florida State University, Tallahassee, FL, USA

David R. Henderson Hoover Institution, Stanford University, Pacific Grove, CA, USA

Randall G. Holcombe Department of Economics, Florida State University, Tallahassee, FL, USA

Janet T. Landa Department of Economics, York University, Toronto, ON, Canada

Dwight R. Lee Southern Methodist University, Dallas, TX, USA

Richard B. McKenzie Paul Merage School of Business, University of California, Irvine, CA, USA

William F. Shughart II Jon M. Huntsman School of Business, Utah State University, Logan, UT, USA

Randy T. Simmons Jon M. Huntsman School of Business, Utah State University, Providence, UT, USA

Nicolaus Tideman Virginia Tech, Blacksburg, VA, USA

Bruce Yandle Clemson University, Clemson, SC, USA

Richard E. Wagner Department of Economics, George Mason University, Fairfax, VA, USA

Chapter 1
The Impact of *The Calculus of Consent*

J.R. Clark and Dwight R. Lee

The most authoritative thing we can say about the impact of *The Calculus of Consent: The Logical Foundations of Constitutional Democracy* is that it had a big impact on us. And though that hardly makes us unique among readers of this volume, providing a useful answer to the more interesting question about the wider impact of Buchanan's and Tullock's (1965 [1962]) book is a difficult task.

Any attempt to evaluate the impact of a particular book, even one as important as *The Calculus of Consent*, is a daunting task. What kind of impact are we talking about? In the case of a scholarly book such as *The Calculus of Consent*, its impact on education and research is obviously relevant. There are different ways to measure this impact, however, and in the case of *The Calculus of Consent,* the measures do not always point in the same direction. Also relevant in the case of the book is the impact on the political process, which is influenced by far more things than scholarly advances. Of course, ideas have important practical consequences, but there are generally long lags between the ideas and the consequences. Certainly the appropriate time frame for political changes of the type considered in *The Calculus of Consent* (fundamental constitutional changes) can be expected to extend far beyond the 50 years since it was published. Even when, and if, constitutional changes do occur, when judging their effectiveness, one should recall Henry Simons' (1951, p. 20) observation:

J.R. Clark (✉)
The University of Tennessee,
Suite 313 Fletcher Hall,
Chattanooga, TN 37403-2598, USA
e-mail: j-clark@utc.edu

D.R. Lee
Southern Methodist University,
6212 Bishop Blvd,
Dallas, TX 75275, USA
e-mail: leed@cox.smu.edu

D.R. Lee (ed.), *Public Choice, Past and Present: The Legacy of James M. Buchanan and Gordon Tullock*, Studies in Public Choice 28, DOI 10.1007/978-1-4614-5909-5_1,

> Constitutional provisions are no stronger than the consensus that they articulate. At best, they can only check abuses of power until moral pressure is mobilized, and their check must become ineffective if often overtly used.

So another important measure of *The Calculus of Consent*'s impact is the influence it has had on public opinion, an influence that would be primarily indirect, if it exists at all.

Obviously, any attempt to assess the impact of *The Calculus of Consent* will necessarily be largely conjectural. But there are some things that can be said at the onset with a reasonable degree of confidence. Buchanan and Tullock clearly made a major intellectual contribution in their book by using economic analysis to challenge dominant views of the democratic process that constituted the intellectual dogma of the day among political scientists, and other social scientists, including economists. Among these views were two that received particular attention from Buchanan and Tullock. The first was that increasing the substantive and procedural constraints on democratic processes would hamper the ability of government to provide for the general welfare by limiting its ability to respond to the desires of voters. The second was that an important function of government is to correct the failures which supposedly characterized real-world markets. The implicit assumption behind these two, as well as other prevailing understandings of the democratic process, was that political agents were motivated primarily by the desire to promote the public good and had the ability to effectively do so.

To mount their challenge, Buchanan and Tullock examined the implications of two powerful propositions that almost all of the leading political scientists of the day had either never considered or had dismissed. First, the most fundamental political choices are not concerned with what government should do but are choices on the rules political agents follow when making decisions that determine what government actually does. Second, the appropriate level for analyzing political choice is the individual, and when making political decisions, individuals are no less influenced by self-interest than when they are making market decisions. After the book was published, these propositions were rejected aggressively by most orthodox political scientists and accepted only reluctantly by many economists, if accepted at all. There is no denying, however, that *The Calculus of Consent* had an immediate intellectual impact, albeit one limited primarily to a small subset of economists and to an even smaller subset of political scientists.

Obviously, the appeal of *The Calculus of Consent* depends to a large degree on the political philosophy of the reader. Those with classical liberal, or libertarian, leanings find the book more appealing than those favoring a more active role for government. But though the book makes a case for strong constitutional limits on government and points to the importance of balancing criticisms of markets with a realistic consideration of political alternatives to market allocation, it also emphasizes the importance of the complex exchanges involved in the provision of public goods that require collective action of the type facilitated by government. So it is not surprising that some on the left have recognized the contribution of

The Calculus of Consent to deeper understandings of the political process. Still, some obvious insights have been largely ignored by most of the economics profession.

In Chap. 5, for example, economists found out, many for the first time, something that should have been obvious for a long time—that political activity generates negative externalities that are at least as pervasive and persistent as those generated by market activity. This has made it difficult, at least for economists, to discuss market failure without, at a minimum, feeling mildly embarrassed if they did not at least hint at the possibility of government failure. And economists could no longer claim explicitly that market failures were sufficient to justify government policies to correct those failures, although this claim was, and still is, often suggested implicitly. Maybe it is not surprising that Bator (1958) wrote "An Anatomy of Market Failure" before the publication of *The Calculus of Consent*. One can hope that an economist with the reputation of Bator would have written this article with more qualifications after 1962, or if he had not, *The Quarterly Journal of Economics* would have refused to publish it without the qualifications. There may be some basis for hope and for seeing the impact of *The Calculus of Consent* as the primary justification for it. Yet, as we shall see, at best, this hope needs to be qualified far more than academic discussions of market failure have been qualified since 1962.

The Impact on Economic Education

When looking for the impact of *The Calculus of Consent*, and public choice more generally, on the teaching of economics, the evidence is disappointing. In an admittedly quick and dirty sampling of 11 widely used economic principles texts, we found few pages containing a discussion of public choice. Based on an index search, the least number of pages containing a mention of public choice was 2, the median number was 4, the average number was 6.5, and the top two each had 18 pages. Those top two were Gwartney et al. (2010) and Arnold (2010), which is not surprising since Gwartney et al. contains "public choice" in the title and Arnold received his Ph.D. in economics from Virginia Tech in 1979 when the Public Choice Center was still there. Also, based on index references, market failure was discussed in all the economics principles text, with government, or political, failure discussed far less, if discussed at all. We want to emphasize that our "research" here was crude. A textbook can provide a public choice perspective on a wide range of issues without making use of the term public choice or government failure. We know this to be the case with Gwartney et al. (2010) and Arnold (2010). We doubt it is nearly as true with the other texts.

Our impression on the coverage of public choice in most principles text is consistent with that of Gwartney and Arnold. In private correspondence, Gwartney stated that

> The failure of the profession to integrate public choice into principles of economics and economic analysis more generally is one of my biggest disappointments. I thought this would happen to a larger degree after Jim Buchanan won the Nobel Prize, but it did not. I believe that this omission is the most important shortcoming of modern economic analysis. As a result, we are leaving still another generation of students with a misleading impression about how the political process really works and failing to explain to them why it often results in outcomes that are inconsistent with economic efficiency and dynamic progress.

Arnold stated, also in private correspondence, that

> Most of the leading principles texts do very little when it comes to public choice. What they do on public choice is usually quick and brief. Substantive content is missing. Market failure is discussed much more and usually in a "this is something that is really important" tone. For every 1 page on public choice and government failure, there are probably 6–8 pages on market failure.

Further information on the coverage of public choice in economic courses comes from Gwartney (2012), which is based on a paper he presented at the 2012 American Economic Association. His paper, titled "What Should We be Teaching in Basic Economics Courses," examines the Advanced Placement economic courses taught in high school—which are structured to conform to what is being taught in macro and micro at the college level—and concluded that "the gravest omission of the current teaching of basic economics is the virtual exclusion of the economics of public choice." Advanced Placement economics was examined further by Ferrarini et al. (2011, pp. 71–72) and concluded that

> Students are presented with a highly imbalanced view of market versus government. Market failure is covered, but government failure is totally omitted. Students are left with the false impression of how the political process works and a lack of understanding of why government intervention often leads to outcomes that are dramatically different than those promised by politicians. The cause of economic enlightenment is poorly served by these omissions and imbalances.

This suggests that our expressed hope that Bator would have been unable to publish his article "The Anatomy of Market Failure" in the *Quarterly Journal of Economics* after 1962 may have been naïve. As further evidence in support of this view, Bator's article has been described as "the standard reference to the approach [that] now forms the basis of textbook expositions in the economics of the public sector."[1] The hope that *The Calculus of Consent* and the academic development of public choice that followed have had a significant effect on the teaching of economics, particularly at the principles level, is one that has yet to be realized.

[1] See http://www.hks.harvard.edu/about/faculty-staff-directory/francis-bator.

Research: The More Select, the Greater the Neglect

We are persuaded that the neglect of government failure, and public choice more generally, in principle text books is found at all levels of economic education, with this extending, though to a lesser degree, into research as well. It is also our impression that the tendency to emphasize market failures and conclude that these failures are sufficient to justify government action to correct them, while largely ignoring the insights of public choice, is more pronounced in the more prestigious or select universities. This impression is just that, an impression, based on general observations and examples, such as the following.[2]

One of the authors was asked recently to comment on a talk titled "Markets and Government" given by a Nobel Prize-winning economist from an elite American university. His first slide was on the importance of government functions without which markets could not perform well—certainly a reasonable point. The second slide was on four causes of market failures: (1) lack of competition, (2) externalities, (3) incomplete markets, and (4) asymmetric information. Again this is quite reasonable except for not mentioning that each of the four also causes government failures. The economist then acknowledged that while government can improve economic performance, they can also pursue policies that are harmful to economic performance, with the role of economic analysis being to determine what government does well, what it does poorly, and what it is not currently doing to improve the economy that it should be doing. After this introduction, however, the presentation consisted of an argument that the best hope for solving our current economic problem is higher taxes and more government spending and regulation. From conversations at a reception and dinner following the talk, it was obvious that this professor, not surprisingly, knew enough about public choice to have given a talk with a more realistic balance between market and government failures. But one got the impression that he did not quite feel it was in good taste to bring up public choice and government failure in polite company.

There is a plausible argument for why professors at elite universities would be more likely to deemphasize public choice than professors at less esteemed universities. Holding the view that market failures are ubiquitous and government action is justified to correct those failures surely opens more doors to interesting stints in Washington, DC, for the former professors than it does for the latter. This argument is captured in the old joke that "the fastest way for an academic to get to Washington is to go to Harvard and turn left." When at the prestigious London School of Economics, Hayek (2007, p. 37) noticed a tendency for professors at elite universities

[2] We recognize that this impression may be biased by the fact that it is the writings and presentations of economists at the more prestigious universities that we, and other economists, are more likely to encounter. So even if the neglect of public choice were evenly spread over all economic departments (and the influence of economists at the elite universities on the rest of the profession certainly pushes in that direction), it could easily appear that it is concentrated in the most highly regarded universities.

to favor active government when in the first edition on *The Road to Serfdom* he wrote:

> I am always told by my socialist colleagues that as an economist I should occupy a much more important position in the kind of society to which I am opposed—provided, of course, that I could bring myself to accept their views.

Another example of the neglect of public choice by prestigious professors from select universities comes from the relatively new subfield in economics known as behavioral economics. The early work in what developed into behavioral economics was done in the early 1970s by Daniel Kahneman, a professor of psychology at Princeton, who received the Nobel Prize in economics for this work in 2002 (sharing it with Vernon Smith for his work in experimental economics). The main thrust of behavioral economics, briefly stated, consists of identifying decisions people systematically make under experimental conditions that are inconsistent with the rationality assumption of standard microeconomic models. As examples, the negative value people assign to a loss is greater than the positive value they assign to a gain of the same magnitude, the value people are willing to pay for an item they do not own is less than they require to give it up as soon as they own it, and people will drive 5 miles to reduce the amount paid for a good from \$10.00 to \$5.00 but will not drive 5 miles to reduce the amount paid for another good from \$1000.00 to \$980.00.[3]

These results are interesting, though some scholars, such as Plott and Zeiler (2005), have argued that they are not as robust with respect to how the experiments are designed as suggested by behavioral economists. Also, see others such as McKenzie (2010) and Glaeser (2006) for broader critiques of behavioral economics. But assuming that such irrationalities are pervasive, there are still reasons to question the willingness of behavioral economists to suggest public policy implications, either implicitly or explicitly, from their results without giving serious thought to public choice considerations or considerations from any well-thought-out model of political behavior. This is a rather serious omission since behavioral economists commonly suggest that since people are not rational, they cannot be depended upon to effectively pursue their own interest in response to market incentives without the guidance of government.[4] One is left wondering why the same irrationalities that

---

[3] See McKenzie (2010, Chap. 6) for an extensive discussion of the different experimental results upon which behavioral economists base their critique of rationality.

[4] Ariely (2008, p. 48) is more explicit than most in recommending that government step in to correct market failures due to irrationality. He states that "[i]f we cannot rely on the market forces of supply and demand to set optimal market prices, and … help us maximize our utility, then we may need to look elsewhere. This is especially the case with society's essentials, such as health care, medicine, water, electricity, education, and other critical resources. If you accept the premise that market forces and free markets will not always regulate the market for the best, then you may find yourself among those who believe that the government (we hope a reasonable and thoughtful government) must play a larger role in regulating some market activities, even if this limits free enterprise."

plague market decisions are not also discussed when political decisions are being suggested.[5]

Behavioral economists are ignoring an insight of Buchanan's that was critical to the development of public choice. In recalling his year (1955–1956) in Italy on a Fulbright grant to read the Italian classics on public finance, Buchanan (2007, p. 7) observed that "[t]his Italian year was critical in the development of my ideas on the importance of the relation between the political structure and the positive and normative of economic policy." Even confining ourselves to just Buchanan's contribution to public finance, we see this insight still paying dividends 24 years later when Brennan and Buchanan (1980) teamed up to write *The Power to Tax* in which they upended several long-standing normative conclusions about taxation by incorporating an explicit model of politics into the analysis. If behavioral economists applied the irrationalities found in their experiments to both market and political agents and compared the results, some of their policy suggestions would surely be upended, but whether upended or not, their policy discussions could be taken more seriously. Since they have not, we have yet another example of resistance to public choice theory in the academy.

Although it may seem that this section has been pessimistic regarding the impact of *The Calculus of Consent* on teaching and research, we do not see it that way. Indeed, we see the reaction to the book and the scholarship that followed from it as exactly what one would expect from any work that mounts a serious challenge to the entrenched wisdom in any academic discipline. Our view that the reaction has been most pronounced in the elite economic and political science departments is not surprising since it is in those departments that we find those with the most to lose from the threat public choice poses to their human capital.

There is also a measure of academic success that clearly points to the powerful positive impact of *The Calculus of Consent*. In the 24 years from the beginning of 1988–2012, *The Calculus of Consent* received 25,699 citations listed in the social sciences index, with this number of citations per year steadily increasing over these years (Thomson Reuters 2012). By way of comparison, over the same time *The Monetary History of the United States: 1857–1960*, by Milton Friedman and Anna Schwartz published in 1963, had 12,109 citations in the same index (Thomson Reuters 2012). It is widely accepted that Friedman and Schwartz (1963) had a big impact on monetary policy. Even if the citation numbers are to be believed, they do not mean that Buchanan and Tullock's book had more impact than Friedman and Schwartz's. But there can be no doubt that both books had a large impact on academic research.

[5] Thaler and Sunstein (2008, Chap. 17) consider some objections to using behavioral economics findings to nudge (with government often doing the nudging) decisions in more rational directions, with some of these objections being based on concerns that government decisions are likely to make things worse instead of better. Their response focuses on the argument that government will do something about the problems they discuss, and it makes sense to offer good advice. No mention is made of the case for constitutional limits on government as a way of preventing government action that does more harm than good.

The Political Impact

The impact of *The Calculus of Consent*, and the literature it spawned, on economic education and research has not been as positive as we would have liked, but it would seem to be more encouraging than the impact, or lack thereof, on political decisions. Of course one can argue that disappointment in this regard is moderated by the fact that much of public choice analysis contained in, and followed after, *The Calculus of Consent* suggested strongly that it would not have much influence on "politics as usual." As Buchanan (2007, p. 106) writes, "positive public choice theory suggests that the rent seekers are indeed to inherent our earth." But this pessimistic view is based on only one of the two analytical threads running through *The Calculus of Consent*; that when people are making decisions within existing rules of the political game, they are concerned primarily with their narrow self-interest. The other analytical thread develops the insight that when considering which rules of the political game would be best, people are more concerned with the general long-run benefits that can be expected to emerge from rules that are chosen. Buchanan has long expressed the view that the hope is not in getting voters to elect better politicians who will put the public interest above those of the rent seekers because it is the right thing to do but in getting agreement on constitutional rules that will increase the political payoff from elevating the general interest above those of the rent seekers. But even here, Buchanan (2007, p. 106) is at best only cautiously optimistic, as reflected in his comment:

> Constitutional reform offers the only escape from this gloomy prediction [of the rent seekers inheriting the earth]. But until and unless the rent-seeking potential embodied in the nonconstrained institutions of governance is fully appreciated, it remains impossible to secure the requisite constitutional attitude or constitutional wisdom that will make reform a realistic alternative.

In other words, in order to achieve effective constitutional reform, it is necessary to develop a public awareness of the collective harm resulting from a political process that is no longer sufficiently disciplined by constitutional constraints. This takes us back to the observation by Henry Simons (1951, p. 20) that "[c]onstitutional provisions are no stronger than the consensus that they articulate." The problem is that [see Buchanan quotation in previous paragraph] "the rent-seeking potential embodied in the nonconstrained institutions of governance" has already been largely realized, with virtually everyone, either as an individual or a member of a group, benefiting from a government program and the rent seeking that allows it to be maintained or expanded. Almost all of us are now trapped in a prisoners' dilemma in which government spending has expanded well into the region that leaves us collectively worse off but with each recognizing that he or she would be harmed by a unilateral surrender of their government largess. This prisoners' dilemma explains both why the United States Congress has an approval rating only slightly higher than swine flu and why congressional incumbents have high reelection rates. People are not happy being surrounded by pirates, but they understandably hesitate to get rid of their own pirate when they are.

It is difficult not to give in to pessimism when hoping the growth in government will be halted and then reversed by constitutional reform. Perhaps this is why Buchanan has expressed somewhat mixed feelings about the impact of his academic work. On the one hand, he states "I should reject, and categorically, any affinity with the preacher who writes or speaks for the express and only purpose of persuading others to accept his prechosen set of values."[6] On the other hand, he writes a few pages later "I have often stated that I feel a moral obligation to hope that such [constitutional] reform can indeed take place."[7] So it is difficult to classify Buchanan as either a pessimist or an optimist. As he has been known to say, and we paraphrase here, I am a pessimist when I consider the future because there are so many problems on the horizon, but an optimist when I consider the past because things have always worked out better than I thought they would.

Is Reversing Government Growth a Reasonable Hope?

How reasonable is the hope that we can achieve constitutional reform that will make government more responsive to the public interest by reducing its discretionary power? And if such reform does take place, what, if any, role will *The Calculus of Consent* and public choice have played? We shall consider the question on hope first and speculate on the second question in the following section.

We believe there is a darkness-before-the-dawn argument that having hope that government can be beneficially reduced in size with constitutional reform is not delusional.[8] We begin with Bastiat's (1995, p. 144) observation that "[t]he state is the great fictitious entity by which everyone seeks to live at the expense of everyone else." People can disagree as to whether ordinary politics driven by the rent-seeking prisoners' dilemma described earlier has already made Bastiat's state a reality in America. Even if we have not arrived at that state, however, we are rapidly headed in that direction with federal transfers in the form of Social Security, Income Security programs (means-tested programs not including Medicaid), Medicare, and Medicaid making up over 60% of the federal budget in 2012. The inevitable result, if this trend continues, is that an increasing number of people will be receiving less value from the government benefits than they are paying for the government benefits of others[9].

---

[6] Buchanan (2007, p. 81).

[7] Buchanan (2007, p. 106).

[8] This section will draw on a more complete argument made in Clark and Lee (2011).

[9] See Office of Management and Budget (2012, Table 3.1, p. 47). Keep in mind that much of the federal government transfers of income and wealth are not recorded in the federal budget. It cost very little to enforce federal regulations and import restrictions that protect some industries from competition. Yet these regulations and restrictions transfer large amounts from consumers and potential competitors to those being protected. Furthermore, the federal transfers that are found in the budget will soon accelerate rapidly since the baby boomers have just begun to become eligible for Social Security and Medicare.

A point can eventually be reached when forming a controlling coalition that favors shrinking government transfers and government spending in general becomes politically feasible. Of course, depending on how the costs and benefits are distributed, the transfers could become very large, with a majority still receiving more than they are paying or believing they are if they do not consider the largely hidden costs of what the transfers are costing them. But, given political reality, it is unlikely that a majority will remain net beneficiaries of transfers (even ignoring the hidden costs) if they expand much, if any, beyond current levels—the political reality being that the net gains (or losses) from taxes and transfers are more evenly distributed, as a percentage of income, over different income levels than the political rhetoric about transferring from the rich to the poor would have us believe.

Of course, even if most are net losers from government transfers, there would remain at least two serious problems with forming a politically effective coalition in favor of reducing those transfers. First, even if everyone were willing to scale back his transfers in return for others doing the same, there is the problem of reciprocity. As with any prisoners' dilemma, no one is willing to choose the cooperative solution (give up some of her benefits) without assurances that others (or at least large numbers of others) will do the same. Second, even if it is in everyone's narrow interest to sacrifice some of her transfers in return for others doing the same, people regularly ignore their narrow interest when voting. Since the probability that any one vote will determine the outcome of a state or federal election is literally less than that of being killed by jellyfish, the opportunity costs to disregarding one's private advantage to vote in favor of advancing broad social concerns are effectively zero. So, if people are ideologically convinced that government transfers promote such objectives, such as helping the poor or protecting American jobs from foreign competition, many will vote against a general reduction in government transfers (or politicians who support such a reduction) even if they recognize that they would personally benefit from such a reduction.[10] This has become known as expressive voting.

Buchanan and Tullock contributed to understanding these two problems in ways that suggest insightful responses to them, both together in *The Calculus of Consent* and in separate writings. As emphasized in their book, it is easier to get agreement on rules of the game than on the outcomes that will emerge from those rules. To pick an obvious example, the teams in the National Football League are able to agree on the rules of professional football (and occasional changes in those rules), even though they could never agree on the next season's won-lost record of each team that will result from the rules they do agree on. One can think of constitutional rules as a way of providing reciprocity in the sense that we can each agree to subject ourselves to the restrictions imposed by those rules with the understanding

[10] Voting is a good way to achieve a sense of moral virtue at low cost. But this does not always result in people voting against their narrow interest since people have a natural talent for convincing themselves that government policies that are good for them (e.g., high pay for teachers if you are a teacher) are essential for promoting the general interest (e.g., improving the education of our children).

that others will be doing the same. So if enough people want to restrict government transfers and spending collectively, constitutional reform is a way of overcoming, or at least diminishing, the reciprocity concerns that would otherwise prevent getting it done.

But this still leaves the problem of expressive voting—people supporting government actions for ideological reasons even when aware that those actions make them worse off. Most discussions of expressive voting use it to explain how it reduces the responsibility of voters for the costs of what they vote for and therefore why they tend to vote for more government than they would if their political votes in the ballot box were as decisive as their dollar votes in the market place. For example, the first discussion we know of what would later become known as expressive voting was published in 1954 when Buchanan (1999 [1954], p. 80) wrote the following:

> It seems quite possible that in many instances the apparent placing of "the public interest" above mere individual or group interest in political decisions represents nothing more than a failure of the voters to consider fully the real costs of the activity to be under-taken. It is extremely difficult to determine whether the affirmative vote of a nonbeneficiary individual for a public welfare project implies he is either acting socially in accordance with a "nobler" ordering of alternatives or is estimating his own self-interest in accordance with a "collective-action" preference scale, or whether it suggests that he has failed to weigh adequately the opportunity costs of the project.[11]

Tullock (1971) also makes use of expressive voting (again, before that label was coined) to explain why voting for expensive government programs to help others is not as charitable as it seems. If it is charitable at all, it is charity on the cheap since casting a vote either for or against increasing government spending has no meaningful effect on the voter's personal cost. Of course, expressive voting can motivate support for more government spending on noncharitable activities, such as war, as discussed by Brennan and Lomasky (1993, pp. 49–51), who do use the term "expressive voting" and may have originated it. And Caplan (2007, Chap. 2) considers how expressive voting magnifies the support for what he discusses as four "systematic biased beliefs about economics"—antimarket bias, antiforeign bias, make-work bias, and pessimistic bias—all of which can be used to justify more power for, and spending by, government.

However, expressive voting can cut both ways, either for or against larger government. This means that political ideology is the critical factor determining the direction of government growth, far more important than financial interest.[12] The political ideology that has prevailed at least since 1930 has, with minor and short exceptions, been sympathetic to government growth to address a host of problems

---

[11] A similar observation is made on p. 38 in *The Calculus*.

[12] If the probability that a vote will determine the outcome of an election is 1 in a million (which is on the high side of a reasonable estimate of the probability in most state or federal elections), then the voter who realizes a penny's worth of ideological satisfaction from voting for a policy that will cost him $10,000 if it passes will be indifferent between voting yes or no. In other words, political ideology is a million times more influential than financial interest in the voting booth.

that, though once seen as private or local concerns, are now widely seen as national concerns demanding action by the federal government. The current ideology represents a major shift from that which prevailed over the first 142 years of United States history, during which the federal government peace-time expenditures averaged less than 3% of GDP. If such a major ideological shift occurred once, it seems plausible that a reversal is possible, at least a partial one. But is there any reason to expect that *The Calculus of Consent* and public choice will deserve any credit for such an ideological reversal if it does occur?

The Long-Run Importance of *The Calculus of Consent*

It is easy to dismiss the influence on public opinion of ideas that are almost entirely confined to the work of a few academics. But is also takes little effort to trot out Keynes's (1936, p. 383) famous, but generic, statement in support of the argument that obscure ideas can have big consequences and then assume that this makes a serious case that particular ideas are consequential. It is no doubt true that "[p]ractical men who believe themselves to be quite exempt from any intellectual influences, are usually the slaves of some defunct economist." But what is it about the ideas propagated by *The Calculus of Consent* and public choice that suggests that they will have much, if any, influence on the prevailing political ideology? There are, no doubt, a number of public choice insights that scholars in the field can think of in consideration of this question. But the one we feel deserves emphasis is taken from the title of Buchanan's (1999 [1979]) article "Politics without Romance."

Much of the *resistance* to public choice is a function of the fact that it strips away the romantic notions about the political process that make it so appealing to many. Consider the moral satisfaction that many realize from voting for noble-sounding government programs or for politicians who support them, despite (or because of) their high cost. That moral satisfaction depends on voters' belief that their votes represent their willingness to sacrifice personally to promote virtuous objectives. But the messages people receive from public choice are that (1) their votes do not represent a meaningful sacrifice since their individual votes have no noticeable influence on whether or not the programs they vote for are enacted, (2) those with the most influence on the details and implementation of the noble-sounding programs that are enacted will use their influence to promote their own interests by undermining the achievement of the noble objectives intended, and (3) many of the programs they vote for will end up harming the very people who were intended to be helped no matter how the programs are designed and implemented. If a person accepts these conclusions, there is not much left in the act of voting, or the political process in general, to feel particularly virtuous about.

There is a continuum of reactions to the above public choice messages that can be expected from those who value the righteous feelings they receive from their political "generosity." At one extreme, the reaction is to dismiss belligerently the nonromantic view of public choice and become more attached to a pro-government ideology. The reaction becomes less hostile as an intermediate position along the continuum is approached at which point the public choice messages are simply ignored, leaving a person's pro-government ideology neither strengthened nor weakened. Beyond the intermediate point, the reaction ceases to be hostile and finds people becoming increasingly open to and convinced by the public choice messages until at the other extreme people are immediately converted to the view that morality would be best served by reducing the power and spending of government. Our belief is that, at any point in time, the hostile half of the continuum contains more people, probably far more, than the nonhostile half. Assuming this is correct, then if public choice were considered only by those who have an emotional attachment to the romantic view of government as a means of expressing their morality, it would have had an impact, but not the one Buchanan and Tullock would prefer.

But the impact of public choice is not limited to those with an emotional stake in the romantic view that the political process is a means of expressing their moral superiority. That number is surely no larger, and probably smaller, than the number who either do not think much about the proper role of government one way or the other or believe, with different degrees of passion, that government has become more destructive than constructive. The latter number has certainly been increasing in recent decades as confidence in the competence of government (the federal government in particular) has diminished along with government's increasingly clumsy and expensive attempts to solve a host of social problems that are inherently less amenable to centralized solutions than winning a war, building an interstate highway system, or putting men on the moon. Of course, it is this experience with government, not the influence of public choice scholarship, that is primarily responsible for increasing the number of people who have given up their romantic views of politics. But this still leaves an important means for public choice to have an impact that Buchanan and Tullock can be proud of.

It is one thing to believe that government should be smaller and less intrusive in our lives. It is quite another to have a coherent understanding of why government has become increasingly excessive and what to do about it. Probably the most common belief is that better people need to be elected to public office, meaning people who understand that the public welfare would be improved if government were reduced in size and scope and are willing to act on that belief independently of their personal advantages. Almost none of those who believe this have ever heard of public choice, much less read an article or book on it. But a few will read a popular piece by someone who does know something about public choice, or will talk to, or hear a discussion by, someone who has. And the academic influence of *The Calculus of Consent* and the public choice literature on constitutional economics it spawned make it likely that many of those desiring the downsizing of Leviathan will hear about the futility of attempting to achieve that objective by changing politicians, without changing the incentives they face. To these people, the stress on the importance of constitutions, and the need for constitutional reform, can lead to a sharper understanding of what is required to impose tougher restraints on the political process and a stronger commitment to support such reform. Furthermore, recalling Simons (1951, p. 20) once again, such commitments increase the restraint imposed by our existing constitution by strengthening the consensus that its provisions articulate.

In addition, the impact created by the intellectual respectability of *The Calculus of Consent* and subsequent contributions to public choice, though being narrowly confined initially, can gradually grow over time to exert a powerful, but largely unnoticed, influence on the prevailing political ideology. Like many social phenomena, political ideology is subject to a network effect—meaning that as the number of people who have a particular political ideology increases, the more value others receive from having the same or similar ideology. The result is that a critical number of adherents of an ideology can reach a point, often referred to as a tipping point, which motivates a bandwagon effect in favor of that ideology. This obviously does not mean that everyone in the country, or even a small community, will end up with the same political ideology, but it is common for a particular ideology to dominate within groups made up of people who identify with each other for any number of reasons, such as being members of the same academic discipline. And even in groups as large as nations, it is possible to identify differences in the prevailing political ideology between nations and across time. As discussed earlier, it is obvious that the prevailing political ideology in America is currently more hospitable to a larger and more active government than it was during the nineteenth and into the twentieth century. So it is possible that work by Buchanan and Tullock published 50 years ago as *The Calculus of Consent*, and the intellectual movement that it initiated, is now nurturing a broader ideological movement that will eventually shift the prevailing political ideology back toward that which prevailed in the United States for well over half of its history. And the power of political ideology, as magnified by expressive voting, suggests that a small shift in that ideology, leading to a small increase in the value voters place on expressing themselves in favor of smaller government, can have a large impact on political decisions.

We recognize that our arguments do not assure a more restrained and disciplined political process that is more responsive to the general welfare than our current political arrangements. Indeed, when making our arguments, we often thought of Samuel Johnson's characterization of second marriages as the triumph of hope over experience. But in the end, we are more inclined to agree with Alfred Marshall's (2009 [1924], 164n) observation that "without hope there is no enterprise." We like to think Buchanan and Tullock join us in favoring Marshall's view as well.

References

Ariely D (2008) Predictably irrational: the hidden forces that shape our decisions. HarperCollins, New York

Arnold RA (2010) Economics. South-Western College, Cincinnati

Bastiat F (1995) In: de Huszar GB (ed) Selected essays on political economy. The Foundation for Economic Education, Irvington-on-Hudson

Bator FM (1958) The anatomy of market failure. Quart J Econ 72(3):351–379

Brennan G, Buchanan JM (1980) The power to tax: analytical foundations of a fiscal constitution. Cambridge University Press, Cambridge

Brennan G, Lomasky L (1993) Democracy and decision: the pure theory of electoral preference. Cambridge University Press, Cambridge

Buchanan JM (2007) Economics from the outside in: better than plowing and beyond. Texas A&M University Press, College Station

Buchanan JM (1999 [1954]) Individual choice in voting and the market. In: Brennan G, Kliemt H, Tollison RD (eds) The collected works of James M. Buchanan: the logical foundations of constitutional liberty. Liberty Fund, Indianapolis, pp 75–88

Buchanan JM (1999 [1979]) Politics without romance. In: Brennan G, Kliemt H, Tollison RD (eds) The collected works of James M. Buchanan: the logical foundations of constitutional liberty. Liberty Fund, Indianapolis, pp 45–59

Buchanan JM, Tullock G (1965 [1962]) The calculus of consent: logical foundations of constitutional democracy. Ann Arbor Paperbacks, Ann Arbor

Caplan B (2007) The myth of the rational voter. Princeton University Press, Princeton

Clark JR, Lee DR (2011) Shrinking Leviathan: can the interaction between interest and ideology slice both ways? Indep Rev 16(2):221–236

Ferrarini TH, Gwartney JD, Morton JS (2011) Advanced placement economics: the good, the bad and the ugly. Econ J Watch 8(1):57–75. http://econjwatch.org/articles/advanced-placement-economics-the-good-the-bad-and-the-ugly

"Frances M. Bator" profile on Harvard Kennedy School website. http://www.hks.harvard.edu/about/faculty-staff-directory/francis-bator. Accessed 8 June 2012

Friedman M, Schwartz AJ (1963) A monetary history of the United States, 1867–1960. Princeton University Press, Princeton

Glaeser EL (2006) Paternalism and psychology. Univ Chic Law Rev 73:507–548

Gwartney JD (2012) What should we be teaching in basic economics courses. J Econ Educ 43(3): 300–307

Gwartney JD, Stroup RL, Sobel R, Macpherson DA (2010) Economics: private and public choice. South-Western College, Cincinnati

Hayek FA (2007) Preface to the first edition of The road to serfdom: text and documents, edited by Bruce Caldwell. The University of Chicago Press, Chicago

Keynes JM (1936) The general theory of employment, interest and money. Harcourt, Brace and World, New York

Marshall A (2009 [1924]) Principles of economics, 8th edn. CosimoClassics, New York

McKenzie RB (2010) Predictably rational?: in search of defenses for rational behavior in economics. Springer, Heidelberg

Office of Management and Budget (2012) Historical tables, budget of the U.S. Government. http://www.whitehouse.gov/sites/default/files/omb/budget/fy2012/assets/hist.pdf

Plott CR, Zeiler K (2005) The willingness to pay—willingness to accept gap, the 'endowment effect', subject misconceptions, and experimental procedures for eliciting valuations. Am Econ Rev 95(3):530–545

Simons HC (1951) Economic policy for a free society. University of Chicago University Press, Chicago

Thaler RH, Sunstein CR (2008) Nudge: improving decisions about health, wealth, and happiness. Yale University Press, New Haven

Thomson Reuters (2012) Social sciences citation index. http://webofknowledge.com/wos. Accessed 8 June 2012

Tullock G (1971) The charity of the uncharitable. West Econ J 9:379–392

Chapter 2
Institutions and Constitutions: The Economic World of James M. Buchanan

Randall G. Holcombe

James Buchanan, surely best known as one of the scholars who established the subdiscipline of public choice, was awarded the 1986 Nobel Prize in economics "for his development of the contractual and constitutional bases for the theory of economic and political decision-making."[1] That statement by the Nobel committee suggests a contribution that is considerably broader than public choice, if one thinks of public choice as the use of economic methods to analyze political decision-making but at the same time appears to leave out much of the subject matter of public choice, if one characterizes the subject matter as the type of research that appears in *Public Choice*, the journal. The broad nature of the Nobel committee's statement is very appropriate, in that it references a particular approach that Buchanan's work has consistently taken when analyzing private sector and public sector economic activity. Buchanan's work has always focused on the institutional framework within which people exchange, whether that exchange is a bilateral market exchange or a more complex exchange made through collective decision-making. Within the sphere of collective decision-making, an important part of the institutional framework is the set of rules within which collective action takes place – that is, the constitutional rules. This is just as true for market exchange. Buchanan's work has consistently recognized that whether one is analyzing market exchange or political exchange, the outcomes depend critically on institutions and constitutions.

[1]This statement is taken from www.nobelprize.org/nobel_prizes/economics/laureates/1986, "the official Web site of the Nobel Prize."

R.G. Holcombe (✉)
Department of Economics, Florida State University,
288 Bellamy Building, Tallahassee, FL 32306, USA
e-mail: holcombe@fsu.edu

D.R. Lee (ed.), *Public Choice, Past and Present: The Legacy of James M. Buchanan and Gordon Tullock*, Studies in Public Choice 28, DOI 10.1007/978-1-4614-5909-5_2,

The Subject Matter of Economics

Buchanan (1979) notes that modern economic analysis focuses on the way that individuals choose among various alternatives, with a heavy emphasis on maximization. Individuals make choices that maximize their utilities, firms are managed to maximize profit, and economic policies are designed to maximize social welfare. Economic problems become technological problems, and even the idea of an economic problem suggests that there is some solution. Buchanan (1979: 26, emphasis in original) says that economics should "... concentrate on *exchange* rather than *choice*." Comparing an analysis of an individual choosing among alternatives to a group of individuals engaging in economic activity, Buchanan (1979: 28) says, "The fact of association requires that a wholly different, and wholly new, sort of behavior take place, that of exchange, trade, or agreement." Buchanan critiques the framework of competitive general equilibrium, where all are price-takers and no participant can influence the outcome by noting that all social content has been eliminated from the model, so every firm and every individual views the economy as a set of constraints within which they make choices, rather than seeing themselves in a situation within which they can engage in mutually beneficial exchange with others.

Buchanan criticizes Samuelson (1954) for depicting the market as a mechanism, a calculating machine, that generates aggregate outcomes. Rather, Buchanan sees it as an arena within which individuals can engage in exchange for the purpose of accomplishing their own ends. Sometimes, Buchanan notes that bilateral exchange will be insufficient for individuals to achieve their ends and collective action will be required. Buchanan (1979: 34) says, "Economics is the study of the whole system of exchange relationships." That would include collective action taken by government. "What I should stress is the potentiality of exchange in those sociopolitical institutions that we normally regard as embodying primarily coercive or quasi-coercive elements." Economists can analyze politics as exchange. Economics, as Buchanan sees it, studies exchange, not choice.

Buchanan (1962) notes that when applying the Pareto principles in economic analysis, little insight is gained by viewing them as descriptive of exchanges of goods and services. Individuals have an incentive to engage in mutually advantageous exchange, so with a given institutional framework, a Pareto optimum is produced almost tautologically. Buchanan (1962: 341) says, "... the Pareto criterion is of little value when employed solely to classify 'results' defined with respect to the orthodox economic variables... the criterion must be extended to classify social rules which constrain the private individual behavior that produces such results."

If people have an opportunity to engage in mutually advantageous exchange, they will, as long as transaction costs are not too high. If transaction costs are too high, then because of those costs, the exchange would not be mutually beneficial. The Pareto concepts make more sense when applied to rules and institutions. If a group of people can change the institutional constraints so that exchanges that are not mutually advantageous because of transaction costs become so, then the rules can be changed and a Pareto improvement can be made. Buchanan's vision of economics as the study of exchange, rather than choice, points directly toward the institutional environment within which exchange takes place.

Buchanan (1962: 353) notes that "… the operation of alternative rules can only be evaluated in terms of predicted results, and the Pareto construction can be helpful in this process. At the level of application to the social constitution, to the evaluation of the 'rules of the game,' the Pareto criterion serves, however, a function that it cannot possibly serve in the more standard usage. Unless the observing economist is assumed to be omniscient, his classification of a final position as nonoptimal can never be more than a conjectural hypothesis that is impossible to test." He goes on to note that it is an agreement among individuals involved, whether in a market setting or in collective decision-making, that provides the evidence on whether outcomes are welfare enhancing.

Buchanan (1962: 348) notes that optimal institutions may at times produce specific results that appear nonoptimal when removed from the context of the institution, using the example of traffic signals. If a driver comes upon a red light and no other traffic is approaching the intersection, it appears suboptimal for the driver to have to stop. Yet in the larger context, where traffic signals provide order for potentially conflicting traffic, the institution provides results that enhance welfare. Thus, analyzing an individual outcome, such as the driver stopped at the light with no conflicting traffic, misrepresents the value of the institution that caused the driver to stop. Buchanan's institutional approach stands in contrast with outcome-based approach taken by a general equilibrium approach to evaluating welfare. Buchanan consistently takes a procedural view, perhaps most evident in Buchanan (1975), where outcomes are judged by the processes that produce them. An optimal institutional structure produces an optimal outcome, and the outcome can be judged by the process that produces it rather than looking at the outcome itself. As Buchanan notes, unless the economist judging the outcome is omniscient, there is no way to take the abstract ideas of welfare economics and apply them to judge the efficiency of specific real-world outcomes.

Buchanan's Institutional Approach

Throughout his career, Buchanan has taken an institutional approach to economic analysis. Buchanan (1949) argues that rather than viewing government as a mechanism for maximizing some measure of social welfare – taking Samuelson (1947) as an example of the approach he recommends against – government should instead be viewed as an institutional setting within which individuals can agree to accomplish ends collectively that could not be undertaken individually. Buchanan (1949: 496) objects to analysis that views the state "… as a single organic entity…" and says, "… the state is represented as the sum of its individual members acting in a collective capacity. … These two approaches have not been clearly separated or distinguished in the literature of government finance."

Buchanan references Wicksell (1967) as a proponent of this approach, as he often has in his work.[2] Buchanan criticizes the traditional theory of taxation, noting that taxes are treated as paid to the government with nothing given to citizens in return. Buchanan (1949: 497) notes that the revenue and expenditure sides of the government's budget are typically analyzed independently of each other and says, "… that the optimum values for the tax variables cannot be determined independently except for given values for the expenditure variables." Indeed, even in the twenty-first century, most analyses of taxation treat taxes that way, looking at how tax revenue can be extracted from taxpayers at least cost, with no analysis of how that revenue will be spent. "Fiscal analysis has proceeded as if all taxes were net subtractions from social income, never to be returned." (Buchanan 1949: 500) In keeping with Buchanan's vision of politics as exchange, Buchanan argues that any theory of optimal taxation must weigh the costs and benefits and that because there is no independent measure of benefit, agreement among citizens must be the benchmark. Buchanan's individualistic approach to fiscal theory relies on political institutions to weigh the costs and benefits of collective action, rather than envisioning a Pareto optimal outcome as a goal and then designing policies to get there. Only through the process of exchange are the individuals' values that are assumed to exist in the aggregate model actually revealed.

Buchanan (1949) also shows that the foundations of modern public choice were a part of Buchanan's research program from the beginning. Buchanan (1949: 498) says, "The state has no ends other than those of its individual members and is not a separate decision-making unit. State decisions are, in the final analysis, the collective decisions of individuals." He goes on to link the revenue and expenditure sides of the fiscal state by noting "The income of the state represents payment made by individuals out of their economic resources in exchange for services provided." Much of this article is devoted to a critical analysis of theories of government finance that depict government revenue as a cost imposed on citizens without looking at the benefits those revenues generate for those who pay for them. For example, it makes little sense to depict a tax system as progressive or regressive without at the same time examining the distribution of benefits those taxes finance. One can see in this article published more than 60 years ago the blueprint for Buchanan's research career.

Buchanan (1954a) writes a review article of Arrow (1951) in which he argues that Arrow's "impossibility theorem" is less relevant to social choice issues than at first it appears. Buchanan begins by questioning the idea of a "socially rational" decision-making process and notes that majority rule, a commonly-used decision-making rule, can never be viewed as resulting in some kind of optimal outcome. It is only a mechanism for making collective decisions. Buchanan (1954a: 116–117) says, "… the individual is the only entity possessing ends or values. … A social value scale as such simply does not exist. … Arrow's analysis appears to consist … in proving that the decision-making processes themselves define no social welfare function…"

---

[2] The reference to Wicksell (1967) is Buchanan's translation of Wicksell's 1986 essay that originally appeared in German.

Buchanan also notes that when people's preferences differ, collective choices are rarely going to give any one individual outcomes that individual most prefers all the time. In this context, a cyclical majority may even be a desirable outcome. Buchanan (1954a: 119) says, "... majority rule is acceptable in a free society precisely because it allows a sort of jockeying back and forth among alternatives, upon none of which relative unanimity can be obtained." Normally, votes are over candidates, not policies, and a cyclical majority would give various groups the opportunity to see their preferred candidates elected, rather than have a majority permanently dominate a minority. Even there, the election of different candidates to office does not necessarily mean that different policies will be enacted as a result. Political outcomes are driven by political institutions, and elections are only one of many political institutions at work. A cyclical majority in candidates will not necessarily produce a cyclical majority in policies.

Buchanan (1954a: 120) notes, "The attempt to examine the consistency of majority voting requires the assumption that individual values do not themselves change during the decision-making process. ... The definition of democracy as 'government by discussion' implies that individual values can and do change in the process of decision-making." People are open-minded to the extent that the process itself can change their political preference orderings. The political process is not a mechanism for revealing a social welfare function; it is an institutional structure within which people act collectively to produce outcomes they could not produce individually.

Buchanan (1954b) extends these ideas by comparing collective choice through voting with individual choice in the market. He offers a series of now-familiar arguments for why individuals are more likely to find their preferences satisfied though market exchange rather than through voting for an outcome that is imposed on everyone in the collective. This reinforces the idea that government action is beneficial when individuals want to accomplish ends that require collective action and cannot be accomplished through individual exchange.

Buchanan's (1965) theory of clubs takes an institutional approach to public goods theory. Public goods theory following Samuelson (1954) defines a public good as a good that, once produced, additional consumers can consume the full amount of the good without reducing the consumption of any additional consumer. Buchanan takes an institutional approach by looking at the conditions under which groups would form to produce goods collectively rather than relying on individual exchange in the marketplace. Arguing that few goods are purely public in the Samuelsonian sense, Buchanan (1965: 2) says, "The central question in a theory of clubs is that of determining the membership margin, so to speak, the size of the most desirable cost and consumption sharing arrangement." Buchanan's approach has the advantage of taking into account the possibility of congestion of public goods, such as when additional traffic causes a road to become congested, and impure public goods that straddle the line between Samuelsonian public and private goods. Buchanan's article laid the foundation for a literature on what has been called club goods, but Buchanan's emphasis is on the "club" that produces those goods – that is, on the institutional framework that provides them – rather than on the goods themselves.

Buchanan and Musgrave's (1999) book is an interesting volume that offers a series of lectures by the two scholars, subtitled "Two Contrasting Visions of the State." Buchanan's institutional approach clearly comes through there, in contrast with Richard Musgrave's. He notes (Buchanan and Musgrave 1999: 118) "Knut Wicksell's … emphasis was on rules … Gordon Tullock and I were working in the Wicksellian paradigm, and that book's argument may be summarized as a plea for replacing majority rule by more inclusive rules, at least for critically important collective actions." Recognizing the normative strength of majority rule, Buchanan goes on to note, "… we are left with possible limits on the domain of permissible outcomes as the only means of constraining political discrimination." Further analyzing institutions, Buchanan (Buchanan and Musgrave 1999: 125) says, "With a two-house legislature, an executive veto, and independent judicial review, any collective action presumably requires the equivalent of considerably more than majority support." This volume contrasts Buchanan's views with Musgrave's but notes the even more stark contrast with Arrow (1951), who analyzes social choice by looking at preferences without considering the institutional structure under which preferences will be aggregated. Institutions constrain political decision-making and often direct the outcome of collective decisions.

Brennan and Buchanan (1985: 2) note, "If rules influence outcomes and if some outcomes are 'better' than others, it follows that to the extent that rules can be chosen, the study and analysis of comparative rules and institutions become proper objects of our attention." They go on to discuss the importance of the institutional and constitutional framework – the rules – to the ability of a society to operate for the well-being of its members. This volume shows the institutional approach that Buchanan takes to public choice, that is, his constitutional approach.

Buchanan (1962) makes perhaps the clearest statement of his institutional approach to economics by noting that individuals will exchange for their mutual benefit whenever the opportunity exists, so with a given set of institutions, resources will tautologically be allocated Pareto optimally. Economic analysis takes place by examining alternative institutional arrangements which allow people greater opportunities for mutually advantageous exchange, whether that means bilateral exchange or through collective action. The institutional approach Buchanan takes to economic analysis is apparent even in his earliest work.

The Subjective Nature of Cost

Buchanan (1969) looks at the nature of cost and choice to develop an argument that costs are opportunity costs, so the cost of any choice is the value of the foregone alternative. But because the alternative is not taken and is foregone, the cost is subjective and cannot be known precisely. One cannot know what would have occurred had a different choice been made. Value is only revealed through a market process, where in the process of exchange, values are attributed to goods and services.

Taking this approach, one might in the abstract conjecture that there is some optimal allocation of resources based on an aggregation of individual production and utility functions into a general equilibrium, but the actual values that people place on goods and services are only revealed through the process of exchange. The data needed to compute a general equilibrium cannot be observed. One cannot observe utility functions and production functions but only the prices and quantities that are produced when consumers and producers make choices based on the opportunities they perceive. There is no such thing as social welfare beyond the individual welfare of members of a group, and that individual welfare is only revealed as a result of the exchanges that individuals actually make.

Buchanan (1969: 25, emphasis in original) notes, "*Subjectivist* economics … amounts to an explicit denial of the objectivity of the data that informs economic choice. … Equilibrium is described not in terms of objectively determined 'conditions' or relationships among specific magnitudes, e.g., prices and costs, but in terms of the realization of mutually reinforcing and consistent expectations." Economic measures of value are the result of exchanges that take place within market institutions. Individuals place subjective value on goods and services, and through interaction with others – market exchange – the market places a value on goods and services. That market value can change if individuals' subjective values change, and the individual values underlying market value do change based on many factors, including factors as seemingly insignificant as fad or fashion. When the value purchasers place on goods or services falls, the value of the inputs that produce those goods and services will fall; when purchasers increase the value they place on some goods or services, that causes the value of inputs that produce those goods and services to rise. Thus, costs are subjective, driven by the subjective value consumers place on the outputs produced by those inputs that determine the cost of output.

Buchanan (1969: 25) notes that economics has sometimes been characterized by a fuzziness on the subjective nature of cost and value but says, "With the advent of 'welfare economics,' regardless of how this might be defined, such previously admissible methodological fuzziness no longer passes muster."

Market institutions ultimately determine the prices, and therefore the values at the margin, of goods and services. Buchanan (1969: 78) says, "…neither the marginal evaluations of demanders nor the marginal costs of suppliers … can be employed as a basis for determining prices. The reason is that these are both brought into equality with prices by behavioral adjustments on both sides of the market." Buchanan recognizes the importance of market institutions to the determination of economic value, and ultimately economic welfare, and draws a clear distinction between his view of markets and a "welfare economics" view in which the optimal allocation of resources is determined prior to market activity. The values that go into the computation of a general equilibrium are revealed only as a result of people interacting within market institutions. This is an illustration of Buchanan's approach to economics as the study of exchange, rather than the study of choice, and illustrates the importance of market institutions to reveal cost and value.

The Calculus of Consent

In hindsight, it is easy to say that Buchanan and Tullock's (1962) *The Calculus of Consent* was the book that started the public choice revolution. Earlier works, such as Black (1958) and Downs (1957), are foundational books in public choice, but public choice became an identifiable subdiscipline when Buchanan and Tullock not only added their book but also held a conference on the subject in 1963 that became an annual event and evolved into the Public Choice Society. *The Calculus of Consent* clearly fits the theme of "institutions and constitutions" that characterizes Buchanan's work. Buchanan and Tullock took an institutional approach to their analysis of collective decision-making. In keeping with themes in Buchanan's earlier work, they examine logrolling and vote trading, depicting politics as exchange. They look at the effect of institutions such as a bicameral legislature, and they discuss the effects of special interests on political outcomes.

The idea of politics as exchange emerges early in *The Calculus of Consent* when Buchanan and Tullock (1962: 19) say, "Men co-operate through exchange of goods and services in organized markets, and such co-operation implies mutual gain. ... At base, political or collective action under the individualistic view of the State is much the same. Two or more individuals find it mutually advantageous to join forces to accomplish certain common purposes." In keeping with their analysis of politics as exchange, Buchanan and Tullock (1962: 188) look at the buying and selling of votes and conclude that "...open buying and selling of political votes may actually lead to an 'improvement' for the group, measured in the extremely weak ethical sense of making everyone in the group better off as a result." Institutions matter, and their discussion of a bicameral legislature shows that bicameralism is effectively equivalent to imposing a more restrictive voting rule in a unicameral legislature. Buchanan and Tullock (1962: 235) note that "...the two-house legislature may produce results ranging from those equivalent to simple majority voting in a single house to those equivalent to the operation of the unanimity rule in a single house." While their specific logic is worth studying, the point for present purposes is their emphasis on the way that the institutional design of the legislature affects legislative outcomes.

The Calculus of Consent also lays the foundation for constitutional economics because Buchanan and Tullock explicitly develop a framework for analysis within which decisions on the rules within which people interact are distinguished from the decisions people reach within the constraints of those rules. This idea also comes across in Buchanan (1962), published the same year as *The Calculus of Consent.* Buchanan's work, which has always focused primarily on the public sector and has always taken an institutional approach, focuses on constitutional rules as the embodiment of institutions in *The Calculus of Consent*. The book explicitly focuses on collective action and explicitly develops a framework for analyzing the constitutional framework within which collective decision-making takes place, separately from the decisions that are made within the constitutional rules. While in some sense *The Calculus of Consent* can be viewed as a pivotal point in Buchanan's career, it fits well within the institutional and constitutional framework that has characterized his work both before and after the book was published. Buchanan's work has been remarkably consistent throughout his long career, as Meadowcroft (2011) notes.

Buchanan's Constitutional Economics

Buchanan's work after the publication of *The Calculus of Consent* has taken a consistently constitutional approach to public choice. Buchanan (1975) develops a social contractarian model for identifying optimal constitutional rules. Buchanan's benchmark for evaluating constitutional rules is unanimity, and one might view Buchanan (1975) as providing a more complete foundation for the constitutional framework developed in Buchanan and Tullock (1962). Buchanan (1975: 6–7) says of *The Calculus of Consent*, "The framework for analysis was necessarily contractarian, in that we tried to explain the emergence of observed institutions and to provide norms for changes in existing rules by conceptually placing persons in idealized positions from which mutual agreement might be expected. ... I have come to be increasingly disturbed by this basically optimistic ontology. ... Zero-sum and negative-sum analogues yield better explanatory results in many areas of modern politics..."

Buchanan (1975: 8) then raises a question about the applicability of the politics as exchange analogy, saying "So long as collective action is interpreted largely as the embodiment of individual behavior aimed at securing the efficiency attainable from cooperative effort, there was a natural tendency to neglect the problems that arise in controlling the self-perpetuating and self-enhancing arms of the collectivity itself. The control of government scarcely emerges as an issue when we treat collective action in strictly contractarian terms. Such control becomes a central problem when political power over and beyond plausible contractarian limits is acknowledged to exist." After laying out his social contractarian model, Buchanan (1975: 161) notes that even under democratic institutions, Leviathan government can escape constitutional constraints. "Democracy may become its own Leviathan unless constitutional limits are imposed and enforced."

Brennan and Buchanan (1980) apply this constitutional framework to taxation by examining the constitutional rules that have the potential to constrain a government with the power to tax from using that power to exploit the citizens it taxes. They model government as a revenue-maximizing monopoly and analyze constitutional constraints that may be able to limit the power of a monopoly government. Brennan and Buchanan (1980: 20) justify this, saying "The monopoly-state model of government may be acknowledged to be useful, not necessarily because it predicts how governments always, or even frequently, work, but because there are inherent tendencies in the structure of government to push it toward that sort of behavior implied in the monopolistic model, tendencies that may emerge in settings where constraints are wholly absent." From the more optimistic view Buchanan and Tullock (1962) take of politics as exchange to the view that Leviathan government may extend its reach beyond the constraints of a social contract expressed in Buchanan (1975), Brennan and Buchanan (1980) apply that apprehension about government power to analyze the tax system, not as the product of a benevolent despot, or even as a result of agreement among taxpayers, but rather looking at the public choice alternative of analyzing how self-interested individuals within government might act. This leads them to an analysis of how Leviathan government might be constrained with appropriate constitutional rules. Buchanan's institutional and constitutional approach to economics clearly motivates this volume.

Brennan and Buchanan (1985) further develop their ideas on constitutional economics in a follow-up volume subtitled "constitutional political economy," where they lay out the notion that the constitutional framework provides the foundation for individual interaction and those constitutional rules create a framework that channels individual actions toward their fellows away from predatory zero-sum and negative-sum action toward action that is positive-sum and mutually advantageous. Brennan and Buchanan (1985: 5) reference Hobbes to say that we benefit from a set of rules that govern people's interactions with each other because "...without them we would surely fight. We would fight because the object of desire for one individual would be claimed by another. Rules define the private spaces within which each of us can carry out our own activities." Even half a century after the first shots were fired in the public choice revolution, economists often depict the actions of government as if they are directed by an omniscient benevolent dictator, and Brennan and Buchanan (1980, 1985) are working within an alternative view of government – the view that people in government act in their own interests just as people do in the private sector. Their method of analysis is institutional and constitutional, in that they examine constitutional rules that could be designed to constrain government and examine institutional structures within which people can engage in economic activity for their mutual benefit.

The constitutional framework in Brennan and Buchanan (1985) is the same framework that Buchanan had been developing throughout his career but now is explicitly developed using the constitutional economics, or constitutional political economy, name. The terminology is interesting in light of the fact that public choice, going by that name, was only a few decades old at the time. But, by attracting a following of established academics, a substantial amount of public choice literature fit within the "science of choice" framework, even as Buchanan (1979) argued that economics should focus on the process of exchange, rather than choice. The constitutional political economy framework is the one that Buchanan has worked within his entire career, and his work in public choice clearly falls under the constitutional heading.

Buchanan's Constitutional Methodology

Buchanan's work throughout his career has been very methodologically consistent. Sandmo (1990: 63) notes that Buchanan has published no empirical work. Not only has Buchanan not done any empirical work, but he rarely references the empirical work of others, even though a large share of the articles in the journal *Public Choice* have substantial empirical content. Buchanan's conclusions are derived through historical and theoretical evidence, not statistical results, and Buchanan has always recognized that the institutional structure has a substantial impact on real-world outcomes. What one observes in the real world is not merely the product of utility functions on one side of the market and production functions on the other. Production possibilities are heavily dependent on the institutional environment within which people interact. One reaction to the methodological orientation of much work done in public choice was the creation of a new journal, *Constitutional Political Economy*, in 1990, that would focus more exclusively on the institutional and constitutional framework within which Buchanan worked.

In the first article of that new journal, Buchanan (1990) notes that economic analysis often examines people's choice within constraints. Constitutional political economy focuses on the choice of constraints. The idea that Buchanan puts forward as the foundation for a new journal and a new subdiscipline in social science is the same one Buchanan (1962) had put forward decades earlier. In keeping with his emphasis on politics as exchange, Buchanan (1990: 1) argues that constitutional political economy emphasizes "cooperative rather than conflictual" interaction among individuals.[3]

A short and clear summary of the primary constitutional issue that Buchanan's work deals with is found in the subtitle of his book, *The Limits of Liberty: Between Anarchy and Leviathan*. Buchanan takes a Hobbesian view of anarchy, in that without a government to create and enforce rules, life would be a war of all against all where people would find themselves constantly at risk from the violence of others. However, the government powerful enough to protect people's rights also has the potential to be the worst violator of those rights, an idea that goes back to Thomas Jefferson. No government; no liberty. But at the other extreme, Leviathan government; no liberty. Buchanan's work is probing the limits of liberty that lie between anarchy and Leviathan. The challenge is to develop a constitutional framework that allows people to interact productively and cooperatively with each other but that constrains the enforcer of the rules sufficiently to prevent the enforcer from becoming an exploiter.

---

[3] For a critique of this emphasis, see Yeager (1985, 2001).

Buchanan as a Teacher

James Buchanan's work has had such influence that most readers of this volume would likely be justified in saying they are students of James Buchanan. I am one of many who have learned so much from Buchanan's work, but I lay more specific claim to being a Buchanan student because I was a classroom student in his graduate public finance class, and he was the director of my doctoral dissertation. This chapter gives some indication of what I have learned from him, and this section is a more personal reminiscence of Buchanan as a classroom teacher and mentor.

I have heard Buchanan tell the story more than once about his discovering Wicksell's work in the University of Chicago library and thinking that it made more sense than all the public finance he had learned in the classroom. I can say the same thing about my discovering Buchanan and Tullock's *The Calculus of Consent.* I had the good fortune of taking a special topics course as an undergraduate that used *The Calculus of Consent* as a textbook, and I went to Virginia Tech to study economics specifically because Buchanan and Tullock were there. My indoctrination into traditional public finance was not as long as Buchanan's, because I came across the public choice approach to analyzing public sector resource allocation as an undergraduate, and of course as a graduate student, that approach was the conventional wisdom in a department where much of the faculty were at the forefront of the public choice revolution. This seemed to me to be the appropriate way to analyze the public sector, so much so that I did not recognize at the time how revolutionary it was.

Buchanan's work was often at odds with the conventional wisdom of the time, as I have noted throughout this chapter, but he never presented it that way. At times, he would refer to some issues where he disagreed with the conventional wisdom, but in the main, he presented his ideas in the classroom as straightforward economic analysis. He was not trying to explain why the conventional wisdom might have sometimes been flawed but rather was presenting his ideas as the correct way of viewing things. His focus was on what he believed to be correct, and he rarely mentioned the work of others that his work called into question. One result was that as I was absorbing what he had to say; I did not realize how revolutionary his work was until some years later, when I was able to put his ideas in a broader perspective. An example of this is the theme of my chapter. Many people will recognize Buchanan as a founder of public choice, but his institutional approach further differentiates his work in a way that I rarely see mentioned.

Buchanan's class required many shorter papers on topics he assigned that were due every 2 weeks. He wanted students to develop their own ideas on the assigned topics. My first thought was that it would be difficult to come up with ideas to write that many papers, and my consoling thought was that Buchanan had made these assignments for years and other students had done it, so I probably could too. One lesson I learned from writing those papers was that if I did some background research, I could write a paper on any topic. I might not know what, exactly, the finished product would look like when I started, but after some research, the ideas would come. That has given me the confidence to undertake research in unfamiliar areas with the thought that I could produce publishable work as a result of the research, even if I did not know ahead of time the exact nature of the resulting work.

Buchanan was a very nurturing professor in the classroom, in contrast with Gordon Tullock's classroom style. Those who know Tullock know that he will argue with just about any statement anyone will make, and he was that way in the classroom. Any idea a student had, no matter how brilliant, had to have a fatal flaw that Tullock would ferret out. In contrast, anything a student said in Buchanan's class would have the element of a good idea in it, that Buchanan would ferret out. A student could say something that (to me) sounded out-and-out wrong, and Buchanan would develop a good idea out of it. He would say that if you thought about it a slightly different way, if you brought in this other idea, and if you develop the argument along these lines, this good idea would emerge. Seeing Buchanan work this way provided great insight into the way he would develop good ideas and the way that we as students could develop good ideas. Students could see the thought process that would generate good ideas right before their very eyes. Buchanan was not a dynamic lecturer, but he was a great teacher.

Outside of the classroom, Buchanan was reluctant to talk to students about their ideas, but he would talk with them about their written work. If a student approached Buchanan with a research idea, he would tell the student "write it up" and then would be happy to discuss the resulting paper. It did not have to be long, but it did have to be written down. This is good discipline because writing up an idea helps the writer refine it and see both its shortcomings and ways that it might be further developed. Also, when discussing what is in the paper, if a question comes up and the answer is not in the paper, that shows where the paper needs to be developed. With just an idea, it is too easy to say "here is how I can take care of that," but with a paper, if the answer is not in the paper, that is an indication of what further work needs to be done.

While I was never Buchanan's colleague, my impression was that he worked the same way. He did not chat with colleagues about his ideas; he wrote them down and would discuss with them his working papers. Buchanan always had a huge inventory of working papers. This seems like a productive way to work, and I have followed Buchanan's examples in my own career as a professor. I assign the papers due every few weeks to my own graduate students, and I encourage them to write up their ideas rather than just discussing their thoughts. And, I write up my ideas so I have something tangible to further develop.

As my dissertation director, my work was undertaken just that way. When I approached him about an idea I had for a topic, rather than discuss it with me he said "write it up," and then we discussed what I had written at length. As I completed chapters, I would bring them to him and get almost instant feedback. I would give him a chapter one day, and in the next day or two, he had comments ready.

He was so prompt, despite his own very active research program. He gave his students priority, which was very helpful in moving my dissertation toward completion.

He also told me not to show other committee members any parts of my dissertation before he had approved them. That way he knew he would be in a position to stand behind what I had done. He was a very supportive dissertation supervisor, he offered good and insightful suggestions, and he helped me move rapidly to complete the dissertation. Buchanan's attitude was to get students finished and get them out the door so they could start their careers.

I consider it an honor and a privilege to have been Buchanan's student and to have written my dissertation under his supervision, but I also have learned a huge amount from him after I had graduated and left Blacksburg, from hearing him speak and from reading his work. Those are opportunities that many readers of this volume have had, regardless of where they went to school, and in that sense, I will close this section on reminiscences where I started, by saying that surely most readers of this volume are students of James Buchanan.

Conclusion

James Buchanan is perhaps best known for the pioneering work he has done to establish the subdiscipline of public choice as a part of mainstream economic and political thought. While this characterization of Buchanan's work is not inaccurate, it does not convey the institutional and constitutional orientation that Buchanan's work has had from the beginning of his career. Sandmo (1990) and Meadowcroft (2011) both note the remarkable consistency in Buchanan's work. In hundreds of published articles and dozens of books, Buchanan has consistently focused on the importance of the institutional framework within which people interact. If one looks at economics as studying exchange, the exchanges that people are able to make depend on the institutional structure within which they operate. That institutional structure is a product of collective choice. To equate Buchanan's work with public choice is at the same time too broad and too narrow. Much work within public choice analyzes collective decision-making within political constraints, whereas Buchanan's focus is more narrowly on the constitutional framework within which collective decision-making takes place. Buchanan's work goes beyond the confines of public choice, however, to recognize the importance of the institutional structure to all of economic activity.

Consider as an example a developer who wants to build a shopping center. This development would rely on institutions such as a clear system for recognizing title to the land on which the shopping center would be built, financing institutions, regulatory institutions that could facilitate or stand in the way of such a development, taxing institutions that might determine whether the development would be profitable, institutions that would provide roads and other infrastructure, and even more broadly, institutions that determine the limits of the corporate form of economic organization and legal institutions that can facilitate or inhibit complex transactions like this one. The institutional structure sets the rules under which individuals interact with each other and determines what exchanges are feasible and what exchanges are not. In keeping with Buchanan's (1962) institutional approach, given the rules, people will make all exchanges that are mutually advantageous. Some institutional structures will facilitate more mutually advantageous exchanges than others, so economic analysis should focus on the way societies choose their institutions.

Buchanan clearly recognizes that his institutional approach to economic analysis is at odds with the ideas of some highly visible economists in his generation. He has explicitly taken on and criticized Arrow, Samuelson, and Musgrave, to name just a few well-known economists whose ideas have been at odds with Buchanan's. Looking beyond specific issues to more general reasons for those disagreements, they have not shared Buchanan's institutional and constitutional approach to economics and, in particular, to the analysis of the government sector.

The institutional structure is a product of social interaction, perhaps the result of the strong imposing their preferences on the weak, perhaps as a result of a general agreement among everyone in a society, or more likely some combination of the two. Public choice, while heavily focused on analyzing politics as exchange and therefore emphasizing institutions as a product of agreement, also recognizes the disproportionate influence of interest groups and the rent-seeking activity of some that can impose costs on others. Rent-seeking and interest group politics are examples of some using their (political) power to impose their preferences on others. The point is that the rules under which individuals interact – the institutional structure – are a product of choices that individuals make. Individuals do not choose one entire institutional structure over another; rather, individual decisions and collective decisions work together to produce a system of social rules within which individuals operate.

Constitutional economics analyzes the way these rules are chosen and looks at the consequences of choosing one set of rules over another. It is the institutional approach to public choice. When one looks at Buchanan's contributions to public choice, they fall into the constitutional category. While Buchanan is rightfully credited as one of the founders of public choice, not only has his work been constitutional in nature from the beginning, it has also been what he has argued economists should do. While Buchanan is typically characterized as a public choice economist, he might be more accurately characterized as an institutional economist who has focused on constitutional issues.[4] Institutions and constitutions. That is the economic world of James M. Buchanan.

[4]Along these lines, see Williamson (1990) who places public choice as one of the branches of institutional economics.

References

Arrow KJ (1951) Social choice and individual values. Wiley, New York
Black D (1958) The theory of committees and elections. Cambridge University Press, Cambridge
Brennan G, Buchanan JM (1980) The power to tax: analytical foundations of a fiscal constitution. Cambridge University Press, Cambridge
Brennan G, Buchanan JM (1985) The reason of rules: constitutional political economy. Cambridge University Press, Cambridge
Buchanan JM (1949) The pure theory of government finance: a suggested approach. J Polit Econ 57(6):496–505
Buchanan JM (1954a) Social choice, democracy, and free markets. J Polit Econ 62(2):114–123
Buchanan JM (1954b) Individual choice in voting and the market. J Polit Econ 62(4):334–343
Buchanan JM (1962) The relevance of Pareto optimality. J Conflict Resolut 6(4):341–354
Buchanan JM (1965) An economic theory of clubs. Economica 32:1–14
Buchanan JM (1969) Cost and choice: an inquiry in economic theory. Markham, Chicago
Buchanan JM (1975) The limits of liberty: between anarchy and leviathan. University of Chicago Press, Chicago
Buchanan JM (1979) What should economists do? LibertyPress, Indianapolis
Buchanan JM (1990) The domain of constitutional economics. Const Polit Econ 1(1):1–18, Winter
Buchanan JM, Musgrave RA (1999) Public finance and public choice: two contrasting visions of the state. MIT Press, Cambridge
Buchanan JM, Tullock G (1962) The calculus of consent: logical foundations of constitutional democracy. University of Michigan Press, Ann Arbor
Downs A (1957) An economic theory of democracy. Harper & Row, New York
Meadowcroft J (2011) James M Buchanan. Continuum, New York
Samuelson PA (1947) Foundations of economic analysis. Harvard University Press, Cambridge
Samuelson PA (1954) The pure theory of public expenditure. Rev Econ Stat 36:387–389
Sandmo A (1990) Buchanan on political economy: a review article. J Econ Lit 28(1):50–65
Wicksell K (1896) A new principle of just taxation. In Musgrave RA, Peacock AT (eds) Classics in the theory of public finance. St. Martin's Press, New York (1967), pp 92–118
Williamson OE (1990) A comparison of alternative approaches to economic methodology. J Inst Theor Econ 146(1):61–71
Yeager LB (1985) Rights, contract, and utility in policy espousal. Cato J 5(1):259–294
Yeager LB (2001) Ethics as a social science. Edward Elgar, Cheltenham

Chapter 3
On Some Neglected, But Profound, Contributions of Gordon Tullock

Roger D. Congleton

Introduction: Gordon and the *Calculus of Consent*

The thesis of this chapter is that Gordon Tullock's contributions are often more profound than (even) he recognizes. This series of profound contributions may be said to have begun in 1959, when Gordon Tullock prepared and circulated a mimeographed research paper while a fellow at the Thomas Jefferson Center for Studies in Political Economy at the University of Virginia. The paper was entitled "A Preliminary Investigation of the Theory of Constitutions." That working paper served as the foundation of Chap. 6 of the *Calculus of Consent*: "A Generalized Economic Theory of Constitutions." Probably the most often referred to part of the *Calculus*, this chapter has played an important role in subsequent theoretical literature on voting rules that emerged after the *Calculus*. Indeed, that working paper can be given credit for launching the entire field of constitutional political economy, as it was the first systematic effort to use rational choice models to evaluate the relative merits of alternative voting rules.

However, even if one accepts this argument, it does not in any way diminish Buchanan's contribution to the *Calculus*. Buchanan is, of course, a very talented and creative man in his own right—and one of his rare gifts is the ability to recognize good ideas when he hears them. Most scholars are so fascinated with and focused on their own ideas that they have a hard time giving the ideas of others serious attention. Jim differs from most scholars in that respect. Indeed, he often appreciates more about such good ideas than the originator him- or herself.

My hunch is that it was Jim, rather than Gordon, who first appreciated how profound a contribution Tullock's working paper actually was. If true, it was Jim's appreciation of the profound, given Gordon's working paper, that caused two very

R.D. Congleton (✉)
BB&T Professor of Economics, West Virginia University,
1601 University Avenue, Morgantown, WV 26506, USA
e-mail: roger.congleton@mail.wvu.edu

D.R. Lee (ed.), *Public Choice, Past and Present: The Legacy of James M. Buchanan and Gordon Tullock*, Studies in Public Choice 28, DOI 10.1007/978-1-4614-5909-5_3,

bright and busy men to write a path-breaking book that created an entirely new methodology for constitutional analysis. Both men were prominent scholars before the book was written, but it was the *Calculus* that made both men famous.

Underappreciation of one's own ideas seems often to be the case with Gordon, although not because of an excess of modesty.[1] Rather, it seems more because he is so busy showing how existing arguments can be rebutted and/or improved that he does not take the time to think very long or deeply about his own contributions. Gordon generates so many new ideas that he does not have time to evaluate them fully before moving on to the next. Indeed, that is partly what makes Gordon's work so interesting to read. Tantalizing nuggets and half-baked thoughts interweave with profound ideas every few pages. (Of course, readers will often disagree about which is which, but most of his readers recognize both Tullock's creativity and his ability to deliver penetrating insights.)

In this short chapter, let me point out two of many instances in which his analysis appears to be more profound than Gordon appreciates.

Missing Generalizations of the Rent-Seeking Contest Success Function

The first example is another paper that demonstrates the importance of the rules of the game, namely, Tullock's 1980 paper on "Efficient Rent Seeking." In 1980, Robert Tollison (with Buchanan and Tullock) assembled a collection of papers on rent seeking that included both "classics" papers and new research. In Buchanan et. al. (1980), Tullock's second paper on rent seeking criticizes his own classic 1967 "full dissipation" model, arguing that it is really a special case, rather than the general one suggested in his 1967 paper.[2] The extent of dissipation, it turns out, is not always 100%, but is shown to vary with the number of participants and the technologies applied.

His characterization of rent-seeking contests as lottery games has become known as the Tullock contest success function (or simply as the Tullock payoff function). The lottery representation provides a powerful and simple mathematical

[1] This conclusion is based on several decades of conversations and arguments with Gordon Tullock. I took Gordon's graduate public choice course at Virginia Polytechnic University in 1976, where Gordon was, in his own way, very generous with students. He was my colleague at George Mason University many years later for more than a decade.

I was the director of the Center for Study of Public Choice when Gordon returned to George Mason University in 1999. Upon his arrival, I invited Gordon to join my Friday "visitor's lunch," which he did nearly every week until he retired. As a consequence, the visitor's lunch rapidly became Tullock's lunch, as the Center for Study of Public Choice's visiting scholars and I were challenged and entertained by Gordon's wry humor, insights, and argumentative style of discourse.

[2] It bears noting that Hillman and Samat (1987) and Hillman and Katz (1987) show that the original Tullock (1967) complete dissipation case is more general than it appears if contest prizes are always awarded to the high bidder.

representation of the contest among rent seekers. It has an equally simple (although far from obvious) Nash equilibrium that can be used to characterize the extent to which participants will invest in a given rent-seeking contest. It rapidly became one of the most widely used models for analyzing rent-seeking and other contests. Together the game and equilibrium allow theorists, including Tullock, to say a good deal about the extent to which resources tend to be invested in winner-take-all contests by rational participants in settings where the winner is not necessarily the high bidder.

Given prize Π and personal effort R_i costing C per unit, the expected net rents, R^e, are:

$$R_i^e = [(R_i)/\Sigma R_j]\,\Pi - R_i C$$

At the Nash equilibrium, player i's competitive effort (and that of i's rivals) is:

$$R_i{**} = [(N-1)/N^2][\Pi/C]$$

And the total resources invested are:

$$(NC)R_i{**} = [(N-1)/N]\Pi$$

Both the model and the equilibria of such contests have a variety of broad implications. Among the properties developed by Tullock (1980) are that total investments and deadweight loss increase with the number of contestants and with economies of scale. In the simple case developed above, the full dissipation case occurs as N approaches infinity. The theoretical literature inspired by Tullock's paper shows that similar conclusions can often be reached for somewhat more complex contests. The applied literature suggests that the contest and rent-seeking concepts can be used to analyze a wide variety of social settings. (Congleton, Hillman, and Konrad provide a thorough overview of those conclusions, and others linked to his first paper in *40 Years of Research on Rent Seeking* published in 2008.)

However, several profound conceptual features of the game and equilibrium seem to have passed by largely unnoticed. For example, the Austrian critique of the neoclassical economic paradigm suggests that the usual model of competition does not really characterize competition per se. In the usual model, there are no resources devoted to competition and no competitive activity that persons engage in. Rather, competition is normally characterized by mere numbers of persons engaged in the activity of interest (usually buying or selling).

Clearly, mere numbers are not sufficient to characterize competition in any meaningful sense. For example, a Greyhound bus depot with thousands of passengers and dozens of sales agents is not a competitive market in any normal sense of the word, although there are lots of participants buying tickets and passing through the depot's hallways and doors and lots of buses leaving for many towns. With the exception of an occasional mishap in seat assignment or crowded passageway, there is no conflict and no rivalry. Similarly, the number of persons standing on a tennis court is not a very good indicator of the competitiveness of a particular set of tennis. Indeed in that case when there are more than 2 or 4 persons on court, the competitiveness of the tennis match normally diminishes, rather than increases.

The Tullock contest has two indices of competition: the number of players and the level of investments made in the contest. The latter is an excellent indicator of the intensity of the competitive process. The commitment made to the contest (R_i**) captures far more of the ordinary meaning of the term competition than the number of players. It also bears noting that the outcomes of Gordon's competitive contests are stochastic; as a consequence, "the best man or organization does not necessarily win," regardless of his or her effort level.

Because of its clear and tractable structure and equilibrium, the Tullock contest success function (and the rent-seeking contest itself) when properly generalized provides a natural vehicle for thinking about the intensity and net benefits of competition under alternative rules.

The equilibrium outcomes of Gordon's game challenge a number of intuitions and conclusions used by economists, social Darwinians, and biologists: *Competition is not always good.* In the contests that Gordon focuses on, competition reduces social welfare (increases social deadweight loss). His examples include two interest group activities: efforts to obtain monopoly privileges and predictive tariffs. It also includes one private example: efforts to steal private property. In all three cases, the greater the efforts, the lower are social net benefits. The private case implies that rent-seeking losses are not products of government policies alone.

Investments in contests in which resources are merely transferred from one person to another, or in which ordinary (Harberger) deadweight losses are produced, tend to reduce social welfare. Resources are consumed, but little or nothing of value is produced. The more resources invested in such contests, the smaller social welfare (in the social net benefit sense) tends to be. Competition in such cases is a "bad," rather than a good. Such results undercut naive libertarian, liberal, economic, and biological arguments that "openness is always good" and "competition is always good."

Whether competition is good or bad depends on the rules of the game. *The rules of the game matter.* Excluding entry to contests that produce net losses can be socially advantageous, as can limiting the use of resources in such contests. Blocking entry in unproductive contests and/or limiting competition tends to increase social welfare, rather than reduce it.

The usual conclusions about openness and competition rely on implicit assumptions about the types of rules in place for the game of interest. Some forms of competition are good because they are framed by what might be called "efficiency-enhancing" rules. That many, perhaps most, forms of market competition are value increasing is strongly indicated by a variety of economic models. However, the benefits of price and quality competition cannot be taken for granted; rather, they vary with the rules of the contest. Both fraud and theft must be curtailed to reach the conclusion that consumers benefit more than firms lose from competition for their favor. Similarly, some, but not all, forms of political competition are also good, because public policies are improved by them, rather than worsened.

These points are not directly discussed or emphasized in Tullock's 1980 paper or in much of the rent-seeking literature, but Tullock's analysis of the lottery model makes it clear that the rules and technologies for seeking a prize (rents) clearly matter: They affect the level of resources committed, the types of resources committed, and how they are used by competitors. Essentially all competitive contests consume resources, but not all of them are wasteful.

The losses from rent-seeking activities arise for three reasons: The process used to influence one's probability of winning a prize (or share of a prize) is costly. Equilibrium efforts (investments) are greater than zero. Those efforts produce zero or negative net value (negative externalities) for those outside the contest. Other contests neglected in Gordon's papers and most of the rent-seeking literature generate external benefits, as with contests for patents, market share, scientific breakthroughs, and major sporting events. In such contests, the process used to increase one's probability of success generates value directly or indirectly for others outside the contests of interests (for other producers, for consumers, for future generations, etc.).

Much of the rent-seeking literature stresses the redistributive consequences of such political games, but not all contests are redistributive in the narrow zero-sum sense of the word. Nonetheless, in such cases, both for those in and outside the game of interest may benefit when investments in rent seeking are reduced. In the standard Tullock contest, a uniform reduction in competitive effort frees resources for other uses without reducing any player's probability of winning the prize.

Revolutionary Pessimism

Tullock's interest in conflict, rather than cooperation, led him to focus on a wide range of topics normally outside the range of economics: criminal law, anarchy, revolution, bureaucracy, and science itself. In nearly every case, Tullock's work is original, insightful, and penetrating. And, it can be argued again that his insights are often more profound than appreciated by Gordon himself. His somewhat depressing work on popular revolution (1971, 1974) is used below as a second illustration.

There is a long tradition in America and elsewhere that popular revolutions can and do happen with some regularity. The masses rise up and throw out the tyrants. Many movies and historical narratives rely on such events to motivate great historical changes. Here, one may note that the various wars of succession waged in North and South America are often termed revolutions. In such cases, it is often argued that political revolutions have occurred because a popular revolt has caused one system of government to be replaced by another.

The term revolution is also applied to science and to technological advance, although with a somewhat different meaning. A revolution may also be said to occur when one theory is replaced by a new one or some new production technique radically reduces the cost of production and so makes natural resources more useful and outputs more widely available. Indeed, a series of such improvements may also be termed a revolution, as with the Industrial Revolution of the nineteenth century. Note that this use of the term revolution may involve rather modest changes.

However, the use of the term revolution, as applied to politics, tends to imply radical change. For example, the *Merriam-Webster Dictionary* defines political revolutions as "a fundamental change in political organization, especially, the overthrow or renunciation of one government or ruler and the substitution of another by the governed." Note that there are several important parts to this definition: "fundamental" meaning large or major changes, "overthrow" suggesting violence or at least the threat of violence, and "by the governed" suggesting that a broad range of citizens participate in the revolution.

Tullock's paper on revolution (1971) and his short books on the *Social Dilemma* (1974) and Autocracy (1987) argue that popular revolutions are essentially impossible and therefore extremely rare. Collective action problems and the efforts of those already in power to resist being overthrown imply that few if any popular revolutions will get off the ground. Tullock uses his theory to explain why dictatorships, rather than democracies, are historically the most common form of government.

As commonplace in Gordon's work, a breathtaking (ingenious) series of simplifying assumptions allows him to cut to the core of a variety of fundamental issues. There are two key assumptions: The first is simply an application of Olson's logic of collective action. Organizing a revolution that broadly supports the interests of ordinary persons (e.g., those not already in government) is a public good problem because the activity of producing a revolution is privately costly and the benefits are diffuse and realized both by those who do and do not participate in the revolt. Potential revolutionaries will free ride rather than participate. As a consequence, revolutions will not emerge spontaneously.

This is not to say that popular revolts are impossible, only that they will not occur spontaneously. They require organizations of some kind. It bears noting that the facts are largely, although not entirely, consistent with this conclusion. In most revolutions, as in the case of the recent Egyptian revolts, there is a significant organization (the Muslim Brotherhood) that encourages revolutionaries to turn up at certain times in certain places and behave in certain ways (armed or not, signs, etc.).

Gordon's more profound insight is that revolutions are not simply one-sided events organized by revolutionary cadres. A well-functioning state can head off revolutions in a variety of ways. Many proponents of revolutionary theories suggest that an authoritarian state may do so by being a productive state, that is, a state that produces many desired public services. Tullock, following Machiavelli, suggests that authoritarian states can often avoid being overthrown by being repressive, rather than productive.

Taking Olson's argument in a new direction, Tullock suggests that authoritarians may avoid revolution by *increasing collective action problems* for revolutionaries. That is, collective action problems are not entirely determined by exogenous organizational costs, as assumed by Olson (1965). Many of those costs are endogenous and so can be manipulated by government to make collective action problems more difficult for their opponents and less so for their supporters.

Authoritarian governments reduce the likelihood of popular revolts in a number of ways, including the use of spies and secret police; imposing severe punishments on revolutionary publications, participants, and organizers; and organizing demonstrations that indicate "broad" support for their regimes. All these steps make revolutions less likely by increasing collective action problems. Tullock does not point out the connection to Olson explicitly but notes that revolutionary activity can be suppressed by increasing the costs of revolting.

The latter helps explain why tyrannical regimes tend to be more robust than popular revolt theories suggest. He also suggests that "palace coups" are more difficult to discourage and so far more common than "revolutions." This, in turn, implies that authoritarian institutions are more stable than the persons occupying seats in the upper echelons of government.

In this case, it is clear that Gordon understands the importance of his contribution to constitutional political economy, if not to the broader issues that concern collective action in general. And his arguments should be, but have not been, taken into account by the revolution-driven literature on constitutional reform that has emerged in the past decade or so (Acemoglu and Robinson 2005), which ignores collective action problems. So, his theory of counter-revolutionary policies remains relevant and provides a persuasive explanation for an important historical phenomenon (the prevalence of dictatorship or at least nondemocratic states) neglected by much revolution-based research.

His theory can also be criticized in various ways. For example, dictators may differ in important ways neglected in his analysis (Wintrobe 1990, 1998), or they may have more complex internal structures than assumed by Tullock (Bueno de Mesquita et al. 2004; Congleton 2011). But these can be taken into account without significantly affecting Tullock's main conclusions.

His broader point about the role of government decisions for organizational theory and related issues concerning economic and political freedom has also received less attention than it deserves from others (and by Tullock himself). That collective action problems are partially endogenous has broad implications that are not articulated in his work on revolution or elsewhere (as far as I know). Olson also mentions such endogeneity in passing but fails to focus much attention on it or on the incentives for government officials to actively encourage and discourage various forms of collective action.

Yet, it seems clear that both democratic and authoritarian governments have good reasons to encourage antirevolutionary and other status quo–preserving collective activities (e.g., demonstrations in support of national holidays, leaders, and policies) that encourage law-abiding behavior—what Wintrobe terms loyalty-building activities. Moreover, the endogenous component of organizational costs has broad implications for both market and governmental stability and evolution. Civil and constitutional law both affect the extent and kind of collective action that we observe in a wide variety of economic, political, and religious areas of life. They do so by affecting the costs (and benefits) realized by all sorts of organizations, not simply revolutionary and politically active interest groups.

Indeed, the manipulation of organizational costs may be said to determine the extent to which individuals are "free to choose" as well as "free to organize." Again, as indicated by the rent-seeking case, complete freedom to organize may cause problems. Rent-seeking organizations should be discouraged to avoid social losses. However, the formation of organizations that produce net benefits should be encouraged by reducing their collective action costs. Groups lobbying for peaceful reforms may improve public policies, but it is not obvious or easy how to encourage the latter but discourage rent-seeking groups or whether this should be done in every case. It bears noting that corporate law attempts to both encourage the formation of productive enterprises and constrain them in a manner that reduces the ability of corporate governments to extract rents from their stockholders (through rules on fiduciary interests).

That liberty itself is partly endogenous is acknowledged by all students of government; that liberty in the long run is substantially the result of manipulating the costs of collective action is not nearly as widely understood.

Is Underappreciation of the Profound a Problem?

Buchanan in his Nobel speech (1986) spoke eloquently about how equality before the law tends to increase both economic and political efficiency. By doing so, with quotes from Wicksell, he was both honoring his hosts and connecting modern constitutional political economy with the liberalism of the nineteenth century. This ability to recognize the profound, the essential, and the enduring is one of Buchanan's great strengths as a political economist.

Gordon, on the other hand, somehow seems to lack this perspective, and so many of his truly profound observations pass unnoticed by his readers (and evidently himself), because he does not emphasize them. Yet, his creative, contrarian approach to social science has generated an impressive body of work that includes numerous original insights and much that is profound. That work can be argued to have begun with the *Calculus of Consent.* It clearly continues through his work on rent seeking, anarchy, and the law.

In this short piece, I have suggested that Tullock has made more profound contributions to constitutional political economy and other related fields than he is recognized for, in part because he himself has failed to recognize them. Gordon is not self-consciously pursuing the profound but simply pushing out the frontiers of knowledge in as many directions as occur to him, more or less as rapidly as possible for a very insightful active man. Carefully integrating his research and plumbing its depths has largely been left to others.

This is not entirely a loss for his readers or for the fields of research in which he has engaged. It can be argued that by pressing on with his research, rather than carefully working out the implications of a few key ideas, he has produced a far larger body of interesting research than would have been produced had he self-consciously attempted to plumb the profound. Although Tullock occasionally waxes philosophically, he normally simply attempts to amaze and confound those engaged in more conventional work. He does so by showing how many implicit assumptions (and blinders) conventional work has relied on.

Now that Gordon's work has itself become conventional, perhaps it is time to see what blinders and implicit assumptions have grounded his work. In some cases, this will lead us to honor his work for being more penetrating—more profound—than he seems to have understood. This chapter has provided a few examples in which this may prove to be the case. In others, his work may prove to be wrong in significant ways, and research will head off in entirely new directions as his assumptions are replaced with different or less restrictive ones. However, much in his work is likely to prove both correct and very durable because it is more deeply grounded than it may appear on first impression.

Fortunately for the rest of us, even after Gordon's and Jim's extensive research on constitutional issues, there are many questions that remain, many of which are latent in their great bodies of research. The institutions examined in the *Calculus* were the mid-twentieth-century American ones, which had long functioned tolerably well. Their work attempted to show why that was the case. On the other hand, a few years later, Tullock's work on rent seeking suggested that not all is well with American governance.

Clearly, both cannot be entirely true. If rent seeking (interest group politics) is omnipresent and very costly, how did we get such good institutions and so many reasonably good policies, rather than the efficient rent-extracting machines that one might have anticipated?

Even though Jim and Gordon provided us with much that may prove essentially final upon further reflection and investigation, much of their work needs extension, review, and correction. As Jim has often been heard to say, "onward and upward."

References

Acemoglu D, Robinson JA (2005) Economic origins of dictatorship and democracy. Cambridge University Press, Cambridge

Buchanan JM, Tullock G (1962) The calculus of consent, logical foundations of constitutional democracy. University of Michigan Press, Ann Arbor

Buchanan JM, Tollison RD, Tullock G (eds) (1980) Towards a theory of the rent-seeking society. Texas A & M Press, College Station

Bueno de Mesquita B, Smith A, Siverson RM, Morrow JD (2004) The logic of political survival. MIT Press, Cambridge, MA

Congleton RD (2011) Perfecting parliament: constitutional reform, liberalism, and the rise of western democracy. Cambridge University Press, Cambridge, MA

Congleton RD, Hillman AL, Konrad K (2008) 40 years of rent seeking research, vol 2. Springer, Heidelberg

Hillman AL, Samet D (1987) Dissipation of contestable rents by small numbers of contenders. Public Choice 54:63–82 (also reprinted in Congleton, Hillman, and Konrad 2008)

Hillman AL, Katz E (1987) Structure and the social costs of bribes and transfers. J Pub Econ 34:129–42 (also reprinted in Congleton, Hillman, and Konrad 2008)
Olson M (1965) The logic of collective action. Harvard University Press, Cambridge, MA
Tullock G (1967) The welfare costs of tariffs, monopolies, and theft. Econ Inq 5:224–32 (also reprinted in Congleton, Hillman, and Konrad 2008)
Tullock G (1971) The paradox of revolution. Public Choice 11:88–99
Tullock G (1974) The social dilemma: the economics of war and revolution. University Publications, Blacksburg
Tullock G (1980) Efficient rent seeking. In: Buchanan JM, Tollison RD, Tullock G (eds) Toward a theory of the rent-seeking society. A&M Press, College Park (also reprinted in Congleton, Hillman, and Konrad 2008)
Tullock G (1987) Autocracy. Martinus Nijhoff, Dordrecht
Wintrobe R (1990) The tinpot and the totalitarian: an economic theory of dictatorship. Am Polit Sci Rev 84:849–872
Wintrobe R (1998) The political economy of dictatorship. Cambridge University Press, New York/Cambridge, UK

Chapter 4
Buchanan on Freedom

Geoffrey Brennan and Michael Brooks

Apologia

The occasion for this chapter is the fiftieth anniversary of the publication of Buchanan and Tullock's *Calculus of Consent*. However, that work will not represent the primary object of our attention here. We shall instead be concerned with 'liberty' and specifically with Buchanan's thoughts on this subject—essentially because liberty is expressly mentioned in much of Buchanan's work (even though, as we shall argue, his treatment of it remains tantalisingly elliptical).[1]

In choosing this topic, we ought to confess at the outset to an independent research agenda of our own. And it may help to locate our concerns to explain something of the nature and origins of that agenda.

One of the legacies of the behavioural economics 'revolution'[2] has been an interest in a variety of so-called 'soft' policy instruments—instruments that depend for their effects on certain systematic 'irrationalities' in people's behaviour (framing

[1] This should not be taken as in any way denying the distinctive qualities of Tullock's genius. It is, however, simply a fact that Tullock's work is much less directly focused on liberty than Buchanan's is.

[2] Just how much of a 'revolution' the behavioural move represents is a debatable question. But that debate is not one we enter here.

G. Brennan (✉)
Philosophy Program, Research School of Social Sciences, Australian National University, Canberra, ACT 0200, Australia

Political Science Department, Duke University, Durham, NC, USA

Philosophy Department, University of North Carolina-Chapel Hill, Chapel Hill, NC, USA
e-mail: geoffrey.brennan@anu.edu.au

M. Brooks
School of Economics and Finance, University of Tasmania, PO Box 85, Hobart, Tasmania 7001, Australia
e-mail: Michael.Brooks@utas.edu.au

D.R. Lee (ed.), *Public Choice, Past and Present: The Legacy of James M. Buchanan and Gordon Tullock*, Studies in Public Choice 28, DOI 10.1007/978-1-4614-5909-5_4,

effects, anchoring biases and the like). Part of the justification for reliance on soft policies involves the claim that, in many instances, these soft policies are more friendly to liberty than their 'hard' alternatives (like taxes and subsidies)—hence, the idea that 'libertarian paternalism is not an oxymoron'. But whether soft policies are indeed more accommodating to the requirements of liberty is a somewhat tricky question, and one that has generated its share of controversy. To analyse that question would seem to require not just a better understanding of how exactly soft policies operate (and whether indeed their 'softness' is all of the same type) but also a clear conception of how liberty is properly to be understood and what exactly its requirements are. Of course, much of the latter work might be finessed if it could be shown that liberty was systematically related to other more familiar normative concepts in the economist's kitbag. And so the particular question of how liberty and Pareto optimality relate is one piece of this larger agenda. As it turns out, the systematic analysis of policies (and actions and institutions) in terms of a normative scheme that includes liberty *as such* as an independent value is a demanding exercise and frankly is still in its infancy.

Buchanan is an obvious resource in this connection. Two of his books bear 'liberty' in their titles—the 1975 *Limits of Liberty* and the 1977 collection *Freedom in Constitutional Contract*.[3] Moreover, Buchanan is clearly one of the most interesting and thoughtful exponents of the Pareto framework in modern economics. In that sense, it is natural for us to look to Buchanan's writings to help us sort out our own ideas about freedom/liberty and how freedom/liberty fits into a broader constitutional contractarian scheme.

Even this more modest task is daunting. Buchanan's *Collected Works* run to 20 volumes, and those volumes cover only the work written before 2000. Some of Buchanan's writings since that time have been concerned with his attitude towards and conception of liberty—and we will want to include that more recent material. We will deal mainly with the work that seems to us most relevant, but there is clearly a danger of omission or misrepresentation and/or of bending Buchanan's views to suit our own prejudices. In that spirit, caveat emptor.

Introduction

If one were to ask where to locate Jim Buchanan in the standard catalogue of political positions, we think the answer would be clear enough. Certainly, he self-identifies as a classical liberal, as his most recent collection of articles (with its subtitle *The Normative Vision of Classical Liberalism*) makes totally clear. When, for example, he describes the 2002 London meetings of the Mont Pelerin Society[4] as a 'gathering

[3] For the purposes of the current exercise, we shall treat 'liberty' and 'freedom' as interchangeable terms for the same concept. Perhaps, this usage does violence to certain subtleties, but we think that it is obedient at least to Buchanan's practice.

of the clan' (or perhaps of the 'tribe'), it is clear that this tribe is one to which he sees himself as belonging. And it is also clear that, for him, the defining feature of the 'gathering' lies in its classical liberal commitments, and specifically *not* its conservative ones.[5]

Of course, Buchanan is a classical liberal of a somewhat distinctive stripe. For one thing, the normative position with which he is most clearly associated amongst those who know his work is 'constitutional contractarianism'—so there is a natural question as to whether he sees this constitutional contractarianism as deriving from his classical liberalism (or perhaps vice versa). Moreover, he concedes that popular perceptions of his political commitments may diverge from how he sees them himself. As he puts it (Buchanan (2001 [1992]), p. 26):

> ...the public's image of me ... is that of a right-wing libertarian zealot who is anti-democratic, anti-egalitarian and anti-scientific. [But,] I am... none of these things... Properly understood my position is both democratic and egalitarian, and I am as much a scientist as any of my peers in economics.

In the egalitarian connection, for example, he carries a strong distaste for second- and later-generation wealth—is indeed a supporter of essentially confiscatory estate duties (and presumably analogous gift duties). In a late essay (2005, p. 101), he defines classical liberalism by reference to a 'predisposition'[6] the characteristic feature of which is indeed egalitarian:

> by a 'liberal predisposition' I refer specifically to an attitude in which others are viewed as moral equals and thereby deserving of equal respect, consideration and ultimately equal treatment.[7]

And he has consistently declared a 'strong affinity' (Buchanan 2005, p. 100) with the work of John Rawls and identified the Rawlsian project as close to his own 'although our two efforts have been interpreted quite differently' (Buchanan 2005, p. 100).

Taking Buchanan's classical liberalism as given, one might expect that Buchanan's work might begin with a clear definition of liberty and proceed to spell out the implications of that definition for institutional arrangements. But that is not how Buchanan proceeds. If some clear definition is required as to how liberty is to be understood (and measured, at least in broad comparative terms), we think it fair to say that Buchanan does not provide it. He does make strong claims about what is *necessary* for the realisation of freedom/liberty—but that is on the face of things a downstream question.

---

[4] In Buchanan (2005), p. 62.

[5] Much of Buchanan (2005) is concerned to distinguish classical liberalism from conservatism and to allow Buchanan to identify himself firmly with the former position.

[6] And interestingly, not an institutional order.

[7] The Kantian redolence of this statement is notable and further evidence of the Rawlsian 'affinity'. See Kliemt (2011) for a more extended discussion of the Kantian elements of the Buchanan project.

Consider, for example, Buchanan's introduction to the collection *Freedom in Constitutional Contract* (Buchanan 1977, p. x):

> Individuals can secure and retain freedom in constitutional contract; they cannot do so in any other way. This statement summarizes my argument in this book and elsewhere. But what sort of freedom? And what kind of constitutional contract? These are relevant and important questions, but they are not answered here. Before we can begin to approach such questions, it is necessary to lay the ground rules for discourse and it is to this purpose that my efforts here are devoted.

And in a later essay in the same book (Buchanan 1977, p. 288):

> There should be relatively little dispute about the proposition that individual freedom, in any meaningful sense, is possible only under law, along with the implied consequence that the rules, "the law", must be enforced by some collective entity, some state.

If these remarks are to be taken at face value, we think they have quite strong implications for how liberty is properly to be construed, and our aim in what follows is basically to spell out those implications. But the remarks also reveal something about how Buchanan views his own task in the analysis of freedom—a matter of 'setting the ground rules for discourse', of creeping up on the central issue of freedom somewhat indirectly.

We shall by necessity follow suit. We will here be concerned with four questions, on which we think Buchanan's work throws interesting light:

1. Is liberty intrinsically social?
2. What is the status of 'anarchy' in Buchanan's liberal scheme?
3. At the individual level, what is the relation between exchange and liberty?
4. At the collective level, what is the relation between unanimity, majority rule and liberty?

Our engagement with these questions forms the five substantive sections of this chapter. Section "A Tentative Summing Up" offers a brief conclusion.

Liberty in/Through Society?

In the two quotations provided, Buchanan tells us (a) that individuals *can* secure freedom through constitutional contract and (b) that they can *only* do so in that way.

It is not totally clear whether these are empirical or conceptual claims. If empirical, the idea could be that, though we might imagine individuals enjoying greater freedom in some circumstance other than 'through constitutional contract', such circumstances are simply infeasible. Such circumstances are not accessible to people of 'our kind'.[8]

[8] In general, Buchanan's work is obedient to a foundational principle that the analyst should eschew all 'romance' and treat people as they are (and laws as they might be). However, to the extent that the liberal order requires a significant number of individuals to hold the 'liberal predisposition' already mentioned, he seems to retreat from the 'antiromantic' method.

If conceptual, the idea would be that, at the basic level, freedom/liberty is intrinsically an objective to be pursued in association with others. Some normative concepts have this character—they are intrinsically relational. Equality is an example, so, perhaps relatedly, is 'justice'. Imagine, for example, Robinson Crusoe on his island (before Friday's arrival). We cannot speak of Crusoe acting 'justly' or living under 'conditions of justice', because there is no one to be just to—no one with whom Crusoe's relations can exhibit justice.

Perhaps, liberty is like justice and equality in this respect that, as it were, the properly specified *domain* of 'liberty' is alternative institutional arrangements under which the interactions between individuals exhibit the right 'free' character, rather than free individuals as such. If that is so, then it raises a conceptual problem in discussing freedom in the Robinson Crusoe economy. One might think that individuals *could* be free in isolation—and indeed, that Crusoe on his island is by definition free simply because he is not and cannot be coerced by any other agent. On the other hand, if noncoercive *relations* are thought of as the essence of liberty, then Crusoe cannot enjoy noncoercive relations because he enjoys no relations at all.

It is important to note that the idea of liberty as noncoercive relations rules out the idea of liberty as 'freedom from interference'—at least unless 'interference' is given a thick normative interpretation. Put another way, we would need some principled way of distinguishing between 'interference' and 'interdependence' if we are to define liberty in non-interference terms. When Friday arrives to share the island with Crusoe, there becomes scope for a degree of specialisation and attendant mutual benefits from exchange. Friday and Crusoe become thereby mutually dependent: actions undertaken (or not) by Friday influence Crusoe's well-being. If Friday decides not to go fishing on a particular day, this can leave Crusoe worse off than Crusoe would otherwise be. In that sense, Friday's decision has 'interfered' with Crusoe. In the absence of some fairly heavy duty concept like 'rights', it is not easy to see how one can distinguish between actions by Friday that reduce Crusoe's liberty and those that do not.

When the interdependence is writ large—when Crusoe, Friday and thousands of others are knit together in the kind of large-scale trading nexus that Adam Smith envisages as 'commercial society' [say in Chap. 1 of *The Wealth of Nations*]—each individual will be dependent on 'the assistance and cooperation of many thousands' for 'what we very falsely imagine, [is] the easy and simple manner in which he is commonly accommodated' (1976 [1776], I.i.11). Yet, precisely because each is so heavily dependent on others, he is vulnerable to changes in those others' behaviour. So when Mr Duke contracts with the inventor of a machine that makes 'ready-rolled' cigarettes, he thereby renders obsolete the human capital acquired by the workers who hand-rolled cigarettes. Schumpeter was right to see that the free market order is a process of 'creative destruction',[9] and though the victims of that

[9] But it is wrong not to acknowledge Smith as the obvious source of the underlying logic. Indeed, it is ironic that Schumpeter was rather dismissive of Smith's role in the history of economic thought, since it is the 'human capital' aspects of Smith's account of markets that supplies Schumpeter with his most obvious examples of market 'destructiveness'.

'destruction' may not have had their rights violated, they are surely made worse off. Dependence implies vulnerability to the actions of others. And if our definitions of 'interference' involve actions by one person that leave another worse off, then individuals are indeed 'interfered with' in market process. Duke and his inventor colleague may not have violated any rules of market conduct, but between them their actions certainly leave some others worse off.

We shall have cause to return to some of the questions raised by these observations in later sections. At this point, we want to offer a clarification. To say that freedom is first and foremost a property of institutions is not to deny that freedom is enjoyed by individuals. When Buchanan talks of 'free institutions', the institutions are deliverers of freedom to the individuals who operate within them, not independent bearers of freedom. A free society is one whose *subjects* are free—not one that is, in some Hegelian sense, *itself* free. Nevertheless, the individuals are connected via social structures—not isolated. In Buchanan's view, '[e]conomics is, or should be, about individual behaviour *in society*' (Brennan and Buchanan 1985, p. 1, emphasis added).[10] In this sense, we think the picture of freedom in terms of 'non-coercive social relations' makes most sense of Buchanan's position. If, as Buchanan claims, an essential feature of classical liberalism is, indeed, a disposition to see others as moral equals, then the presence of those others is an intrinsic feature of the concept.[11] This in itself may not tell us a great deal substantively: we still have to flesh out what is meant by coercion. But it does serve to establish that liberty is intrinsically a social concept and that there is no one-to-one connection between liberty and independence from others.[12]

The Status of Anarchy

Buchanan's most extended and most explicit treatment of freedom/liberty is that developed in *The Limits of Liberty,* and the conceptual framework in that book relies heavily on a constructed contrast between anarchy and civic order. Accordingly,

[10] This remark follows immediately on observations about the limits of appeals to 'Robinson Crusoe' analogues.

[11] To say, this is not to claim that sometimes securing reduced dependence among persons may not be a mechanism for securing greater liberty. What it is to deny is that securing greater independence is *prima facie* to secure greater liberty. The identification of liberty with social independence is, on this view (our own), just a mistake. And we think the best interpretation of Buchanan endorses that view. However, the case is not entirely crystal clear. In the Preface to *Limits of Liberty,* he remarks that 'men and women … want to be free but… recognize the inherent limits that social interdependence places on them' [1975, p. xv], suggesting that social interdependence does indeed restrict freedom.

[12] To reject the Crusoe possibility in relation to liberty is to meet one aspect of Philip Pettit's (1997) critique of conventional classical liberalism. In fact, Buchanan's definition of the 'liberal predisposition' suggests that he might be sympathetic to some aspects of Pettit's alternative 'republican' version—though to explore this possibility would carry us well beyond the scope of this chapter.

Buchanan's picture of the status of freedom in anarchy presents itself as a natural point from which to explore his understanding of freedom more broadly.

Buchanan offers, as a kind of point of departure, the following remark: 'To the individualist, the ideal or utopian world is necessarily anarchistic in some basic philosophical sense' [Buchanan 1975, p. 2]. Since Buchanan has in the previous pages identified *himself* as an individualist, it is reasonable to interpret anarchy as descriptive of Buchanan's *own* 'ideal or utopian world' (though it is not exactly clear what work the 'basic philosophical sense' proviso is doing). Moreover, it soon becomes clear what it is about anarchy that is attractive:

> This world is peopled exclusively by persons who respect the minimal set of behavioural norms dictated by mutual tolerance and respect. Individuals remain free to "do their own things" within such limits, and cooperative ventures are exclusively voluntary. Persons retain freedom to opt out of any sharing arrangements which they might join. No man holds coercive power over any other man and there is no impersonal bureaucracy, military or civil, that imposes external constraint. (Buchanan 1975, pp. 2–3)

In this situation, individuals are, so the encomium goes, entirely 'free'. But immediately, Buchanan proceeds to distance himself from this 'ideal'. Although

> "the anarchist utopia" has a "lingering attractiveness", that attractiveness "must be acknowledged" to be "spurious.... Little more than casual reflection is required ... to suggest that the whole idea is a conceptual mirage." (1975, p. 3)

Conceptual mirage? Buchanan's arguments are as much pragmatic as conceptual. The relevant considerations are as follows: that individuals are extremely unlikely to exercise the forbearance that such an order requires; that despite the many arenas in which human interactions operate in obedience to rules without external enforcement, deep disputes are bound to arise in the absence of formal dispute resolution processes (with enforcement teeth) and these disputes are likely to create violence; and so on. The anarchy 'utopia' will, on such grounds, predictably descend into the Hobbesian war of all against all.[13] As we say, these are empirical claims. However, Buchanan does hint at a more conceptual argument. The thought is that, in anarchy, it is not so much that rights are *violated* as that there *are* no rights.

[13] Recent work on the economics of anarchy suggests the possibility that there may be more order under anarchy than depicted under the Hobbesian viewpoint. Eighteenth-century pirates (see Leeson 2009, Chap. 3 for details), for example, created constitutional contracts that created order on the high seas, at least for some. We are not aware of what Buchanan makes of such research. Perhaps one can recognise that on board the pirate ships there was not a war against all—that it is not too romantic to observe that significant amounts of order are possible without the formal apparatus of government.

But that observation overlooks the obvious point that the pirates set out to prey on the crew and resources of other ships. Freedom of entry on the part of individuals to form a pirate crew does not extend to freedom of exit on the part of the prey. In short, the order under the pirates is not a liberal order that extended to all. Nevertheless, the research does raise interesting questions. See, for example, Leeson and Coyne (2012).

> Without some definition of boundaries or limits on the set of rights to do things and/or exclude others from doing things, an individual as such could scarcely be said to exist. (Buchanan 1975, p. 15)[14]

For someone taking an 'individualist' point of departure, this is a significant claim. If rights can only be *defined* in the context of collectively agreed and enforced rules, then the whole idea of an individualist anarchic utopia is misconceived: it is somewhat akin to the fantasy that most of us pursue as children, imagining that we might have been born to other parents, without the realisation that if we had been born to other parents we would not be us!

One might have anxieties too that, in any ordered anarchy, there would be other institutions of enforcement of whatever norms happened to emerge. Regimes of strong conformity might be imposed—with the lynch mob, or the 'tyranny of popular opinion' that so concerned John Stuart Mill, operating in lieu of the institutions of the law. Or perhaps in the spirit of our earlier Crusoe example, people would respond to the presence of others by self-protection, seeking out insulated islands from which all others were totally excluded. Then, individuals would not be coerced, but neither would they or could they enjoy noncoercive relationships. Life may not be quite as 'poor, nasty, brutish and short' as otherwise, but it would surely be 'solitary',[15] and as we argued earlier, liberty as Buchanan takes it to be is meaningless for the totally solitary life!

In a discussion of Hobbes elsewhere,[16] Buchanan seems to concede to Hobbes at least one claim that we think, on his own grounds, Buchanan ought to reject. The Hobbesian proposition is that '*the* state of nature affords maximal natural liberty' (Buchanan and Lomasky 2000 [1984], p. 381). The immediate implication, given Hobbes' diagnosis of life in the state of nature, is that 'the leap into order can be accomplished if people trade-off natural liberty for security'. In this context, a definition of liberty is offered '... as the absence of constraints on the individual's choice among options' (Buchanan and Lomasky 2000 [1984], p. 385).

Now, taken on its face, the definition of liberty as absence of constraint is intrinsically dubious because *all choice is by necessity constrained*: if there were no constraints, choice would be unnecessary—all options would be available. The obvious response to this quibble is to see the constraint-based conception of liberty as a *metric* of liberty: the less constrained the chooser is, the more liberty she has. This notion—what we might term the 'opportunity set' approach to liberty—has received a certain amount of attention in the literature on liberty measurement, and some scholars seem to take it seriously.[17] However, it does not sit easily with the Buchanan

---

[14] For Buchanan, as he earlier puts it, '... there is really no categorical distinction to be made between that set of rights normally referred to as human and those referred to as property' (1975, p. 14).

[15] In Chap. 8 of Leviathan, Hobbes refers to life in the state of anarchy as 'solitary, poor, nasty, brutish and short.' For some reason, many references to this claim seem to register only the final three elements of this lamentable quintet.

[16] In a collaboration with Loren Lomasky. See Buchanan and Lomasky (2000 [1984]), pp. 381–4.

[17] See Pattanaik and Xu (1990); Carter (2004); Sugden (1998, 2006); Dowding (1992); Van Hees and Wissenburg (1999).

conception as elaborated elsewhere. Nor incidentally does it support the liberty/security trade-off claim.

Consider the latter issue first. Given Hobbes' picture (broadly endorsed by Buchanan) of how life in anarchy goes, the opportunity set confronting individuals in the state of nature lies well inside that confronting individuals within a well-ordered society—even one ruled by an arbitrary despot. This indeed seems to be precisely Hobbes' point. So the idea that liberty is maximised in the state of nature—and the related idea that the leap out of the state of nature involves giving up liberty for some other valued thing (order/security/well-being)—simply cannot be sustained on the basis of an opportunity set metric of liberty. To be sure, Buchanan and Lomasky restrict the claim about maximal liberty to '*natural*' liberty—to be distinguished from 'civic' liberty—but it is simply unspecified what 'natural liberty' can be, other than the liberty enjoyed in the state of nature!

Moreover, elsewhere [in *Cost and Choice,* 1969, p. 54], Buchanan implicitly rejects the opportunity set metric. He argues there that a possible advantage of excise taxation over income taxation is the former may give the taxpayer 'greater liberty', in that any individual is 'free' to pay the tax or not in the excise case (and more so than in the income tax case). Setting out the analytics of this case here would involve us in unnecessary complications, but it can be verified that, under aggregate equi-revenue assumptions, the conclusion cannot be established on the basis of opportunity set comparisons.

We think there are, in any case, good independent reasons for rejecting the opportunity set metric. As emphasised by Hayek (1960),[18] infringements of liberty in the political sense can only come from the actions of other humans. The opportunity set metric does not distinguish between constraints imposed by other persons and constraints *simpliciter*. It has the effect of treating, say, bad weather (surely a constraint) as an assault on one's liberty, as if the weather were, on this inclement occasion, exercising 'coercive power' over the agents subject to it. Our own inclinations strongly follow Hayek here. And we believe that in general Buchanan also follows Hayek in this.

If we do reject the opportunity set metric, might there still be some sense in which a Hobbesian state of nature *is* a situation of maximal liberty? One clear possibility here is that the interactions that characterise the Hobbesian state of nature, though they involve general mutual harms, are not *coercion*. In order to have coercion, so the thought might go, one must have prior *rights*: coercion is precisely the violation of those rights. So, no rights means no coercion, and no coercion means no violations of liberty. And if there are no such violations, then individuals are maximally free.

Note though that this line depends on a certain semantic obfuscation. If there are no violations of liberty in the state of nature, there are no instantiations of it either. If liberty is the enjoyment of noncoercive relations, then there is no liberty in the state of nature because noncoercive relations are conceptually impossible.

[18] Though it has a long history in the literature on liberty and claims, many distinguished advocates.

We do not want to become mired down in semantic issues here. But there is a matter of substance at stake. Do 'rights' exist in the state of nature, prior to civil order, or are rights actually constructed *by* civil order? If the former, then there is a meaningful concept of 'natural liberty'; but the interactions that occur in Hobbes' state of nature will involve violations of it. If the latter, then there is a sense in which the state of nature involves zero coercion—but as we have said, it is a pretty uninteresting sense.

There is a related question as to the terms in which 'rights' are conceived—whether as legal (i.e. instantiated in some institutional order), however exactly enforced, or as purely 'moral'. Put another way, the constitutional exercise of making/choosing rules can be thought of either as *constructing* rights, or as fine-tuning and institutionally embedding them. Of course, the distinction is one of degree rather than categorical. The 'moral law' might be a vague shadowy thing whose substance only becomes clear in its institutional instantiation. Or (as most scholars in the 'natural rights' tradition—including Locke specifically had it) the moral law may be fairly clear, and the role of laws and institutional rules is to *enforce* it.

Where in this spectrum Buchanan lies is not always clear. But we think the evidence suggests something pretty close to the constructivist end of the spectrum. Buchanan self-proclaims a kind of moral scepticism,[19] reluctant to offer his own (substantive) normative judgements. As he states, at the outset of *Limits of Liberty* (1975, p. 3):

> Those who seek specific prescriptions of the "good society" will not find them here. A listing of my own private preferences would be both unproductive and uninteresting.

The clear implication is that prescriptions (of the good society) are essentially 'preferences' and that Buchanan's normative judgments have no more status than his (or anyone else's) tastes for apples. There is, we think, some ambiguity here between two different distinctions that might be in play—one relating to the epistemic status of normative judgments (realist vs. nonrealist), and the other relating to 'constitutional' versus 'in-period' prescriptions. We think Buchanan tends to run these two distinctions together and believe that the former is less relevant to his overall position than the latter. In any event, the insistence that 'individual liberty is only possible under law' (and related quotations offered earlier) suggests the constructivist position.

However, we ought to reserve as a placeholder the possibility of two potentially different concepts—'in-period or substantive liberty' (which on our argument presupposes a *moral* theory of substantive rights) and 'constitutional liberty' (under which the domain of normative evaluation concerns the processes applied for constitutional decision-making.) The weight of Buchanan's understanding of classical liberalism is we think heavily oriented towards the latter. But whether he entirely dispenses with the former is an open question which we will want to pursue in what follows.

[19] See, for example, the essays in *Moral Science and Moral Order* vol 17 of the Collected Works.

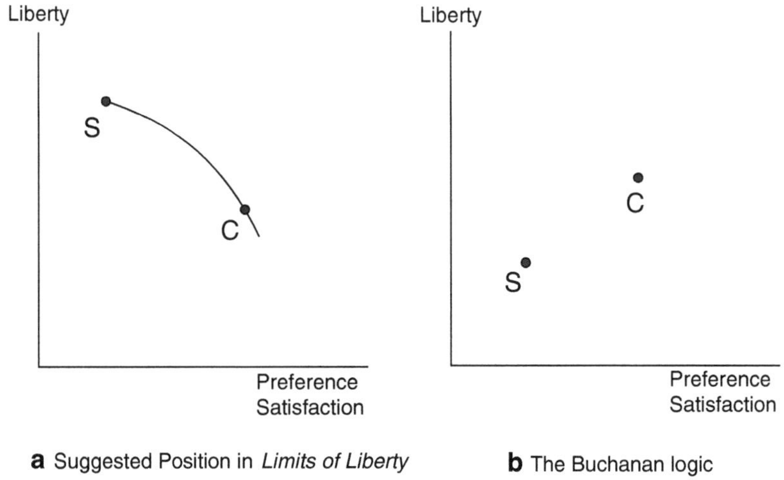

Fig. 4.1 A contrast of expression and underlying logic

In order to underline the differences exposed by our interpretative exercise here, consider Fig. 4.1, which sets out the contrast between Buchanan's position in the *Limits of Liberty*—panel a—with the *logic* of his work on liberty—panel b. The two panels share a common set of axes with liberty on the vertical and the degree of preference satisfaction represented on the horizontal. The status quo for an individual under a thick veil of uncertainty is represented by S, and the outcome expected from the constitutional rules is suggested by C.

A cursory examination of the two panels suggests a stark contrast between the two lines of argument. In panel *a*, there is a trade-off between liberty and preference satisfaction. The notion that there is such a trade-off is perhaps made no more clearly than noting that the subtitle of the *Limits of Liberty* was *Between Anarchy and Leviathan*.[20] Evidently, the stated line of argument in the *Limits* is that a constitutional set of rules lies between the maximal liberty of anarchy and the coercion of a Leviathan government. But our view is that it is panel *b* that represents the relation consistent with Buchanan's account of the nature of liberty. There is no trade-off—the constitutionally chosen set of rules results in the emergence of an economic order that normatively dominates the status quo on both the liberty and preference satisfaction margins. Manifestly, the two visions of the leap from anarchy are worlds apart. Of course, panel *a* would represent the true relation between S and C if any and all government action were intrinsically coercive. But that is a position that, though hardly unknown in libertarian circles, Buchanan explicitly rejects.

[20] It is on the public record (Brennan 2000, p. 1) that Buchanan created titles for his works with the utmost care—not any set of words would do—the title and subtitle had to capture the principal thrust of the work and do so with a certain pizzazz.

Exchange and Liberty

For most classical liberals—and certainly the variant that inhabits the Mont Pelerin Society—market exchange is taken to be the paradigmatic case of noncoercive relations amongst individuals. Just what the connection between exchange and liberty is, however, is an interesting question and becomes especially interesting when viewed through Buchanan's constitutional contractarian lens.

There are two ways in which we might view the connection between markets and liberty. One is via 'instantiation', the other via 'constitutional choice'. Consider instantiation first. Most economists feel a natural affinity with Adam Smith when he remarks that, '... the obvious and simple system of natural liberty ...' is one when '[a]ll systems of preference or of restraint [are] completely taken away...'. For Smith, liberty (natural or otherwise) is realised when '[e]very man... is left perfectly free to pursue his own interest in his own way...—... as long as he does not violate the laws of justice...'. (Smith 1776 IV. ix. 51, 1976, p. 687). But, as Buchanan observes in 'The Relevance of Pareto Optimality',[21] every man *will* pursue his own interest in his own way, within the confines of whatever constraints he finds himself confronting. Therefore, the chief question arising from the Smithian position is what the laws of justice may contain. If, for example, justice were conceived in broadly Rawlsian terms and included the imposition (say) of a revenue-maximising income tax regime,[22] then that revenue-maximising tax would constitute no barrier to 'natural liberty' as Smith defines it as under that tax regime, each *would* be free to pursue his own interest in his own way, subject to the laws of justice. The worry here is that the content of justice is really doing all the work: exchange and its relation to liberty are pushed out of the picture. And in particular, depending on what justice requires and what agency is entitled to enforce it, the Smithian definition of the system of natural liberty might prove accommodating to all kinds of government 'interventions'.

Buchanan's strategy in establishing the liberty credentials of markets is structurally very akin to Rawls'. That is, he appeals to the constitutional level of decision-making, where the basic institutions of society are to be chosen by unanimous consent amongst all citizens. It is that unanimity rule applied here where exchange makes its prime appearance. Following in the spirit of Wicksell,[23] the thought is that unanimity has a special relation with the Pareto criterion: whatever object of choice emerges from a process in which all affected players can exercise a veto is prima facie one in which all gains from exchange are exhausted. On this basis, it is the institutional choices—the rules of the game—that are endorsed unanimously at this

---

[21] The year 1962 was a 'bumper year' in Buchanan output. It saw not just the publication of the *Calculus* but also of the important 'externality' paper with Stubblebine, and this 'relevance' paper in which he attempted, for the first time, to spell out the contractarian imperative for the constitutional move.

[22] As Phelps (1973) argues, is required by maximin.

[23] The status of Wicksell as a Buchanan hero is legendary.

constitutional level that possess the relevant contractarian normative authority. And the institutional rules so endorsed possess that authority *uniquely*.

Consider specifically the contrast between market choices and unanimous constitutional choices. In the latter, all affected parties are given a right of veto.[24] In market choices by contrast, at least some affected parties effectively have no voice at all. That is, individuals who are not party to a transaction can be made worse off. It is common in the face of this possibility to make a conceptual distinction between 'technological' and 'pecuniary' externalities in market transactions, and a related distinction between Pareto relevant and Pareto irrelevant externalities. And we can admit that, if transactions costs were zero, all parties *would* have a voice because any affected parties could seek to compensate agents for refraining from actions by which they would be harmed. But as Buchanan takes it, the distinction between pecuniary and technological externalities—and indeed the identification of the latter in the presence of significant transactions costs—are epistemically overwhelming tasks. On this basis, the appropriate arena of contractarian norms lies at the constitutional level. If decisions about the proper scope of markets are taken at that constitutional level under conditions of unanimity, then markets to that extent carry the imprimatur of contractarian endorsement. Market exchange gains its contractarian credentials, on this view, not so much from securing Pareto optimality in each instance but because the market system is the object of unanimous choice at the constitutional level.

But of course, it is an open question just how extensive the reliance on markets will be under such a constitution. The unanimously decided rules of the game will include three elements, at least:

1. A specification of the rules for exchange and the scope of decentralized market decision-making.
2. A corresponding specification of the rules for and scope of collective decision-making.
3. A specification of the precise property and personal rights regime on the basis of which markets and political processes will operate.

There seems to be an interesting difference between Wicksell and Buchanan here. In the Buchanan scheme, these three elements are determined simultaneously and have similar contractarian status. Wicksell envisages (quasi)-unanimity to be employed for in-period political decisions about public goods supply (and taxes). But in the Wicksellian scheme, the underlying property rights system, determining the incomes on the basis of which those in-period taxes are to be levied, has to be decided at a separate and prior level. That is, the prior property rights system in Wicksell has to be 'just', but there is no presumption that the justice thereof is

[24] In Brennan and Lomasky (2000 [1984]), a distinction is drawn between ex ante and ex post veto—and the possibility that what emerges from unanimous choice among large numbers of individuals acting collectively might not actually be 'efficient'. But this is a quibble we finesse here.

settled by unanimous consent under 'veil of ignorance' conditions. In the Buchanan scheme, however, it seems as if the questions of mine and thine—the precise details of the personal and property right law—are settled as part of the rules of the game *alongside* choices about the domain of collective decision-making and the rules by which those 'political' decisions will be made. Many commentators (of a free market kind) complain that by assigning the determination of the basic property rights structure to a unanimous decision process effectively collectivises the starting point for property rights determination. Doubtless, some move to private property will be endorsed under the conditions of constitutional choice as Buchanan envisages them. Constitutional contractors will, Buchanan believes, recognise the enormous benefits that accrue from the institutions of private property and will, behind the veil of ignorance, seek to maximise those benefits. But the agreements they secure will take place from a position of equal standing. In that sense, Buchanan's classical liberalism is an expression not just of a disposition towards 'moral equality': the institutional decisions are drawn from a fundamental position of equal standing—albeit equal standing in a context, by stipulation, of considerable ignorance about one's future personal location in the economic/political structure. The affinity here between Buchanan and Rawls is quite notable, even if predictions about the ultimate constitutional preferences differ.

Given that Buchanan's perspective on markets is itself constitutional, one interesting question relates to Buchanan's attitude to Coase's analysis of property rights. Coase (1960), it will be recalled, considers the question of how courts should allocate property rights in cases where there are (significant) positive transactions costs. Coase's conception of property rights is exclusively as an instrument to further exchange—and specifically not to 'secure justice' (however exactly justice is construed). Coase reckons that judges should[25] decide cases according to the Learned Hand rule of minimising social cost—allocating title to the higher-value user. Buchanan (2001 [1974]) is clearly uncomfortable with this scheme. On Buchanan's picture, the basic property rights structure is determined as a constitutional level matter, and whatever the parties to the constitution decide in relation to property rights is normatively decisive. Presumably, parties at the constitutional level will have an eye to the gains from exchange likely to be available from the entire range of transactions relevant in any class of cases and will determine property rights with such considerations in mind. But in the Buchanan view, it is the entire *class* of cases—not the particular tort case subject to judicial discretion—that is the basis of property right determination.[26] And for Buchanan, there is, we think, no necessary presumption that the considerations that weigh in property rights determination will be exclusively 'efficiency oriented'.[27] But determination of the relevant property

[25] And arguably largely *do*.

[26] This appears to be the normative framework that undergirds the line of argument employed in Buchanan and Faith (2001 [1981]), where a *general* case is made for liability as opposed to property rights.

law is for Buchanan a constitutional matter: and the role of judges is to interpret and implement the law so determined. Judges should enforce the constitutional outcome and in so doing they will administer 'justice'—not seek 'efficiency'! In any event, rights are a matter for constitutional determination—and once set, the role of the courts is to enforce them, independent of the efficiency implications. Following the Buchanan logic, a judge who assigned rights according to the Learned Hand rule, would in at least some cases be acting unjustly, violating the existing rights structure—and in that sense *coercing* the losing party. In other words, such judicial action would be violating the *liberties* of citizen litigants. In that sense, in the relevant transaction-costs world, the objects of preserving liberty on the one hand and simulating market outcomes on the other would be in tension. Buchanan supports the former, and Coase, the latter.

Unanimity, Majority Rule and Liberty

We said in the previous section that, in Buchanan's constitutional scheme, there are three distinguishable elements. In the *Calculus*, the primary focus of analysis is on one aspect of the second of these elements—and specifically, the proportion of the citizenry who must agree for an in-period collective decision to be implemented. The conceptual status of unanimity at the constitutional level is indisputable, but Buchanan's insight is that unanimity is subject to a kind of self-defeatingness: unanimity as a rule for *in-period* collective decisions would be unanimously rejected at the *constitutional* level. What would be unanimously accepted depends amongst other things on the precise domain of collective decision-making—a more restrictive rule would apply to decisions bearing heavily on rights issues and a less restrictive rule for decisions relating to public goods provision.

Later, in the *Limits*, Buchanan distinguishes explicitly between the 'protective' and the 'productive' state—the former associated with the enforcement of the basic rights (3 above) and the latter concerned with government action under 2 above.[28] As Holmes and Sunstein (2000) emphasise, the protective state will require resources—so even at this level, rudiments of 2 obtrude. That is, there will have to be rules specifying the terms on which such resources can be acquired—something

[27] If, for example, there are prevailing norms about 'mine' and 'thine' that pre-exist in the constitutional contract (however vague and disparate those norms might be), then these might well play a role in determining the content of the 'rights' which the constitutional contractors settle on. And certainly, the constitutional bargains will reflect the particular distribution that emerges in the Hobbesian state—even though that distribution may have no intrinsic normative authority (no authority that is beyond the fact of being the point from which constitutional bargaining begins).

[28] It might be thought that research in the new institutional economics, which finds that exchange relationships occurred without the formal apparatus of government, disproves the need for a protective agent, at least in the domain of market exchange. Not so. All it shows is that *some* trade could be governed by the trade associations.

like a 'fiscal constitution' or, more accurately perhaps, elements of the constitutional contract dealing with 'the power to tax' (and perhaps the 'power to regulate').

Broadly, the considerations relevant to 2 will track the welfare economics literature on public goods, market failures and externalities. An activity will be assigned to the market if the degree of 'market failure' is less than the degree of 'political failure' associated with the provision of that good. In-period politics will 'fail' because the relevant collective decision rule will fall short of unanimity—because, at the in-period level, there are very significant 'transactions costs' in forming unanimously acceptable proposals. But markets will also fail and for much the same reason—because there are significant transactions costs in organising contracts to which all citizens are effectively party. Politics and markets, on this picture, are alternative ways of organising exchange, and the institution that does better in a particular case is the one to which that activity should be assigned.[29] In some ways, the language of 'failure' here is unhelpful, because the benchmark against which 'failure' is measured is an infeasible benchmark in both cases. Constitutionally viewed, markets and politics are equally exercises for the pursuit of gains from exchange, or to put the point in Rawlsian terms, society is a 'cooperative venture for mutual advantage'[30] whether one has its political or its market operations in sight. And if the constitutional compact *is* consistent with the requirements of unanimity at that level,[31] then *neither market process nor political process involves a violation of liberty*. Property rights themselves and exchange on the basis of them are *optimally* protected via the unanimously constructed constitutional rules. What is optimal here involves something that falls short of what would be ideal if, say, transactions costs were zero—there will be majoritarian interventions that would not occur in an ideal world. There will be market transactions that reduce aggregate preference satisfaction and some activities that would involve benefits for everyone that will not be pursued. And there will be explicit violations of the rules that it will cost too much to determine and rectify. But within all that 'failure', the in-period outcomes will over the long haul be not only the best that can reasonably be expected but also involve individuals living with the most liberty that this world offers.

But of course, things are quite otherwise if the constitution is *not* chosen under unanimity at the constitutional level. And one way of interpreting the Buchanan agenda (both in the *Calculus*, with Tullock, and in other works, some of them in other collaborations) has been to indicate general considerations why it seems implausible to think that the *actual* constitution satisfies this unanimity test. So, for

---

[29] The point applies generally and not just to questions of welfare failures—if there is liberty that has coevolved under the natural equilibrium, then a proper comparison of relevant alternatives (perhaps with in-period liberty in a democratic setting) would have to take that fact into account.

[30] In A Theory of Justice (1972, p. 4).

[31] The astute reader will detect a shift of position in this formulation. It is one thing for the constitutional order to be the object of explicit unanimous choice—something that can presumably be observed—and another for it to be 'consistent with the requirements of unanimity' which sounds like an analytic requirement waiting to be explicated by the social scientist/philosopher. There is of course a well-known critique of the entire 'social contract' tradition based on just this issue. Neither Buchanan nor we have anything to contribute to this critique.

example, in the *Calculus*, the claim is that the widespread use of simple majority rule for collective decisions flies in the face of the recognition that simple majority rule is but one possibility amongst many—and one with no obviously compelling features. The failure of most constitutions to specify the dividing line between political and market processes effectively assigns to in-period political process the power to settle that issue for itself, with perhaps predictable biases. The failure of most constitutions to include clear rules for the terms on which resources can be appropriated by the fisc—effectively assigning to majority rule decisions on taxing procedures that ought to be determined by relative unanimity—seems a clear violation of constitutional contractarian requirements. And so on. In such cases, the in-period rules can be said to be illiberal.

Accordingly, Buchanan is able to identify within the prevailing order lots of scope for violations of liberty, as he conceives the notion, where the process or lack thereof provides the dividing line between constitutional and in-period liberty. Of course, as he himself claims, he has no privileged view as to what would emerge from a genuinely unanimous constitutional contract. As viewed through his paradigm, diagnosis is merely a set of suggestions—observations of the kind: surely, this, and that, feature of the way we operate sits oddly with what we would plausibly agree to in constitutional contract? Surely, this particular outcome is an instance of coercion—a violation of liberty—viewed through the constitutional contractarian lens?

Whether in the real world there is any necessary presumption that such violations of liberty (rights violations under a nonoptimal constitution) are more likely to occur in political process than in market process is an open question—perhaps so. But it is to be emphasised that the benchmark that Buchanan offers—his own version of a 'feasible utopia'—is a rather abstract animal. Ultimately it depends on the values and preferences and beliefs (about the world and about institutional operations) that ordinary people carry into the constitutional process with them. In his scheme, the 'classical liberal' elements appear in terms of the insistence that the constitutional determination process must secure agreement from all affected parties. Beyond that requirement, everything else is ultimately just whatever emerges.

Constitutional Reform

Of course, what individuals will choose in their constitutional deliberations depends on their beliefs about the working properties of market and political processes under various specifications. And the vast bulk of Buchanan's work has been devoted to giving an account of those working properties. But it is a central part of our message in this chapter that he has done so with an eye to institutional effects on preference satisfaction—not with an eye to liberty. Liberty has entered the normative scheme at the more abstract level of specifying the requirements of constitutional decision-making.

We want to close our discussion with some observations about Buchanan's remarks on 'reform'.

First, a general point. When Buchanan talks of the constitution, it is in the spirit of formal constitutional documents—at least in one important sense. Alternative 'constitutions' are for Buchanan explicit objects of choice—and it is important for his scheme that they be so. They cannot be unwritten codes that have merely evolved and remained exempt from explicit endorsement. And yet, at many points—often in final chapters, when the issue of 'policy upshots' is in view—what emerges is something else: a plea for a new (or renewed[32]) 'constitutional awareness'. Recall in this connection, Buchanan's presentation of classical liberalism, with which we began, with its emphasis on a specific 'predisposition'. There is an interesting question as to whether such awareness or predispositions or 'civic religions', as in Brennan and Buchanan (1980), are matters of choice in any ordinary sense. Presumably, for example, people view others as moral equals not out of an act of explicit collective choice, but because that view is normatively compelling.

In discussing what can be done to ensure the viability of the liberal order, Buchanan (2005, p. 19) claims that '[m]an must be educated, both in ethics and in political economy...'. Presumably a collective decision will be taken on the lesson that can be taught. The nature of the institutions that best gives expression to that predisposition and the processes by which such institutions are appropriately selected may be issues of intellectual persuasion and 'reasoned speculation'. But it is not obvious that the underlying ethical impulse is appropriately modelled as an exercise in broadly rational choice. That impulse seems better thought of as given to us by evolution and history.

Relatedly, there is something of a tension in the Buchanan scheme that can be perhaps best seen by considering the following scenario. Suppose a group of individuals come together under the veil of uncertainty and in fact manage to unanimously agree on this or that rule. One might be inclined to claim that all is well and good—individuals were free to veto any proposal, and if there is an agreement, then the Pareto criterion and constitutional liberty have been instantiated. But suppose that many of the individuals at the forum are of a conservative disposition and create hierarchical rules, under which individuals are not treated as moral equals. If constitutional liberty is just a matter of the instantiation of unanimous decisions, then one would seem hard-pressed to criticise this feature in the rules. On the other hand, if liberty is more than a procedural issue, it must also have substantive content. Think of the issue this way. If Buchanan himself as participant in the constitutional forum has constitutional preferences over the set of rules, those 'preferences will presumably be classical liberal ones'.[33] But if that is so, then classical liberalism must have

[32] The distinction between 'new' and 'renewed' here is interesting. The picture often suggested by Buchanan is of an earlier period in US history when the 'constitutional consciousness' was more vibrant than currently. The constitutional 'revolution' is often described as an exercise in discovery.

[33] When discussing constitutional outcomes, Buchanan (2005, p. 4) raises the possibility that '... some persons ... [may] not simply place much value, if any at all, on individual liberty ...', and goes on to observe '[c]ontinuing frustration with the apparent failure of members of the body politic to understand what seems genuinely to be in their own enlightened self-interest may tempt the classical liberal either to join the ranks of those who would impose changes even in the absence of consensus or to acknowledge, with the conservatives, that a hierarchical classification, ... must be made. ... The dilemma for the contractarian classical liberal cannot be resolved'.

substantive content at the in-period level. Some in-period rules will be more coercive than others in terms of the extent to which they violate the basic precepts of the classical liberal order.

Two questions follow directly. First, what is the relation between in-period liberty so specified and preference satisfaction? They cannot be coterminous. That would be to reduce liberty to whatever people happen to want and to rule out by fiat the possibility that they may not desire liberty.

Second, is there not an intrinsic tension between the procedural liberal and the classical liberal?

Actually, we think that there are, hovering in the Buchanan corpus, three separate notions of liberty. First (and not necessarily in order of importance to the liberty agenda) is the procedural liberalism instantiated by unanimity at the constitutional forum. Second, there is in-period liberty, which exists at the post-constitutional stage when various agents use their power to impose outcomes under rules that are *not* consistent with the requirements of unanimity at the constitutional level. Third, there is classical liberalism, which is the substantive expression of the '… attitude in which others are viewed as moral equals and thereby deserving of equal respect, consideration and, ultimately, equal treatment' (Buchanan 2005, p. 101).

Buchanan (2005, p. 19) has recently claimed that individuals '… must be educated, both in ethics and in political economy…'. The idea that education, rather than persuasion, is appropriate to ethics sits oddly with Buchanan's claims elsewhere—and we do not know exactly how to interpret the claim. But education in political economy is a different matter. What exactly they need to be educated *about,* though, is an important issue. One thing they may want is to know how institutions map into future expected well-being. But another they may want is to know how alternative institutions affect their *liberty*. And here they seem more likely to have substantive than procedural liberty in mind. Unfortunately, however, we cannot see that Buchanan's work makes much progress on that question.

One additional remark worth making is that, if liberty has substantive normative value, then it will actually affect the way the analytical tools should be applied by the constitutional economist.[34] It is common knowledge, for example, amongst the public choice cognoscenti that, in the analytics of the *Calculus,* decision-making costs and external costs are the essential ingredients of reckoning the 'optimal collective decision-making rule'. But Buchanan and Tullock's perspective implicitly adopted the normative position that in the construction all that matters is the relative positions of the two cost curves and that costs should be minimised.

But as we have attempted to explain, participants at the forum may have moral positions over liberty (and for the record we are open to the view that they may have yet other ideals that do not mesh with the notion of preference satisfaction) that are distinguished from 'preference satisfaction' as conventionally interpreted in economics. And to the extent that the participants do have constitutional preferences over liberty—that consent/voluntariness in transactions plays some independent role and that coercion is a *prima facie* bad—then external costs are different from

[34] See Brennan (forthcoming) for a slightly different formulation of the argument about what ought to be counted for the purpose of designing optimal rules.

decision-making costs along the liberty dimension. Decision-making costs are made voluntarily. The citizen is generally free to opt out of participating in the political process at the post-constitutional stage. External costs are costs that are imposed on the citizen involuntarily.[35] It then follows that external costs should either be weighted by a liberty infringement factor greater than unity or there should be a 'coercion' cost curve added to the ordinary external cost curve to reflect the full costs of in-period rules. 'Optimal' decision-making rules should become more inclusive than the argument in the *Calculus* suggests.

One might respond that any preference the agent has for liberty/antipathy to coercion is already embedded in the external cost curve. That Buchanan with Tullock foresaw our point when they argue that the expected external costs curve will be higher and the decision-making rule more inclusive when the domain of in-period decision-making is over rights as opposed to other affairs of the state. If, however, Buchanan simply lumps antipathy to coercion into all other external costs—that coercion is just a matter of measuring the expected costs to the agents at the forum—then liberty has no independent normative status from other matters conventionally interpreted under preference satisfaction category. But for the classical liberal, liberty is not just a matter of preference satisfaction. The fact that individuals may be 'willing' to sell themselves into slavery will not be decisive in dissuading the classical liberal that the enforcement of such arrangement is anything but illiberal. The protective state cannot use its resources to enforce a contract, even one voluntarily agreed to, that prevents the slave's ability to exit without losing its claim to be part of the liberal order. And if that is so, the classical liberal will not be content with a mere adding up of the expected costs the participants expect to bear under various rules.

A Tentative Summing-Up

The Buchanan project is a normative project.[36] Unlike many economists who conceive their enterprise as essentially a science, Buchanan has always viewed his enterprise as halfway between true science and art[37]; as he puts it (2001 [1992], p. 22):

> The social science works in the hope that improvement in the processes of social interaction will emerge upon agreement both on diagnosis and on effective reform.

---

[35] We are assuming that externalities exist because transaction costs are positive. In such a setting, individuals will use political resources to capture other agents' resources and the interaction is coercive.

[36] As we indicated elsewhere, Buchanan's writings are extensive and wide ranging. In this chapter, we admit that we have not been able to follow or comment on all of the trails marked by Buchanan's various observations, some quite extensive, on the matter of liberty. We think we have raided the obvious works. Nevertheless, our final remarks should be interpreted as a speculative summary for the simple reason that there is no reason to believe that Buchanan has finished with the topic himself.

[37] See, for example, the essay 'From the Inside Looking Out' where this distinction is explicitly explored and Buchanan's conception of his own location within it clearly stated.

And though Buchanan has sometimes been reluctant to own the normative element, almost all commentators see it and remark upon it. Of course, his normative project involves a substantial amount of purely positive analysis—shrewd observation and substantive theorising. But the core commitments to individual liberty and a preoccupation with 'precepts for living together' (Buchanan 1975, p. xv) are never far from view.

Our object in this short piece has been to explicate Buchanan's conception of individual liberty and to trace its connection to the 'working themes' in his corpus—contract, constitution, Pareto optimality, 'public choice' and so on. Buchanan has not been interested so much with developing a clear definition of liberty—perhaps he sees that task as being one for the (appropriately informed) philosopher. But he has been concerned to see how individual liberty might be given institutional expression—how it might be thought of within a broad constitutional scheme, in which the relations between individuals are governed by free exchange amongst moral equals. Unfortunately, the focus of his attention in this respect has been rather *too* constitutional to provide much help to anyone interested in the ways in which institutions or policies bear on substantive liberty. The requirement of free exchange amongst moral equals remains in his approach a feature of relations amongst *constitutional contractors*. There remains the question of whether that is enough to satisfy the requirements of classical liberalism, substantively construed.

References

Brennan G (2000) Onwards and upwards: James Buchanan at 80. Public Choice 104:1–18

Brennan G Politics as exchange. Public Choice, Special Issue (forthcoming)

Brennan G, Buchanan JM (1980) The power to tax: analytical foundations of a fiscal constitution. Cambridge University Press, Cambridge

Brennan G, Buchanan JM (1985) The reason of rules: constitutional political economy. Cambridge University Press, Cambridge

Brennan G, Lomasky L (1984) Inefficient unanimity. J Appl Philos 1:151–163

Brennan G, Lomasky L (1993) Democracy and decision: the pure theory of electoral preference. Cambridge University Press, Cambridge

Buchanan JM (1969) Cost and choice: an inquiry in economic theory. Markham Publishing, Chicago

Buchanan JM (1975) The limits of liberty: from anarchy to leviathan. University of Chicago Press, Chicago

Buchanan JM (1977) Freedom in constitutional contract. Texas A&M Press, College Station

Buchanan JM (1999[1962]) The relevance of Pareto optimality. J Conflict Resolut 6:341–54. Reprinted in: The collected works of James M. Buchanan, vol 1. The logical foundations of constitutional liberty. Liberty Fund, Indianapolis, pp 210–229

Buchanan JM (2001 [1974]) Good economics—bad law. Va Law Rev 60:483–492. Reprinted in: The collected works of James M. Buchanan, vol 18. Federalism, liberty, and the law. Liberty Fund, Indianapolis, pp 327–337

Buchanan JM (2001 [1992]) From the inside looking out. In: Szenberg M (ed) Eminent economists: their life philosophies. Cambridge University Press, Cambridge, pp 98–106. Reprinted in: The collected works of James M. Buchanan, vol 19. Ideas, persons, and events. Liberty Fund, Indianapolis, pp 18–27

Buchanan JM (2005) Why I, too, am not a conservative: the normative vision of classical liberalism. Edward Elgar, Cheltenham

Buchanan JM, Faith R (2001 [1981]) Entrepreneurship and the internalization of externality. J Law Econ 24:95–111. Reprinted in: The collected works of James M. Buchanan, vol 17. Moral science and moral order. Liberty Fund, Indianapolis, pp 169–187

Buchanan JM, Lomasky L (2000 [1984]) The matrix of contractarian justice. Soc Philos Policy 2:12–32. Reprinted in: The collected works of James M. Buchanan, vol 17. Moral science and moral order. Liberty Fund, Indianapolis, pp 379–402

Buchanan JM, Tullock G (1962) The calculus of consent: logical foundations of constitutional democracy. University of Michigan Press, Ann Arbor

Carter I (2004) Choice, freedom and freedom of choice. Soc Choice Welfare 22:61–81

Coase R (1960) The problem of social cost. J Law Econ 3:1–44

Dowding K (1992) Choice: its increase and its value. Br J Polit Sci 22:301–314

Hobbes T (1943 [1651]) Leviathan. J.M. Dent, Everymans Library, London

Holmes S, Sunstein C (2000) The cost of rights: why liberty depends on taxes. W. W. Norton, New York

Kliemt H (2011) Bukantianism—Buchanan's philosophical economics. J Econ Behav Organ 80:275–279

Leeson P (2009) The invisible hook: the hidden economics of pirates. Princeton University Press, Princeton

Leeson P, Coyne C (2012) Conflict-inhibiting norms. In: Garfinkel M, Skaperdas S (eds) Oxford handbook of the economics of peace and conflict. Oxford University Press, Oxford, pp 840–860

Pattanaik PK, Xu Y (1990) On ranking opportunity sets in terms of freedom of choice. Res Econ Louvain 56:383–390

Pettit P (1997) Republicanism: a theory of freedom and government. Oxford University Press, Oxford

Phelps ES (1973) Taxation of wage income for economic justice. Quart J Econ 87:331–354

Rawls J (1972) A theory of justice. Oxford University Press, Oxford

Smith A (1976 [1776]) An inquiry into the nature and causes of the wealth of nations. In: Campbell RH, Skinner AS (eds), vol I and II. Liberty Press/Liberty Classics, Indianapolis

Sugden R (1998) The metric of opportunity. Econ Philos 14:307–337

Sugden R (2006) What we desire, what we have reason to desire, whatever we might desire: Mill and Sen on the value of opportunity. Utilitas 18:33–51

Sunstein C, Thaler R (2003) Libertarian paternalism is not an oxymoron. Univ Chicago Law Rev 70:1159–1202

Thaler R, Sunstein C (2008) Nudge: improving decisions about health, wealth, and happiness. Yale University Press, New Haven

Van Hees M, Wissenburg M (1999) Freedom and opportunity. Polit Stud 47:67–82

von Hayek F (1960) The constitution of liberty. University of Chicago Press, Chicago

Chapter 5
Choice Versus Interaction in Public Choice: Discerning the Legacy of *The Calculus of Consent*

Richard E. Wagner

Public choice as a field of scholarly inquiry entered the scholarly lexicon in 1968 when the fourth issue of what had been published as *Papers on Non-Market Decision Making* announced that it had adopted the title *Public Choice*. What had previously been an informal Committee on Non-Market Decision Making became formalized as the Public Choice Society. These changes in titles were followed by establishment of the Center for Study of Public Choice at Virginia Tech in 1969. The rest, to recur to a common expression, is history.

Numerous creative thinkers participated in the meetings of the Committee on Non-Market Decision Making that preceded the establishment of the Public Choice Society and in which I participated in October 1964 as a second-year graduate student. Some of those whose presence I still remember, and whose works will be familiar to anyone versed in the literature on public choice, are James Coleman, Otto Davis, Anthony Downs, John Harsanyi, Henry Manne, Mancur Olson, Vincent Ostrom, John Rawls, William Riker, and Thomas Schelling. Also participating as a third-year graduate student was Charles Plott. Leadership in assembling this group and in initiating the pattern of scholarly interaction that later became known as public choice belonged to James M. Buchanan and Gordon Tullock, and their work in this respect is explored by Wagner (2004).

The Calculus of Consent is undoubtedly the Ur-text that defines the legacy of Buchanan and Tullock with respect to the field of scholarly inquiry that has been described as "public choice" since 1968. Publication of that book was accompanied by a constellation of entrepreneurial and organizational activities that initially preceded establishment of the Public Choice Society and *Public Choice*. Those activities continued in the following years and were surely pivotal in generating the present state of affairs where public choice is universally recognized as a field of scholarly inquiry. But what kind of field of inquiry is public choice these days and

R.E. Wagner (✉)
Department of Economics, George Mason University, Fairfax, VA 22030, USA
e-mail: rwagner@gmu.edu

D.R. Lee (ed.), *Public Choice, Past and Present: The Legacy of James M. Buchanan and Gordon Tullock*, Studies in Public Choice 28, DOI 10.1007/978-1-4614-5909-5_5,

how does it relate to *The Calculus of Consent*? It is this question that I address in this essay. There is clearly contemporary scholarship in public choice and political economics from which it could reasonably be inferred that *The Calculus of Consent* serves the role of Ur-text. But there is equally clearly scholarly work for which that Ur-text status would not be accorded, as Blankart and Koester (2006) recognize in the disjunction they make between public choice and political economics. Yet, this disjunction is a peculiar one to advance in light of the opening line of the Preface to *The Calculus of Consent*: "This is a book about the *political* organization of a society of free men (italics in original)." Whether one describes a body of scholarly inquiry as public choice, political economics, or political economy would seem to be a secondary matter for any scholarly inquiry that seeks to bring economic theory to bear on political activity.

Yet, this is not the case, as can be seen readily by comparing two recent treatises devoted to bringing together politics and economics. The books to which I refer are by Vincent Ostrom (1997) and by Torsten Persson and Guido Tabellini (2000). Any comparison of these books would quickly reveal sharp cleavages in scholarly orientation toward political economy. Analogously, the two parabolas X^2 and $-X^2$ share a common origin and yet point in opposite directions. It is the same with differing orientations toward and approaches toward the application of economic analysis to political phenomena. *The Calculus of Consent* was published a generation before the aforementioned books by Ostrom and by Persson and Tabellini, and it was rendered intelligible in light of the theoretical frameworks and conceptions that were in play at that time. All scholarship has and must have this temporal quality. Yet scholarship can also contain enduring qualities that are independent of the particular conceptual frameworks with which they were conveyed. This is the situation with *The Calculus of Consent*. While the book was conveyed by conceptualizations grounded in choice by a representative or median voter and in representative, two-person interactions, the book nonetheless was fundamentally concerned with the economic logic that lay behind the complex arrangement through which the American republic was constituted. At the time *The Calculus of Consent* was crafted, however, suitable conceptual frameworks did not really exist, as these started to come into play only with subsequent developments in the sciences of complexity. Hence, the themes that were central to *The Calculus of Consent* can take on new life due to these more recent analytical developments.

The appraisal of any economic situation that spans some significant period of time raises the problem of comparability which is addressed through index numbers. The principles that undergird the Laspeyres and Paasche approaches to the construction of indexes pertain as well to the appraisal of scholarly contributions over significant intervals of time. The analogy with index numbers generates two distinct portraits of the legacy of *The Calculus of Consen*t. The Laspeyres analogy shows that legacy to be comparatively narrow and perhaps relatively dated: it is an old text to be admired, but it really does not have much to say to us today. In contrast, the Paasche analogy shows it to be broad and highly pertinent today. While public choice is commonly described in brief as the application of economic theory to politics, which *The Calculus of Consent* clearly exemplified, *The Calculus of*

Consent was animated by a desire to bring to bear an economic logic on the architectural principles that informed the American constitutional founding. Those principles, however, could not be elaborated fully through the simple equilibrium models that were in use at that time, which led to a theoretical reduction that removed much of the complex qualities of the founding constitutional architecture. Conceptual tools now exist to explore more fully those complex qualities than what Buchanan and Tullock had available in 1962. What results is a distinctive approach that can be designated as Virginia Political Economy in contrast to what might be called equilibrated political economy and which, in various efforts at linguistic experimentation, I have designated as conjunctive (2006, 2007), entangled (2009, 2010), and knotted political economy (2011).

Index Numbers and the Appraisal of Old Texts

Any comparison of two economic situations separated by some gap of time involves an arbitrary choice of base in terms of which to make the comparison. Economists face this problem mostly in terms of comparing output across place and time. One can, for instance, seek to compare output between the start and the end of a 50-year interval, say 1962 and 2012. Making this comparison involves numerous problems in the construction of index numbers which Warren Nutter (1966) explores with great cogency. If there were no changes in techniques of production or in the qualities or types of products produced over that interval, it would be simple to measure growth, especially if prices were also unchanged. In this instance, growth would be expressed as $= \frac{\Sigma P_1 Q_1}{\Sigma P_0 Q_0}$, where the $\Sigma P_0 Q_0$ denotes expenditure in the initial year and $\Sigma P_1 Q_1$ denotes expenditure 50 years later.

To be sure, growth is never a simple matter of producing more of the same thing. There will be products that were produced 50 years ago that are no longer produced, just as there will be products produced today that were not produced 50 years ago. It does not follow, moreover, that later products are superior to earlier products. For instance, the digital and programmable thermostats that are used for home heating and cooling today are more difficult to operate than were the mechanical thermostats of 50 years ago: some qualities of those thermostats have been improved (automatic adjustment of temperatures) while other qualities have been worsened (the necessity to program the thermostat). The measurement of growth across intervals where the characteristics and qualities of products change and when new products appear while old products disappear raises questions of selecting just what to compare between the two periods that do not arise when the same products and associated characteristics and qualities are maintained through time.

The Laspeyres approach to the construction of index numbers compares the current situation against a base established in some earlier period. With respect to measuring growth in output between two periods, the Laspeyres approach measures growth as $L = \Sigma P_0 Q_1 / \Sigma P_0 Q_0$. Hence, today's output is compared with yesterday's output based on the prices that prevailed in the past. In contrast, the Paasche approach measures growth as $P = \Sigma P_1 Q_1 / \Sigma P_1 Q_0$. Hence, today's output is again compared with yesterday's output, only those outputs are evaluated with respect to today's prices.

The problem of appraising the present significance of old texts is similar to the problem of measuring the growth of output. The object of examination is the present value of the old text relative to its initial value. But how might that comparison be made? Similar to the measurement of growth, this can be done in two distinct ways. Where the Laspeyres method compares the outputs in terms of past prices, the Paasche method compares those outputs in terms of present prices. But what is the analogue to the prices of products in the construction of output indexes when it comes to the valuation of old texts? At this point, historical judgment must replace price data. This act of judgment, moreover, refers to two distinct ways of reading old texts. One way, the Laspeyres analogue, asks how much insight the old text can add in light of contemporary formulations of similar material. The other way, the Paasche analogue, asks how much insight the old text can contribute in light of new conceptual formulations that were not available when the old text was written. Any scholarly contribution is conveyed using analytical formulations that are in play at the time it is formulated and which renders that contribution intelligible to interested readers. At some later moment, new analytical formulations might have come into play that if they were present at the time of the initial formulation might have led to some alternative formulation. If so, appraisal confronts the problem of selecting between something resembling the Laspeyres-Paasche distinction.

The situation I have in mind is illustrated nicely by Nicholas Vriend (2002) asking: "Was Hayek an Ace?" By "ace," Vriend was referring to an economist who worked with agent-based computational models. Vriend answered his question resoundingly in the affirmative. Yet Hayek never worked with agent-based computational models. He could not have done so because the requisite computer technology necessary to carry those models was not in play then. In posing his question, Vriend was using the Paasche and not the Laspeyres method of reading and appraising Hayek's treatment of the use of fragmented and distributed knowledge in society. Agent-based modeling accommodates open-ended formulations where global patterns emerge through interaction among agents, each of whom acts on the basis of limited knowledge. It is readily apparent that Hayek's treatments of the use of knowledge in society would have taken recourse to agent-based models had that analytical technology been available when Hayek wrote. But that technology was not available, leaving closed-form modeling of some type as the only option for expressing ideas. And yet Hayek's ideas about incomplete and distributed knowledge could not be adequately and accurately conveyed through closed-form modeling because such modeling presents a god's-eye view of its material, whereas Hayek denied that such a perspective existed. So Hayek presented his ideas using closed-form modeling as a point of analytical departure and which confines he subsequently tried to escape through language. In contrast, agent-based modeling offers a direct means of escaping the god's-eye view and yet all the same arriving at formulations about systemic properties of interaction among dispersed agents, none of whom possesses any god's-eye view, as illustrated by Axtell and Epstein (1996), Epstein (ed.) (2006), and Seagren (2011). So Vriend is right to claim that Hayek would surely have embraced agent-based computational modeling in conveying some of his thoughts. And so too Buchanan and Tullock would surely have used some of those insights in developing *The Calculus of Consent*.

The Calculus of Consent: 1962 Versus 2012 as Bases for Appraisal

Joseph Schumpeter (1954: 41) observes that any act of economic explanation starts with a pre-analytical cognitive vision that must subsequently be expressed through a conceptual framework that will render it apprehensible to readers. Those cognitive visions, however, might not be fully or accurately expressible by the theoretical frameworks with which an author is able to work. In this respect, Samuel Johnson once noted that "every man has often found himself deficient in the power of expression, big with ideas which he could not utter, and unable to impress upon his reader the image existing in his own mind" (as quoted by Jacques Barzun (1976: xi)). When authors face this situation, they try to do their best with the modes of expression that are available to them, realizing at the same time that their products must be rendered intelligible in terms of the conceptual frameworks with which their audience is familiar.

Consequently, the problem of Paasche and Laspeyres can arise in appraising the contribution of old texts. This situation faced Hayek with respect to his formulation of fragmented and distributed knowledge, as Vriend explains, and it is likewise present in Buchanan and Tullock's exposition of the "Logical Foundations of Constitutional Democracy," to recur to the subtitle of *The Calculus of Consent*. For the most part, Buchanan and Tullock employed an analytical framework that was readily reducible to the representative agent formulation that later became so common in macro theory and whose public choice equivalent is the median voter formulation. Hence, Buchanan and Tullock's analytical framework appeared grounded in individual choice and representative interaction, as reflected in their various game theoretic exercises. When read in this manner, it is easy to see such a work as Persson and Tabellini (2000) as an extension and amplification of what Buchanan and Tullock began. This appraisal of *The Calculus of Consent* would reflect the Laspeyres-like approach to appraisal where the contribution is evaluated according to the conceptions that were articulated at that time and with that articulation compared with more recent articulations that work with pretty much the same conceptualizations. In comparing Buchanan and Tullock with Persson and Tabellini, for instance, this approach would ask how much of Buchanan and Tullock is still useful in light of the refined articulation of Persson and Tabellini.

In similar vein, and to recur again to Vriend's analysis of Hayek, this Laspeyres-like comparison would compare Hayek's formulation of the use of fragmented and distributed knowledge with subsequent articulations of imperfect knowledge by Sanford Grossman and Joseph Stiglitz (1976, 1980). In making such a comparison, however, the central features of Hayek's cognitive insight would have been lost, as Thomsen (1992) shows. Hayek's precognitive analytical vision rested on a rejection of any god's-eye posture and sought instead to theorize about fragmented and distributed knowledge that through market interaction led to the assembly of such products as pencils (Read 1958), even though no single person could articulate all of the actions necessary to produce a pencil. The production of pencils, Read recognized and so surely did Hayek, was an emergent quality of interaction within a nexus of market interaction. Hayek's formulation was simply incommensurable with the formulations of Grossman and Stiglitz whose formulations of imperfect knowledge were based on comparison with the knowledge possessed by some presumed god's-eye observer.

Something similar affects comparison of Buchanan and Tullock with Persson and Tabellini. While it is meaningful to describe public choice as the application of economic theory to politics, that description nonetheless contains a good deal of ambiguity once it is recognized that economics is a contested discipline (Reder 1999). While there are numerous margins of contestation over the meaning of economics among economists, I focus here only on one such margin: whether economic theory pertains to *states of equilibrium* or to *processes of motion* (Wagner 2010). For roughly a century now, the mainstream of economic theory has construed the theoretical effort as centered on states of equilibrium. In contrast, Boettke (2007) identifies a mainline of economic theory that centers the theoretical effort on processes of motion and on the institutional arrangements that both facilitate and emerge out of that motion. Public choice theory reflects the same distinction between mainstream and mainline as Boettke associates with economic theory. There is a public choice literature associated strongly with states of equilibrium. There is also a literature associated with nonequilibrium processes of development and institutionally governed relationships and interactions. If the former might be identified as closed-form public choice, the latter could be identified as open-form public choice, or Virginia Political Economy.

There is theoretical space for both types of formulation, much as Wagner (2010) locates theoretical space for both equilibrium and nonequilibrium frameworks for economic theory. To be sure, those alternative theoretical frameworks highlight different phenomena for analytical examination. They represent noncommensurable though not necessarily antagonistic conceptual frameworks. Hence, it is possible for an analyst to work with both equilibrium-centered and process-centered frameworks, only not at the same time as Roger Koppl (2011) explains. With respect to Buchanan and Tullock, and particularly The *Calculus of Consent*, it is surely the case that the foreground of their analytical attention reflected a concern with processes of development and not states of equilibrium, though they took recourse to both types of formulation, as many theorists, including myself, have occasion to do. The central concern of The *Calculus of Consent* was with what might be called the architecture of governance. The architecture of governance does not dictate any particular political outcome but rather provides a framework of interaction within which outcomes emerge. A related effort to characterize such an architecture was set forth by Jane Jacobs (1992), who analyzed different patterns of connectivity among carriers of what she described as commercial and guardian activities. Similar to Buchanan and Tullock, she argued that those architectural arrangements had significant implications for the quality of human governance.

Contrasting Visions of Political Economy

There are two contrasting visions by which a theory of political economy, or social science generally for that matter, may be developed. One vision emphasizes the structure of reality conceptualized as a state of being or equilibrium. This is the dominant vision with which economic theory has been practiced since the late nineteenth century. The alternative vision emphasizes reality as a kaleidic process of becoming, which Prigogine (1997) examines luminously. Both visions are capable of logical articulation, though the visions are also noncommensurable. One can work with a theory that holds, like Ecclesiastes, that "there is nothing new under the sun" while also working with a theory that holds, like Heraclitus, that "a person can't step twice into the same river." One just cannot work with both theories simultaneously. Theories of public choice, just like economic theories more generally, are of both types. While Boettke's (2007) distinction between mainstream and mainline involves some unavoidable ambiguity because many theorists have worked with both categories at various times, it is nonetheless possible to classify theorists by Boettke's dichotomy by taking into account the foreground and background of their theoretical efforts.

For instance, Joseph Schumpeter's (1954) analytical foreground was centered on kaleidic processes with a background of equilibrium states. That background attracted attention when he pronounced Léon Walras as the greatest economist for his articulation of general equilibrium, and yet it is clear that Schumpeter worked with processes of development in the foreground of his analytical attention, so would belong to the mainline of Boettke's dichotomy. By contrast, Walras would belong to the mainstream with his focus on equilibrium states. Yet Walras (1954: 377–81) also recognized reality as a process of becoming when he briefly challenged his own equilibrium formulation by positing what he described as a continuous market in place of the annual market with which the rest of the book worked. With the annual market, all activities were coordinated in advance of any actual activity in auction-like fashion, eliminating false trading and the problems this creates for the given conditions necessary for equilibrium theory. In contrast, the continuous market was a nonequilibrium framework that Walras noted briefly but abandoned because its open character was not amenable to the closed-form statements he wanted to derive from his theoretical effort.

Like most theorists, Buchanan and Tullock, both in *The Calculus of Consent* and in their other works whether jointly or severally written, reflected both equilibrium states and kaleidic processes in their theoretical work. Perusal of their bodies of work, however, shows clearly that even their use of equilibrium models is employed as a tool to think about processes of development. Perhaps, nowhere is this relationship between foreground and background made clearer than in Buchanan's (1982) oft-noted remark that order is definable only through the process within which it emerges. This posture stands in stark contrast to the widespread theoretical presumption that a state of equilibrium can be defined independently of any process of interaction among participants. Buchanan is at base a process and not an equilibrium theorist, and so is Tullock as Wagner (2008) explains.

The legacy of Buchanan and Tullock to public choice and political economy is one where the analytical foreground is occupied with processes of societal interaction and with that process played out against a Heraclitus-like background of equilibrium. Consistent with the practice of economic theory around 1960, however, *The Calculus of Consent* was presented largely through a language of equilibrium theory. Representative agent modeling had not come to occupy a central place in economic theory in 1962, but the constitutional calculus that Buchan and Tullock set forth could have been readily assimilated to a representative agent formulation. Indeed, the reduction of political processes to some selection by a median voter is to reduce political activity to a representative agent's optimization problem.

Perhaps nowhere is this representative agent reduction of public choice and political economy expressed so clearly and cogently as it is by Persson and Tabellini (2000). Likewise, perhaps, nowhere is the process orientation that is the true foreground of *The Calculus of Consent* expressed so crisply as it is by Vincent Ostrom (1997). A short comparison of Persson and Tabellini with Ostrom will thus allow proper recognition of the legacy of Buchanan and Tullock, recognizing that these books were published 35 and 38 years after *The Calculus of Consent.*

Persson and Tabellini state that they model "policy choices as the equilibrium outcome of a well-specified strategic interaction among rational individuals (p. 2)." They further note (pp. 6–7) that their "models are always formulated as general equilibrium models to obtain closed-form solutions." Competition between candidates tends strongly to produce an outcome that maximizes utility for the median voter and eliminates rents in doing so, resulting in Pareto efficiency. This happens because of the assumption that the median voter values public output but not political rents. But should the median voter have some preference for one of the candidates, the strength of that preference will both allow political rents while also limiting those rents. In any case, a political outcome is represented as a singular product of an election wherein that outcome is effectively delegated to the median voter.

In sharp contrast to Persson and Tabellini, Ostrom asserts that "majority rule is an inadequate and superficial formulation for constituting viable democratic societies (p. 3)." Part of the reason for this is Ostrom's recognition that "human societies are not determinate systems (p. 11)." Ostrom continues by contrasting a "culture of inquiry" which is open and which is Ostrom's analytical framework with a "culture of command" which is closed and which is Persson and Tabellini's analytical framework. Ostrom subsequently contrasts two forms of sickness: "Tyranny of the Majority … is a sickness of governments … Democratic Despotism is by contrast a sickness of the people … Perhaps the most fatal affliction of a people is a combination of helplessness, envy, and greed (p. 17)."

To recur to an image I have used on several occasions (Wagner 2007, 2010, 2012), equilibrium theory treats society as a form of parade while kaleidic theory treats it as a busy piazza. Parades and piazzas are both orderly social configurations, but ontologically, they are distinct and have different sources of orderliness. A parade is an organization that is directed by a parade marshal. While a parade may be a mile in length, the actions of all participants in the parade are directed by the parade marshal. While parades differ in quality, those qualitative differences would be attributed to such things as the musical and marching skill of the participants and the time given to rehearsal. Furthermore, the parade can be readily reduced to an entity with point mass: nothing of significance is lost by reducing the mile-long line of humanity through which the parade is constituted to a single point that moves through time along some designated route.

In the orthodox theory of political economy and economic policy as set forth by Tinbergen (1952) and continued by Acocella (1994), political power is construed as standing separate from economy and intervening into it. State activity is construed as directed by a single-minded policy maker who, after the fashion of a billiard player, strikes a cue ball to move an object ball to some desired location. Within this formulation, the object denoted as economy is subject to the economic laws that economists seek to articulate, but polity stands outside economy. The initial impetus for public choice theorizing was to bring polity likewise into the ambit of economic law. In ironic contrast, the newer forms of public choice or political economics revert to the old pattern of thought where polity stands apart from economy. Only now the position of policy maker is ascribed to a median voter and with politicians being lackeys who compete for approval from the median voter. The exposition differs from the earlier approach to economic policy, but the effect is the same: a position of economic equilibrium is defined independently of any process by which that equilibrium might have emerged, and political power is used to transform that equilibrium into a new equilibrium. What is described is a parade marshal who suddenly directs the parade to turn left rather than continuing along its previously planned route.

By contrast, a piazza is nothing like a parade even though it is also an orderly social configuration. Most significantly, a parade is not reducible to a point mass entity. The people passing through a piazza at some instant might well contain the same number of people as a mile-long parade; however, the people in the piazza are not all going to the same destination. The orderliness of the piazza does not reside in rehearsal or in marching ability. Rather it resides in such things as conventions of courtesy, a desire to avoid collisions with others, and an ability to make inferences about the intended routes of those nearby so as to avoid collisions. The piazza is a self-ordered, polycentric network of interacting entities, with each entity having its own principles of action. The term “state” likewise denotes a congeries of entities and not a single entity. There is competition among the entities organized within the auspices of state just as there is competition among the entities organized under the auspices of market.

Figure 5.1 represents the idea of an entangled political economy. Shown there is a polycentric arrangement of two types of entity. The entities denoted by circles are

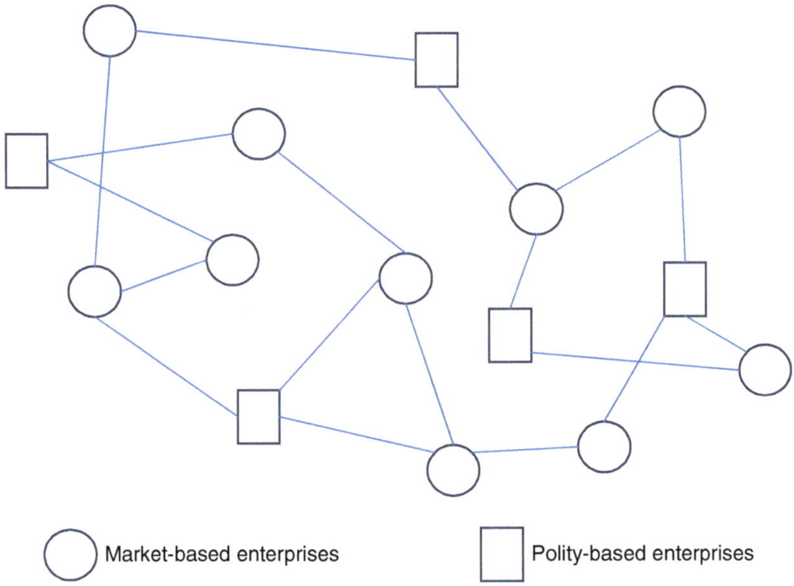

Fig. 5.1 Entangled political economy

market-based enterprises. The entities denoted by squares are polity-based enterprises. All of these entities operate on the same plane and do so through establishing relationships with one another. The principles by which those relationships are established and subsequently operate differ between the organizational forms, as I have explored in such places as Wagner (2007, 2012). The relevant point illustrated by Fig. 5.1 for this essay is that polity is not some entity that stands apart from economy and intervenes into it. Rather, polity denotes first of all a multitude of competing entities and not some unified, singular entity; and it denotes second of all a collection of entities that exists inside the economy, simultaneously imposing on some market entities while at the same time soliciting support from other market entities. What we observe, in other words, is an entangled system of political economy that may be open to different architectures of entanglement, but which remains entangled and polycentric all the same.

The Calculus of Consent was primarily conveyed by equilibrium formulations that had a representative agent look. Accordingly, it would be easy to view such formulations as Persson and Tabellini as a continuation of that line of thought by using a higher level of analytical technology. Indeed, much public choice is consistent with this outlook, as illustrated by the widespread use of the median voter model. To do this would be to take the Laspeyres-based approach to the appraisal of old texts. In this case, the present usefulness of *The Calculus of Consent* would be limited as its formulations have been largely eclipsed by subsequent developments in analytical technology. Doing this, however, would be to reverse foreground and background by treating *The Calculus of Consent* as centered on choices and states of being rather than on interactions and processes of becoming.

Just as I think Vriend is right to treat Hayek as an "ace," so I think it is right to treat Buchanan and Tullock as "aces." At many places within *The Calculus of Consent,* they play up differences among people, which accords better with the image of the piazza than of the parade. True, the members of the parade can differ in other respects but are common in their desire to march in the parade. Having decided to join the parade, they could well participate in choosing their music through some process that would include a vote. In this instance, however, there would be unanimity to participate in the parade and its subsequent vote on the music. This is a long way removed from the willy-nilly application of majority vote and median voters to whatever it is that competition among candidates brings into its grip.

Constitutional Political Economy

In trying to discern the legacy of *The Calculus of Consent*, we should not forget that the subtitle of the book was "Logical Foundations of Constitutional Democracy." *The Calculus of Consent* was written with the American constitutional arrangement in mind and sought to explore the underlying economic logic that was present even if not expressly articulated when that arrangement was established. Within a polycentric system of political economy, there is no singular position from which that system might be modified through conscious choice. There are rather multiple sources from which change can emanate, as Fig. 5.1 illustrates. At the same time, however, it is generally recognized that spontaneous orders can generate systemic features that might be widely if not universally regarded as inferior to alternative features that might be imagined. Thomas Schelling (1978) is a masterful treatment of this theme, and Jane Jacob's (1992) thesis that commingling among carriers of commercial and guardian moralities can result in "monstrous moral hybrids" is a supporting statement that not all patterns that emerge through spontaneous ordering are generally beneficial.

In this respect, *The Calculus of Consent* distinguished between constitutional and post-constitutional levels of activity. Within this conceptual framework, it is meaningful to distinguish between ordinary political activity and the framework of rules through which that activity is governed. As a practical matter, this distinction is not as easy to implement as it is when people choose the rules by which they will play before they start playing whatever it is that they will be playing. Ordinary games are discrete: they can be stopped to revise the rules and with play subsequently resumed. Life is continuous. Yet the distinction between constitutional and post-constitutional activity is a vital heritage of *The Calculus of Consent.*

The American constitutional framework rests upon a fundamental economic logic that people will pursue their interests more vigorously as the intensity of their interest in the matter increases and as their cost of that pursuit decreases. The constitutional question addressed both at the American constitutional founding and in *The Calculus of Consent* is how relationships among a society of interest seekers

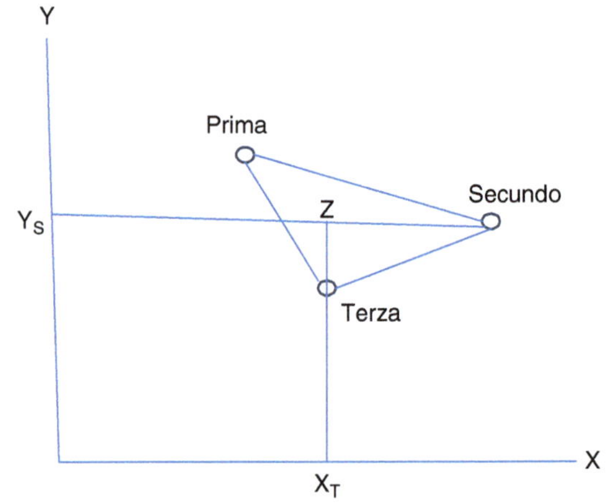

Fig. 5.2 Parliamentary rules and fiscal outcomes

can be ordered so as to promote the general welfare while keeping in check the use of public force as an instrument for factional benefit. There is no easy or final solution to this problem, in part, because constitutional and post-constitutional processes are likewise entangled, leading to constitutional processes sometimes serving to increase the durability of politically generated rents, as illustrated by Buchanan (1959) and Runst and Wagner (2011).

These difficulties aside, *The Calculus of Consent* brought into the analytical foreground recognition that political outcomes are not products of some ruler's choice, whether that ruler is a median voter or a different type of despot, but rather are products of interaction among a multitude of interested participants. In this respect, all political outcomes are catallactical or interactive in nature. With those outcomes being products of interactions as distinct from being choices, they depend not just on the preferences or values of the participants but also on the rules by which those interactions are governed, as Fig. 5.2 illustrates. Shown there are three people who must agree to undertake collectively some amounts of the two activities designated as X and Y. There are, however, numerous particular procedural or constitutional rules by which this three-person interaction might be governed.

Figure 5.2 illustrates two such rules, each of which generates different outcomes; moreover, with larger numbers of people and combinations of interactions, a greater variety of outcomes are possible. One possible framework would allow independent agreement on each activity. This might be accomplished by majority voting on each activity, perhaps with the vote on X preceding the vote on Y. With respect to X, Terza's preferred motion X_T will defeat all other motions. With respect to Y, Secundo's preferred motion Y_S will defeat all other motions. Within this particular constitutional framework, the collective outcome will be (X_T, Y_S) as denoted by Z in Fig. 5.2. An alternative constitutional framework could still require majority approval but would require a single motion to support both activities. Under this institutional framework, all points along any of the three triangular boundaries are possible outcomes, which means in turn that Z is not a possible collective outcome within this framework—though it would be a possible outcome if unanimous approval were required.

When we come to collective action, what is called public or collective choice is not truly any person's choice in the same manner that choice is portrayed in models of choice. Everything that is described as a collective or public choice is a product of some rule-governed process of interaction among interested participants wherein people typically differ in their evaluations and in their influence within that process. Hence, a mapping can be constructed from the rules that govern interactions to the outcomes of those interactions. This is the analytical schema of constitutional political economy that was set in motion by *The Calculus of Consent* and which, at the same time, was recognized inchoately at the time of the American constitutional founding, as Vincent Ostrom (1987) has explained with especial analytical cogency.

One Final Remark

While I have described *The Calculus of Consent* as the Ur-text of Virginia Political Economy, texts do not propagate themselves. People and their activities are required for the propagation of texts. With respect to such propagation, Randall Collins (1998) explains that such propagation is part of a process of open scholarly competition. In Collins's framework, scholars compete for attention space through their articulation of ideas. That articulation takes place within the context of research programs that have both some hard core propositions that are taken as fixed by contributors to those programs and some set of heuristics that serve to direct scholarly energy in directions that extend and strengthen the reach of the research program.

No two scholars, even those with the creative energy of a Buchanan and a Tullock, can create a research program with their pens alone. Other participants must be enlisted in the propagation of that program. In her *Commons of the Mind,* Anette Baier (1997) explains that it is easy for a person to exaggerate how much of a scholar's thought is his or her creation when a good deal of that thought is set in motion through interactions with others. Within contemporary academic settings, that interaction occurs through publications, which other people read, and presentations, which leads to discussion and other forms of interaction. Teaching, in this respect, is one form of presentation.

Scholarly research programs develop as self-organized networks of interested scholars. Organizational entrepreneurship is as much a part of scholarly propagation as are the ideas themselves. Buchanan and Tullock were filled with ideas that provided much analytical material for public choice, but they also pursued a vigorous program of entrepreneurial and organizational activity that expanded interest in their program far beyond what they could have accomplished through publication alone. This is not to say that entrepreneurial and organizational activity can create a research program from just any set of ideas. Not all ideas can be shaped into research programs, and of those that can further entrepreneurial and organizational effort is required if those ideas are truly to emerge into a robust research program. This Buchanan and Tullock accomplished during their period together in Charlottesville and Blacksburg.

In reviewing the organizational and entrepreneurial work of Buchanan and Tullock across their three Virginia venues (Wagner 2004), I offered the ranking: Charlottesville-Blacksburg-Fairfax. Implicit in that essay was a cardinal appraisal that placed Charlottesville and Blacksburg relatively close together, as I ascribed both places as generating abnormally high returns to scholarly effort. In contrast, I placed Fairfax a distinct third by claiming that it offered only normal returns to academic effort. While eight years later I see no reason to change that appraisal, I do see signs that the program in Fairfax might be poised to capture abnormally high returns as did the programs in Charlottesville and Blacksburg. Under the energetic leadership of Peter Boettke, the F. A. Hayek Program for Advanced Study in Philosophy, Politics, and Economics was established in 2012. This program has the potential for carrying forward and deepening the tradition of Virginia Political Economy that James Buchanan and Gordon Tullock set in motion 50 years ago. We should remember in this respect that *The Calculus of Consent* was created within the academic organization denoted originally as the Thomas Jefferson Center for Studies in Political Economy and Social Philosophy. That center was dedicated to multidisciplinary scholarship in the tradition of the Scottish Enlightenment. George Mason's new F. A. Hayek Program for Advanced study in Philosophy, Politics, and Economics aims to carry forward that same multidisciplinary orientation, which, if successful, holds promise for once again bringing abnormally high scholarly returns to Virginia Political Economy (Buchanan 2006).

References

Acocella N (1994) The foundations of economic policy. Cambridge University Press, Cambridge

Axtell R, Epstein J (1996) Growing artificial societies. Brookings Press, Washington

Baier A (1997) The commons of the mind. Open Court, Chicago

Barzun J (1976) Simple & direct. Harper & Row, New York

Blankart CB, Koester GG (2006) Political economics versus public choice. Kyklos 59:171–200

Boettke PJ (2007) Liberty vs. power in economic policy in the 20th and 21st centuries. JPrivate Enter 22:7–36

Buchanan JM (1959) Positive economics, welfare economics, and political economy. J Law Econ 2:124–138

Buchanan JM (1982) Order defined in the process of its emergence. Lit Liber 5:5

Buchanan JM (2006) The Virginia renaissance in political economy: the 1960s revisited. In: Koppl R (ed) Money and markets: essays in honor of Leland B. Yeager. Routledge, London, pp 34–44

Buchanan JM, Tullock G (1962) The calculus of consent. University of Michigan Press, Ann Arbor

Collins R (1998) The sociology of philosophies: a global theory of intellectual change. Harvard University Press, Cambridge

Epstein JM (ed) (2006) Generative social science: studies in agent-based computational modeling. Princeton University Press, Princeton

Grossman SJ, Stiglitz JE (1976) Information and competitive price systems. Am Econ Rev 66:246–253
Grossman SJ, Stiglitz JE (1980) On the impossibility of informationally efficient markets. Am Econ Rev 70:393–408
Jacobs J (1992) Systems of survival. Random House, New York
Koppl R (2011) Pay attention to the physics analogies in Richard Wagner's Mind, Society, and Human Action. Stud Emerg Order 4:156–169
Nutter GW (1966) On economic size and growth. J Law Econ 9:163–188
Ostrom V (1987) The political theory of a compound republic, 2nd edn. University of Nebraska Press, Lincoln
Ostrom V (1997) The meaning of democracy and the vulnerability of societies: a response to Tocqueville's challenge. University of Michigan Press, Ann Arbor
Persson T, Tabellini G (2000) Political economics: explaining economic policy. MIT Press, Cambridge
Prigogine I (1997) The end of certainty: time, chaos, and the new laws of nature. Free Press, New York
Read L (1958) I, pencil. Foundation for Economic Education, Irvington
Reder MW (1999) Economics: the culture of a controversial science. University of Chicago Press, Chicago
Runst P, Wagner RE (2011) Choice, emergence, and constitutional process. J Inst Econ 7:131–145
Schelling TC (1978) Micromotives and macrobehavior. Norton, New York
Schumpeter JA (1954) A history of economic analysis. Oxford University Press, New York
Seagren C (2011) Examining social processes with agent-based models. Rev Aust Econ 24:1–17
Thomsen E (1992) Prices and knowledge. Routledge, London
Tinbergen J (1952) On the theory of economic policy. North-Holland, Amsterdam
Vriend NJ (2002) Was Hayek an ace? South Econ J 68:811–840
Wagner RE (2004) Public choice as an academic enterprise: Charlottesville, Blacksburg, and Fairfax retrospectively viewed. Am J Econ Sociol 63:55–74
Wagner RE (2006) Choice, catallaxy, and just taxation: contrasting architectonics for fiscal theorizing. Soc Philos Policy 23:235–254
Wagner RE (2007) Fiscal sociology and the theory of public finance. Edward Elgar, Cheltenham
Wagner RE (2008) Finding social dilemma: West of Babel, not east of Eden. Public Choice 135:55–66
Wagner RE (2009) Property, state, and entangled political economy. In: Wolf S, Andrea S, Tobias T (eds) Markets and politics: insights from a political economy perspective. Metropolis, Marburg, pp 37–49
Wagner RE (2010) Mind, society, and human action: time and knowledge in a theory of social economy. Routledge, London, p 208
Wagner RE (2011) Municipal corporations, economic calculation, and political pricing: exploring a theoretical antinomy. Public Choice 149:151–165
Wagner RE (2012) Deficits, debt, and democracy: wrestling with tragedy on the fiscal commons. Edward Elgar, Cheltenham
Walras L (1874 [1954]) Elements of pure economics. Richard D. Irwin, Homewood

Chapter 6
Constitutional Change: No Escaping Hayek*

Donald J. Boudreaux

> An attempt to describe the social good in detail seems to carry with it an implied willingness to impose this good, independently of observed or prospective agreement among persons. By contrast, my natural proclivity as an economist is to place ultimate value on process or procedure, and by implication to define as "good" that which emerges from agreement among free men.
>
> James M. Buchanan, *Thee Limits of Liberty* (1975, 167)

In *The Calculus of Consent* (1962), *The Limits of Liberty* (1975), and many of his other books and articles, Jim Buchanan addresses, in a variety of different ways, what can fairly be described as the single greatest theme of his scholarship: the significance of constitutional rules and the necessity of ensuring that these rules are as close to being "right" as is humanely possible. As the quotation above makes clear, for Buchanan, "right" is not a property to be divined and imposed by some great leader (or leaders). "Right" constitutional rules are those that emerge only from an inclusive *process* of bargaining over rules until unanimous agreement on some specific set of rules is achieved.

The ideal constitution-making process, as Buchanan envisions it, is also a conscious one. Each of the many bargainers at the table is aware that he is engaged in a process of making higher – "constitutional" – law for the society that he and his children will inhabit as citizens subject to whatever rules are eventually chosen. Carried out by (Buchanan assumes) reasonably rational beings governed by (hopefully enlightened) self-interest, this process of proposing, altering, pondering, and voting on various constitutional rules will yield a set of rules that as best as possible promotes as much as possible earthly flourishing for as many people as

---

*I thank Dwight Lee for comments and encouragement. I alone, however, am responsible for all of the remaining manifest weaknesses of this paper.

D.J. Boudreaux (✉)
Department of Economics, George Mason University, Fairfax, VA 22030, USA
e-mail: dboudrea@gmu.edu

D.R. Lee (ed.), *Public Choice, Past and Present: The Legacy of James M. Buchanan and Gordon Tullock*, Studies in Public Choice 28, DOI 10.1007/978-1-4614-5909-5_6,

possible in the polity. Importantly, the criteria by which this flourishing is judged are determined only by the preferences of the individuals who are party to the process of choosing constitutional rules.

"Voice" for subjective preferences, equality of individuals, bargaining, and voluntary unanimous agreement are all central to Buchanan's description of his normatively ideal way of making constitutions. This normatively ideal way looks a great deal like the operation of private markets. It involves exchange, gains from trade, and countless individuals each weighing subjective costs and benefits. Buchanan's ideal way of making constitutions also, and importantly, features consumer sovereignty: no one is forced to be party to the bargain. No one is obliged to "buy" until he is satisfied that the value of what he receives exceeds what he gives up in exchange. Requiring unanimous agreement, therefore, ensures that the expected benefits of the constitutional rules are indeed greater than the expected costs, all without any need for a third party to speculate about how some people's subjective benefits compare with some other people's subjective costs.[1]

But although Buchanan's ideal way of making constitutions features many of the attractive features of markets – and features also a *process* whereby people bargain with each other as equals – one attractive feature of markets that is absent from Buchanan's constitution-making picture is genuine, undirected, Hayekian evolution.

Buchanan is not only aware of this absence of Hayekian evolutionary process in his constitution-making scenario, he is glad of it. He rejects as inappropriate such an undirected process for making constitutional rules. As he says about himself, "I have no faith in the efficiency of social evolutionary process. The institutions that survive and prosper need not be those that maximize man's potential. Evolution may produce social dilemma as readily as social paradise" (Buchanan 1975, p. 167).

[1] In Chap. 6 of *The Calculus of Consent* (1962), Buchanan and Tullock explain the logic of weighing decision-making costs against the threat to each individual of having to abide by collective decisions that run against his or her wishes. If decision-making costs were zero, then in a polity whose members wish to accord equal weight to the preferences of each member, a rule of unanimity would always, at every level of political decision-making, be appropriate. There would be no reason not to require unanimous consent before the collective undertakes any action. If a proposal fails to gain unanimous consent, it should be modified until it is acceptable to everyone. The absence of decision-making costs would mean that the process of such modification is itself costless and, hence, should proceed until unanimous agreement is reached. But because such a process in fact is indeed costly – and because the costs of arriving at collective decisions likely rise at an increasing rate the greater is the percentage of voters required for approval – a unanimity requirement for ordinary, day-to-day collective choices would be unduly costly. Decision-making rules requiring less-than-unanimous agreement, therefore, are justified for such quotidian decision-making. But less-than-unanimity decision-making rules (and their outcomes) nevertheless can be said to rest on unanimous consent if they – the constitutional rules themselves – are agreed to unanimously. By unanimously agreeing to abide by decisions taken by (say) simple majority rule under circumstances more or less well specified by the constitution, any decisions reached under the constitution by less-than-unanimity rules will not violate the normative criterion that no one be forced to act against his or her will.

While not denying the truth of this last sentence, I will argue here that Buchanan jumps too quickly to his conclusion that conscious, centralized method of creating and choosing constitutional rules is superior to that of a spontaneous-order process. Indeed, the case for reconsidering the relative merits of relying upon spontaneous-order processes to generate constitutional rules is recommended by Buchanan's (1972) own familiar and proper insistence that sound policy is unlikely to emerge when analysts compare achievable real-world outcomes only with imaginary ideal outcomes.

There is no doubt that evolved constitutional rules might generate social dilemma – situations that are, by almost all normative criteria, inferior to those that would be generated by any number of different sets of constitutional rules that we can imagine being consciously bargained toward and ratified. But our imaginations are not reality. Our imaginations do not set the appropriate standard against which real-world outcomes ought to be judged. My contention in what follows is that Buchanan overlooks an important fact about any plausibly realistic method of conscious constitution-making. And although I will end with a few optimistic words about evolved constitution-making, my conclusion is *not* that Buchanan's rejection of evolved constitution-making is mistaken; rather, my conclusion is only that he has leapt too quickly to that conclusion.

II.

In their pioneering – and still insufficiently appreciated – book *Democracy and Decision* (1993), Geoffrey Brennan and Loren Lomasky distinguish *material* political motives from *expressive* political motives. [2] Material motives have long been the bread-and-butter focus of public-choice scholars. These motives are fueled by each individual's efforts to gain for himself as much material benefit through the political process as possible at as low a cost as possible. "Material political benefit" here can be read broadly. The term obviously includes monetary rents (such as the greater profits domestic producers receive as a result of higher tariffs on imports), lush offices for elected officials, the prospect for such officials to transform their political connections into private-sector jobs that pay high salaries, and inordinate job security for government bureaucrats. But material benefit, as understood here, also includes the psychic enjoyments individuals receive from being famous and from exercising political power.

Expressive political benefits, in contrast, are the satisfactions that a person receives when championing, in one form or another, his political or ethical values *independently of any connection that these values might have to his material well-being.* The free trader who votes against tariffs because he believes in free trade acts on expressive motives, as does the protectionist who votes for tariffs because he believes in (say) the ethical superiority of a national economy that has no commerce with that of any other nation.

[2] See also DeBow and Lee (1988), Boudreaux and Crampton (2003), and, most importantly, Caplan (2007).

While the boundary between material and expressive political motives is fuzzy, the former can be thought of as those fueled by narrow self-interest (or even "greed") while the latter are those fueled, at least partly, by a sincere regard for the welfare of people or phenomena (such as "the environment") beyond one's immediate and narrow personal interests.

Brennan and Lomasky argue convincingly that the fact that no individual voter expects to determine the outcome of an election elevates expressive motives relative to material motives. For example, a steel-company CEO who is ideologically disposed to favor free trade might nevertheless vote for higher steel tariffs if he believes that the outcome of the election turns on his vote, but might well vote against such a tariff if he understands that the outcome of the election will not turn on his vote.

One result of this reality is that each voter's preferences are ambiguous. If the steel-company CEO votes "no" on a ballot proposal to raise steel tariffs, do we conclude that he doesn't want such tariffs? Seems so. But because preferences are informed not only by expected benefits but also by whatever expected costs those benefits entail, a decision-making mechanism that shields a decision-maker from experiencing *at the moment of choice* either the expected benefits or the expected costs (or both) may well prompt that decision-maker to express a preference different from the preference that she would express if she experienced, as a result of *her* choice, the full benefits and costs of that choice.

In the voting booth, the steel-company CEO receives the full benefit of expressing his ideological commitment to free trade by voting against higher tariffs, but he is shielded from the material cost of such a vote. Because the outcome of the election will be unaffected by his vote, the voting booth enables him to express his ideological preferences free of charge. He does not have to consider the full range of consequences – even of consequences that he himself might personally bear down the road – of voting against the tariff.

If, as is plausible, this CEO would have voted for the tariff were he the sole voter in the election – but given that, because he is only one of many voters, he voted against the tariff – it is impossible to say what this CEO "wants." His preference over steel tariffs is unclear.

III.

Significantly, this ambiguity in each voter's preferences doesn't disappear under a rule of unanimity. Unless a voter believes that *all* other voters will vote for a particular option, then that voter is in the same position as he would be in under a simple majority rule: his vote will not affect the outcome of the election. If there are X voters, because each voter understands that no option is likely to receive as many as X–1 votes, no voter's vote will determine the outcome of the election.

Note the parallel between a unanimity rule and a simple majority rule. For a voter to believe that his vote will determine the outcome of the election under a unanimity rule, he must believe that, without his vote, some particular option will receive exactly X–1 votes (where X is the total number of voters or, more generally, the total number of votes that will be cast). For a voter to believe that his vote will determine the outcome of the election under a simple majority rule, he must believe that, without his vote, some particular option will receive exactly *X*/2 votes.[3] In elections with more than a small handful of voters, neither of these beliefs is remotely plausible. Therefore, even under a rule of unanimity, no rational voter will ever reckon that his vote is likely to be decisive.

The significance of this fact for Buchanan's normative theory of constitutional rule-making is that any practicable means of choosing constitutional rules for a polity of thousands (and, certainly, for a polity of hundreds of millions) of citizens, even under a rule of unanimity, will suffer from this ambiguity of each voter's preferences. Neither the knowledge by each citizen-voter that he or she is choosing constitutional rules nor the requirement that all such rules be agreed upon unanimously is sufficient to give each voter incentives to choose realistically rather than romantically. The very real threat of large numbers of citizens-voters going off on flights of perhaps highly irrational fancy as they choose constitutional rules raises the prospect that the process of consciously drafting, bargaining over, and voting on constitutional rules will result in "social dilemma" no less than would reliance upon Hayekian evolution of constitutional rules.[4]

Thus, the possibility that evolved constitutional rules will be worse than consciously chosen rules is insufficient to reject the former route in favor of the latter. The reason is that any practical means of actually arriving at reasonably inclusive agreement on a set of rules will be unable to avoid the problem of ambiguous voter preferences – or what Bryan Caplan (2007) calls "rational irrationality." And there is simply no reason to suppose that the potential problems caused by "rational irrationality" will generally be less troublesome than whatever are the potential problems caused by the failure of evolution to select appropriate rules.

IV.

A related reason counsels in favor of a more positive assessment of relying upon evolved rules relative to consciously chosen ones. At the end of the day, words on parchment, as such, have little power to affect the course of human events.

The range of activities that citizens demand the state to undertake – or will tolerate the state undertaking – ultimately reflects the society's culture. Words on parchment are simply too weak to prevent any government from doing what a significant portion of its citizens want it to do. Likewise, words on parchment will not enable a government to do what a significant portion of its citizens will not tolerate it doing.

History amply supports this proposition. Most infamously, perhaps, is the 1936 Soviet constitution. This document, ratified at the height of Stalin's reign of terror, was filled with glorious words guaranteeing open elections, freedom of religion, and all manner of liberties and privileges for ordinary Soviet citizens. It had no effect.

---

[3] A similar calculus – with only the denominator changed – applies to any other voting rule.

[4] See especially Hayek (1973, 1988).

Likewise, with the US Constitution in the face of the public's demand that the US government deals vigorously with the Great Depression – or, alternatively, with the public's *tolerance* of the US government seizing the opportunity presented by the Depression to greatly expand its power. Whether New Deal legislation resulted more from public demand or public tolerance is here of little relevance. The fact is that President Franklin Roosevelt and the US Congress during the 1930s ramped up significantly Washington's role in the economy. And they did so in ways that Bruce Ackerman (1990) – a scholar quite sympathetic to New Deal policies – agrees are in violation of the actual words of the US Constitution.

Ackerman's legal justification for the New Deal is telling: in his view, the Great Depression was so severe that it created in America a constitutional crisis. The constitution had to be amended, and amended more quickly, than was possible through formal Article V procedures. Roosevelt, the Congress, and the Supreme Court responded positively; they eventually satisfied the public demand for government action of a sort that would have been impossible if the actual words of the written constitutional document were never to be violated. The US Constitution, in Ackerman's telling, was in fact amended.

Proponents of the rule of law, especially as grounded in wise constitutional rules, obviously are uncomfortable with any account of constitutional change such as that offered by Ackerman. If government can do whatever it wants – or whatever a large portion of the public presses it to do – regardless of the words in the actual document, the constitution seems to be meaningless, or at least toothless. This discomfort is understandable. But reality is on Ackerman's side, at least as far as his positive account of constitutional rules goes. Ultimately, words on parchment will be read, interpreted, ignored, unduly amplified, or otherwise construed to mean what citizens and elected officials want them to mean. This description of the reality of constitutional rules might be said to be one of constitutional politics without romance.

This proposition is further supported by Buchanan's own recent and important work (2005) on "parentalism" as a force that drives political outcomes. Insisting that a significant number of people are "afraid to be free," Buchanan argues that the demise of traditional religious belief has prompted people to look instead to government to tell them how to behave. As Buchanan explains, unless citizens themselves reject the demand to be treated like children (which Buchanan thinks unlikely), the public's demand for parentalism will drive the state to intervene evermore intrusively and illiberally into our everyday lives. And this intervention, it is germane to point out here, will occur regardless of what the words of any constitution say.

V.

A Hayekian upshot of this pessimistic assessment of the role of written, formal constitutional rules is that the evolved rules that Buchanan so distrusts and that he wishes to replace with consciously chosen rules are, in the final analysis, impossible to escape. We in fact have no choice but to be governed ultimately by the rules that the political culture imposes – rules that are, at the end of the day, the results of a process of Hayekian evolution.

Recognizing this fact turns our attention from trying vainly to improve political outcomes by changing formal constitutions and toward finding the best avenues for changing political culture. Changing culture for the better, of course, is far more difficult than is drafting and voting to ratify a formal constitutional document. And success at trying to change culture for the better is never assured. These realities frustrate the reformer who wants change to be, compared to relying upon evolution, both easier and more quick to carry out and more certain to succeed. But these *are* the realities behind the romance of constitutional rule-making. We simply have no realistic option for effecting constitutional change other than changing people's perceptions, understandings, and attitudes. At least recognition of this reality might focus our attention on what must be done and inspire us to learn better how to perform this task.

If I may be bold in closing, I suggest that my conclusion is not as much at odds with Buchanan's works as might at first appear to be the case. It was Buchanan and Tullock, far more than any other scholars, who taught us that wishful thinking about politics is far more "wishful" than "thinking." It was Buchanan and Tullock, above and better than all others, who explained the calculus of consent as it operates in collective-choice domains. So it is Buchanan and Tullock whose insights and works form the bedrock on which the conclusion of this chapter rests. In particular, the enormous disconnect between the political choices that each individual makes and the personal consequences of those choices on each decision-maker frees most political decision-makers to rationally behave irrationally. And this rationally irrational behavior manifests itself not only in formal elections but in everyday thinking and talking about politics. For better or worse – it could be either, depending upon the content of the prevailing rhetoric (McCloskey 2010) – words on parchment will always be trumped by the ideas that dominate in society. We can all be thankful that ideas in *The Calculus of Consent* have inspired a significant number of people to think more realistically about politics.

References

Ackerman B (1990) We the people. Harvard University Press, Cambridge, MA

Boudreaux DJ, Crampton EP (2003) Truth and consequences: some economics of false consciousness. Indep Rev 8:27–45

Brennan G, Lomasky L (1993) Democracy and decision: the pure theory of electoral preference. Cambridge University Press, New York

Buchanan JM (1972) Toward analysis of closed behavioral systems. In: Buchanan JM, Tollison RD (eds) Theory of public choice. University of Michigan Press, Ann Arbor, pp 11–23

Buchanan JM (1975) The limits of liberty. University of Chicago Press, Chicago

Buchanan JM (2005) Afraid to be free: dependency as desideratum. Public Choice 124:19–31

Buchanan JM, Tullock G (1962) The calculus of consent. University of Michigan Press, Ann Arbor

Caplan B (2007) The myth of the rational voter. Princeton University Press, Princeton
DeBow ME, Lee DR (1988) Understanding (and misunderstanding) public choice: a response to Farber and Frickey. Texas Law Rev 66:993–1012
Hayek FA (1973) Law, legislation, and liberty: rules and order. University of Chicago Press, Chicago
Hayek FA (1988) The fatal conceit. University of Chicago Press, Chicago
McCloskey DN (2010) Bourgeois dignity. University of Chicago Press, Chicago

Chapter 7
The Bioeconomics of Scout Bees Voting-with-the-Wings Using Less-Than-Unanimity Voting Rule: Can Bees Count, Quorum Sense, etc.?*

Janet T. Landa

Introduction

My 1986 paper entitled "The Political Economy of Swarming in Honeybees: Voting-with-the-Wings, Decision-Making Costs, and the Unanimity Rule," was published in *Public Choice* (Landa 1986). It was my first bioeconomics paper, using economic theory, specifically public choice theory to examine aspects of the swarming of honeybees. I used the Buchanan–Tullock's (1962) cost approach to the choice of Pareto-optimal rules for group decision-making to analyze Martin Lindauer's (1961) pioneering experimental findings that scout bees use the unanimous voting rule to arrive at their collective choice of a new nesting site. More recent experimental findings by Thomas Seeley et al. (2006), however, found that the essence of group decision-making by scout bees is their use of a kind of "quorum-sensing" voting rule, rather than the unanimity rule in arriving at their collective choice of the best new nest site. In light of the new experimental findings, this chapter revises my earlier paper's theoretical conclusion that the unanimity rule is the "best" rule for the scout bees' collective choice of the best new nest site. A novelty in this chapter is my introduction of a hypothesis that although bees cannot count, they are able to "subitize," hence are able to sense when a collective decision of a new nest site has been reached by a quorum of scout bees.

---

*I dedicate this paper to my professors, James M. Buchanan and Gordon Tullock, on the occasion of the 50th anniversary of the publication of their seminal book, *The Calculus of Consent: Logical Foundations of Constitutional Democracy*. Ann Arbor: The University of Michigan Press, 1962.

J.T. Landa (✉)
Department of Economics, York University,
4700 Keele Street, Toronto, ON M3J 1P3, Canada
e-mail: jlanda@yorku.ca

D.R. Lee (ed.), *Public Choice, Past and Present: The Legacy of James M. Buchanan and Gordon Tullock*, Studies in Public Choice 28, DOI 10.1007/978-1-4614-5909-5_7,

The rest of this chapter is organized as follows: I discuss, in the first part of the chapter, the socio-economic organisation of a honyebee colony as a firm and as a superorganism. This is followed by several sub-sections where I discuss honeybee swarming and scout bees democratic voting process in the collective choice of a best new nest site, comparing Martin Lindauer's (1961) experimental findings that scout bees use a consensus/unanimity voting rule with Thomas Seeley et al.'s (2006) empirical findings that scout bees use a quorum-sensing rule. I then discuss Seeley's three hypotheses as to how bees are able to sense when a quorum has been reached. The second part of the chapter is a theoretical section where I use Buchanan-Tullock's (1962) "Calculus of Consent" theory to explain scout bees "voting-with-the-wings" collective choice of a new nest site. Based on Seeley et al.'s (2006) empirical findings, I revise my 1986 bioeconomics-public choice theory that the unamimous voting rule, observed by Lindauer, is the "best" rule for swarming bees' collective choice of a new nest site in favor of the quorum-sensing/less-than-unanimity rule. In the third part of the chapter, I develop the economics and bioeconomics of counting and "subitizing." I offer a new hypothesis that bees, although unable to count, are able to "subitize," hence are able to sense when a quorum has been reached. I end the chapter with some brief conclusions.

Socioeconomic Organization of a Honeybee Colony as a Firm and as a Superorganism

The honeybee, *Apis mellifera*, is a species of bees that are found in temperate and tropical regions all over the world. They live together in a bee colony, consisting of 20,000–30,000 bees (Seeley 2010, p. 33), in a nest constructed of beeswax, beautifully arranged in symmetric hexagon cells.

Biologist Edward O. Wilson (1978, p. 26) describes a bee colony as:

> ...operating somewhat like a factory inside a fortress. Entrenched in the nest site, harassed by enemies and uncertain changes in the physical environment, the colony must send foragers out to gather food while converting the secured food inside the nest into virgin queens and males as rapidly and as efficiently as possible.

Just as in human society, we have factories and firms, so a bee colony can be compared to a factory or a firm, whose output is more bees. The following describes the socioeconomic organization of a bee colony (Landa and Wallis 1988). Analogous to the specialization and division of labor and the coordination of interdependent workers within a firm, there is functional specialization and division of labor among the different castes of bees: the queen—larger in size than her worker daughters—functions as the egg-laying machine inside the nest; the house bees specialize in the activity of building and maintaining beeswax combs; nurse bees feed larvae; foraging bees fly outside the nest to gather food; guard bees, stationed at the entrance of the nest, prevent bees from other colonies from entering the nest to rob honey; and scout bees, former foraging bees, search and vote for the best nest before leading the swarm to the new nest. The only males in the colony are the drones, constituting a tiny minority of the bee population; the drones function is to fertilize the queen during the nuptial flight; once they performed their job, they die. The bee colony is a "family firm."

Communication within the nest are largely through the chemical sense (smell and taste) and by the "dance language of bees" pioneered by Karl von Frisch (1967), resulting in a high degree of cooperation and coordination of the efforts of all members of the bee colony. Hölldobler and Wilson (2009, pp. 110–111) in their study of eusocial insect colonies (ants, bees, termites) characterize these colonies as "superorganisms" because members of these insect colonies work together as teams, functioning as a unit, and are highly integrated by their communication system.

Swarming and Scout Bees Democratic Voting Process in the Collective Choice of the Best New Nest

Swarming is the process whereby a bee colony divides itself into two groups: one group staying behind with the new queen, while the other group (the swarm) flies off with the old queen in order to establish a new colony. Swarming occurs in late spring to early summer in temperate climates when food supplies are plentiful; congestion within the nest appears to be a critical factor leading to swarming.

A swarm contains approximately about 10,000 bees. Half the colony's bees, after leaving the old nest with the old queen, will hang on a nearby object, like a tree; there they will wait for the scout bees to search for their new nest. What is so remarkable about the scout bees' choice of a new home is that they engage in a democratic voting process to arrive at their collective choice of the best new nest, before they fly off to their new home.

Lindauer's (1961) Experimental Findings: Scout Bees Use Consensus/ Unanimity Voting Rule

The pioneer experimental study of swarming in honey bees and of scout bees voting for a new home is by Martin Lindauer (1961), a student of Karl von Frisch (1886–1982), whose most famous discovery was the "dance language of the bees" (von Frisch 1967), i.e., foraging bees are able to communicate to hive nest mates via a waggle dance, to indicate the distance and direction of a food source. The scout bees, experienced former foragers, constitute about 5%, a tiny minority of the swarm. Thus, if the swarm consists of about 10,000 honey bees, about 500 scout bees will be involved in the democratic collective decision-making process. When a scout bee finds a suitable site, it flies back to the swarm where it performs a dance on the outside of the surface of the swarm. Lindauer (1961, p. 50) describes the process whereby the scout bees arrive at an unanimous choice of the best nest site:

> ...the agreement appears to take place in a seemingly simple manner: the better the qualities of a nesting place exhibits the livelier and longer will be the messengers' dance after the inspection. In this way new messengers are recruited in the cluster for this place, which then likewise seek out and inspect this nesting place, and then they too solicit by means of the same lively dances. If those scouting bees which at first had only inferior or average dwellings to announce are persuaded by the livelier dances of their colleagues to inspect the other nesting place, then nothing more stands in the way of an agreement. They can now make a comparison between their own and the new nesting place, and they will solicit in the cluster for the better of the two.

The voting process for the best nest continues until all differences are democratically resolved as scout bees converge to an unanimous choice. Lindauer shows that one particular swarm took 5 days of voting among 21 nest sites until one particular nest—the best nest—becomes the unanimous choice. After consensus is reached for the best nest, the swarm prepares for lift-off to fly to the new nest.

Seeley's Experimental Findings: Quorum-Sensing Rather Than Consensus Voting Rule

In the mid-1990s, Thomas Seeley and his coworkers continued Lindauer's work on swarming bees and how they arrive at their collective decision of a best new nest site.

In a number of experiments conducted on Appledore Island, Seeley et al. (2006) reported their findings: it is *quorum sensing* rather than *consensus* that will *trigger the preparation for the lift-off of the swarm to fly to the new nest.* One of the swarms reached a quorum over 3 days for a nest site after considering a total of 11 sites. See Fig. 5 in Seeley et al. (2006, p. 224).

Once the quorum is reached at one of the sites, the bees at this site will fly back to the swarm and will begin the process of preparing the entire swarm for flying to their new nest. Seeley (2010, p. 71), in his new book, describes their 2006 findings:

> A quorum of scouts at one of the proposed sites, not a consensus among dancers at the swarm, is the key stimulus for scouts to start piping and thereby initiate preparations for takeoff.... [P]reparations for takeoff, which generally take an hour or more, provide sufficient time for the positive feedback process of recruitment to the best site to produce the necessary unanimous agreement among the scouts.

Although consensus is still required for the swarm to fly to their new home, what is important in Seeley et al.'s findings is that the process of lift-off to fly to the new home starts earlier because *preparations for lift-off* begins as soon as the quorum is reached.

Seeley asks the intriguing question: Why don't the swarms use consensus sensing rather than quorum sensing? His answer basically is that bees have difficulty in counting:

> One likely reason is that sensing a consensus among the dancing bees would be extremely difficult for the bees. Presumably, each scout would have to poll the advertisements of her fellow scouts, which would involve travelling over the swarm cluster, reading dances, and keeping a mental tally of these readings. Doing all these things would be especially difficult on larger swarms with more scouts and thus more dances to poll. Quorum sensing however, need not become more difficult with increasing swarm size, because the quorum size, could be fixed, hence independent of swarm size (pp. 171–172).

The other reason suggested by Seeley (p. 173) is that quorum-sensing "enables a swarm to strike a good balance between speed and accuracy in its decision-making" because the swarm is not delayed by the necessity for consensus to be reached before it initiates the start of the fly-off to the new nest. This is important because any delay of the take off after 5 p.m. could force the swarm to spend another chilly night outside its old nest.

Seeley (p. 173) found that the quorum used by the bees is 20–30 scout bees simultaneously at a site (half inside, half outside), which requires that some 75 scout bees are voting for this site.

How Bees Can Sense a Quorum: Seeley's Hypotheses

Seeley apparently dismisses the possibility that bees can count, especially when all the scout bees must come to a consensus regarding the best nest; the larger the size of the scout bee group involved in decision-making, the more difficult counting becomes. Quorum sensing makes counting simpler because of the fixed number of individual bees. Still, Seeley dismisses the possibility that bees can count. The unresolved problem is, in Seeley's (2010, p. 171) words, "Exactly how the scout bees sense a quorum also remains unknown." Instead, Seeley (2010) suggests three hypotheses for future research as to how scout bees sense a quorum, without counting: Bees use:

1. Visual information: "Constantly moving scout bees are easily detected visually outside the cavity and even inside it" (p. 171).
2. Touch/contact with other bees: "It seems entirely possible that a bee could use the rate of contacts with scouts in general, or collisions with buzz-runners in particular, as an indicator of the number of fellow scouts at a particular site" (p. 172).
3. Olfactory information: "It is possible that the level of attraction pheromones rises with increasing numbers of bees at a site" (p. 172).

There is, however, a fourth novel hypothesis which I am offering: bees "subitizing" to sense when a quorum has been reached. This is developed in section "Quorum Sensing: The Economics and Bioeconomics of Counting and Subitizing".

Using Buchanan–Tullock's (1962) "Calculus of Consent" Theory to Explain Scout Bees "Voting-with-the-Wings" Collective Choice of a New Nest

In a paper published in *Public Choice* (Landa 1986), I used the Buchanan–Tullock (1962) theory for the choice of optimal decision-making rule, to explain why for the Lindauer's scout bees, the unanimity rule used by scout bees for their collective choice of a new nest is Pareto-optimal. The theory has two costs curves: the decision-making costs and the external costs; only when decision-making costs are zero would the unanimity rule be Pareto-optimal. But in a large number of instances, decision-making costs are large when the size of the group involved in collective decision-making is large; hence, the majority rule is often the Pareto-optimal voting rule.

Using the Buchanan-Tullock theory, I argued that the scout bees' use of the unanimity rule is Pareto-optimal because the scout bees (1) are former experienced foragers, (2) share a common interest in choosing the best available site, and (3) constitute a very tiny group, 5% of the swarm. These factors make the decision-making costs for the entire group of scout bees negligible, while external costs are reduced to zero when the entire group is involved in the decision-making process.

I was, however, never quite satisfied with my explanation because the famous Lindauer scout bees took 5 days to arrive at their unanimous choice of a new nest. A 5-day voting period can be very risky for the entire swarm in the event that one of the days turned very cold. Until I read Seeley et al.'s (2006) paper, I could not resolve my misgivings about my theoretical explanation that the unanimous voting rule is the optimal rule for Lindauer's scout bees' collective choice of the swarm's best new nest.

On the other hand, Seeley's scout bees, by voting-with-the-wings, using a quorum-sensing rule, means that less-than-unanimity rule is being used. It is more efficient than the unanimity rule because as Seeley puts it: quorum sensing "enables a swarm to strike a good balance between speed and accuracy in its decision-making." In the language of Buchanan and Tullock, here, everything depends on the balance betwen external costs and decision-making costs. Where external costs are especially high, the voting rule will tend to be one of supermajority rule; when decision-making costs are relatively high, the rule will tend to be one of submajority. Majority rule itself may or may not be chosen as the optimal rule. All depends on the vertical summation of the external cost and the decision-making cost functions. The truly significant contribution of Buchanan and Tullock (1962) was that the optimal rule may well be less than or more than simply majority rule. Take Seeley et al.'s (2006) experimental findings that about 30 scout bees out of 75 scout bees at a particular nest site are needed to make a collective choice for the best nest site. This means that about 40% of scout bees at this site make the collective choice for this site for the entire scout bee group at the site as well as for the swarm. Since the Buchanan-Tullock theory considers *simple majority rule* as the optimal decision rule when decision-making costs are positive and the size of group is large, the scout bee's quorum-sensing rule appears to be a less-than-optimal voting rule. How to explain that scout bees appear to use a a less-than-optimal voting rule? Given that I am assuming that (1) scout bees are all equally competent because they were former experienced foragers, (2) each bee independently assesses the quality of the nest sites visited, (3) they all have the same shared interest in finding the best new home, and (4) the risk to the swarm of significant delays (e.g. lengthening the number of voting days) in moving to the new nest if unanimous rule is used, I would argue that the balance between external costs and now the relatively high decision-making costs has resulted in an outcome in favor of a sub-majority rule used by scout bees at a particular nest site. Scout bee democracy, using quorum-sensing rule in the swarming process, now fits perfectly within the public choice theoretical framework of Buchanan-Tullock's 1962) seminal *Calculus of Consent: Logical Foundations of Constitutional Democracy.*

Quorum Sensing: The Economics and Bioeconomics of Counting and Subitizing

Counting and Numbers

Imagine a world without counting and numbers. Such a world would be unthinkable. In the political arena, there can be no democratic governments since counting and aggregating votes in order to declare a winner/winners in an election is an intrinsic part of the voting process in a democracy. In the arena of markets, without counting and numbers there can be no money, no profit-making merchants, no moneylenders, etc. In our personal life, we engage in counting everyday, consciously or implicitly.[1] Fortunately not only numbers exist but also an efficient system of calculation, based upon the 10-digit Hindu-Arabic numeral system: 0,1,2,3,4,5,6,7,8,9 and place values, making it possible to add, subtract, multiply, and divide by easily learned simple procedures.[2]

However, counting objects beyond ten requires some kind of tallying system to keep track of numbers, such as using a stick on which notches are made and devices for adding and subtracting numbers, for example, the use of a calculating device such as a Chinese abacus.

But there is no empirical evidence that bees can count. Thus how can scout bees sense when a quorum of 20–30 bees had been reached? I offer the hypothesis that bees are able to subitize, hence, able to sense when a quorum of 20–30 has been reached.

[1] For a fascinating discussion of counting and numbers, see Brian Butterworth (1999).

[2] See the fascinating book by Keith Devlin (2011) on counting and the introduction of the Hindu-Arabic numerical system by Leonardo Pisano (Leonardo of Pisa), nicknamed Fibonacci, to the Western trading world.

Quorum Sensing: The Bioeconomics of "Subitizing" by Scout Bees

Before discussing scout bees' ability to sense when a quorum has been reached, we need to define the meaning of a "quorum."

According to *Robert's Rules of Order* (pp. 257–8),

> A quorum of an assembly is such a number as must be present in order that business can be legally transacted. The quorum refers to the number present, not to the number voting. The quorum of a mass meeting is the number present at the time, as they constitute the membership at that time. The quorum of a body of delegates, unless the bylaws provide for a smaller quorum, is a majority of the enrolled as attending the convention, not those appointed. The quorum of any other deliberative assembly with an enrolled membership (unless the by-laws provide for a smaller quorum) is a majority of all the members.

For example, the quorum for the United States Supreme Court is *six* judges out of nine judges (chief justice and eight associate justices), hence a two-thirds majority, a supermajority. The quorum for the Supreme Court of Canada is *five* out of nine judges (chief justice of Canada and eight justices), hence is a simple majority.

For scout bees, according to Seeley, 20–30 scout bees comprise a quorum with bees simultaneously at a site (half inside, half outside), which requires that some 75 scout bees are voting for this site. Translated into the language of voting rules, this means that less than a majority—"a minority majority"—of the 75 voting scout bees is needed to make a collective decision for the choice of this particular nest site.

How then can all the scout bees at a particular nest site "know"/sense that a quorum of about 20–30 bees have reached a collective decision regarding the new nest site? I offer the hypothesis that each individual scout bee at the particular nest site is able to subitize that a quorum has been reached.

"Subitizing" is the ability to instantly visualize a small number of objects, ranging from one to six items, without counting. It is a word coined by psychologist E.L. Kaufman et al. (1949) and is derived from the Latin root "subitus" meaning "sudden." I learned of the word "subitize" in November 2010 when I watched a TV lecture on "The Mathematical Animal" given by philosopher Ian Hacking (2010). I was very excited when I learnt of this concept because I immediately saw that this concept is going to be important in the writing of this chapter.

There are two kinds of subitizing: (a) making absolute judgments, for example, when we roll a dice, we can immediately see one, two, three, four, five, six dots, without counting the individual dots and (b) making relative judgments: Hacking said that he can subitize whether there are more people listening to his talk, sitting on the left side of the lecture hall as compared to the right side of the lecture hall. This second example is stated formally by Kaufman et al. (1949, p. 498):

> Suppose that there are two collections or groups of objects--coins, trees, beans, or aircraft--and we do not know how many objects there are. Suppose further that for some reason we cannot count the number of objects in either group. Still, some property of each group makes it possible for a person to say one of these groups is greater-than, less-than, or equal to the other group. It is this property of a collection of objects that we define as *numerousness.*

All human adults are able to subitize. Even newborn infants are said to have the ability to subitize (Butterworth 1999; 2000 paperback, p. 108). In the nonhuman world, there are some empirical evidence that even tiny nonhumans such as birds (e.g., pigeons) are able to subitize in terms of making relative as well as making absolute judgments involving a small number range (Emmerton 2001). Psychologist Jacky Emmerton suggests that birds' numerical abilities have functional significance in that:

> ...there are some situations in which it might be advantageous to be able to differentiate numerosity. One situation that comes to mind is foraging. When an animal has to make feeding choices it may be useful for it to estimate the number of food items available in different patches (VII, first paragraph, e-book)

Emmerton mentioned the experiments done by Otto Koehler (1941):

> ...that a bird, if given a choice between two arrays, should more readily choose the one containing the greater number of items. Such a bias had already been mentioned by Koehler (1941). When he trained a pigeon to choose one of two seed patches, placed at opposite ends of a strip of cardboard, he noticed a spontaneous tendency by the bird to approach the larger amount, even if the 'correct' one for the bird to eat was the less numerous patch. (VII. 3rd paragraph, e-book)

Thus, my hypothesis that scout bees are able to subitize when a quorum has been reached at a particular nest site, can be tested indirectly by testing the following hypothesis: Scout bees prefer to forage in an area with a larger patch of flowering plants compared to an area with a smaller patch of flowering plants. One can do an experiment by placing two boxes at equal distance from a nest site, with more pots of flowering plants placed in one box as compared to another box, and observe whether scout bees from a particular nest fly directly to the box containing more pots of flowering plants.

Conclusions

In my honeybees paper (Landa 1986), I used the Buchanan–Tullock's (1962) cost approach to collective action to explain that Lindauer's (1961) scout bees' use of the unanimous decision-making rule for their collective choice of a new nest site is Pareto-optimal. However, I had misgivings about my conclusion because to reach unanimous consent may take the scout bees too long a time (e.g., one Lindauer bee swarm took 5 days of voting among 21 nest sites to reach their choice of the best new nest site), thus jeopardizing the safety of the entire swarm in the event that cold temperatures suddenly set in. But with the publication of the experimental findings by Seeley et al. (2006) that scout bees use the quorum-sensing rule to reach group decision-making for a new nest site, the Buchanan-Tullock theory is now powerfully able to explain the rationality and the optimality of the "quorum-sensing" rule used by scout bees to arrive at their choice of the best new nest site. Thus, this chapter shows that after 50 years of publication of Buchanan and Tullock's seminal book, *The Calculus of Consent* remains a powerfully insightful and relevant book for all scholars in the social sciences and beyond to evolutionary biology for understanding voting behavior and voting processes in human and nonhuman societies (e.g., ants, fish schools, honeybees).[3]

Because voting always involve counting the results, and bees are unable to count, the novelty in this chapter lies in my introducing E.L. Kaufman et. al.'s (1949) concept of "subitizing"—the instant ability to perceive numbers without counting—in the psychology literature into the public choice and bioeconomics literatures; in this case, my hypothesis that scout bees are able to subitize to sense when a quorum has been reached, hence, they are able to reach a less-than-unanimity decision-making rule for their choice of a new nest site.

Acknowledgments This is a revised version of a paper presented at the Second World Congress of the Public Choice Societies, Hyatt Regency Miami, Florida, 8–11 March 2012. I would like to thank Bernard Grofman, discussant of my paper, Charles K. Rowley, and Anthony Wallis for helpful comments which improved this chapter.

References

Buchanan JM (1965) An economic theory of clubs. Economica 32:1–14

Buchanan JM, Tullock G (1962) The calculus of consent: logical foundations of constitutional democracy. The University of Michigan Press, Ann Arbor

Butterworth B (1999) The mathematical brain. McMillan, London (2000 paperback edition by Papermac)

Devlin K (2011) The man of numbers: Fibonacci's arithmetic revolution. Bloomsbury, London

Emmerton J (2001) Birds' judgement of number and quantity. Avian visual cognition (This is an e-book that I searched via Google)

Hacking I (2010) The mathematical animal. TVO program "Big Ideas": Ian Hacking on the mathematical animal. Aired on 19 March 2011

Hölldobler B, Wilson EO (2009) The superorganisms: the beauty, elegance, and strangeness of insect societies. Norton, New York

Kaufman EL, Lord MW, Reese TW, Volkmann J (1949) The discrimination of visual number. Am J Psychol 62(4):498–525

Koehler O (1941) Vom Erlernen unbenannter Anzahlen bei Vögeln. (On the learning of unnamed numerosities by birds.) Die Naturwissenschaften 29:201–218

[3]See, for example, Landa's (1998) paper on schooling fish, which uses Buchanan's (1965) theory of clubs, combined with Buchanan–Tullock's (1962) "Calculus of Consent" theoretical framework. See also Landa and Wallis (1988), Landa and Tullock (2003).

Landa JT (1986) The political economy of swarming in honeybees: voting-with-the-wings, decision-making costs, and the unanimity rule. Public Choice 51:25–38
Landa JT (1998) Bioeconomics of schooling fishes: selfish fish, quasi free riders, and other fishy tales. Environ Biol Fish 53(2):353–364
Landa JT, Wallis A (1988) Socioeconomic organization of honeybee colonies. J Soc Biol Struct 2:353–363
Landa JT, Tullock G (2003) Why ants do but honeybees do not contruct satellite nests. J Bioeconomics 5:151–164
Lindauer M (1961) Communication among social bees. Harvard University Press, Cambridge
Seeley TD (2010) Honeybee democracy. Princeton University Press, Princeton
Seeley TD, Visscher PK, Passino KM (2006) When 10,000 bees go house hunting, how do they cooperatively choose their new nesting site? Am Sci 94:220–229
von Frisch K (1967) The dance language and orientation of bees. Oxford University Press, London
Wilson EO (1978) The ergonomics of caste in the social insects. Am Econ Rev 68(4):25–35

Chapter 8
James Buchanan and Gordon Tullock: A Half-Century On

William F. Shughart II

Introduction

The Calculus of Consent: Logical Foundations of Constitutional Democracy (Buchanan and Tullock 1962) is a watershed in the economic analysis of collective decision-making. Although the coauthors of that work stood in a very real sense on the shoulders of giants, giants reaching back to the Marquis de Condorcet (1785), Charles Dodgson ("Lewis Carroll") ([1884] 2010), Knut Wicksell ([1896] 1967), and, more recently, Duncan Black (1948a, b, c, 1958), Kenneth Arrow ([1951] 1963), and Anthony Downs (1957),[1] but probably not to Isaac Newton,[2] James Buchanan, and Gordon Tullock's book, published by the University of Michigan Press – and

[1]Appendix 2 to *The Calculus*, written by Gordon Tullock and titled "Theoretical Forerunners" (Buchanan and Tullock 1962: 323–340), summarizes the roots of public choice as seen by that founder in the literatures of economics and game theory. Appendix 1, "Marginal Notes on Reading Political Philosophy," contributed by James Buchanan (ibid.: 307–322), anchors public choice in the literature of political science.

[2]In a letter to Robert Hooke, dated February 5, 1676, Newton famously wrote that, "What Des-Cartes [Rene Descartes] did was a good step. You have added much several ways, and especially in taking ye colours of thin plates into philosophical consideration. If I have seen further it is by standing on ye sholders [sic] of Giants." Newton's unsaid, but implied "seen further than you" may have reflected the fact that in the fields of optics and of other natural sciences, he and Hooke were lifelong rivals and, perhaps, enemies. Source: http://en.wikipedia.org/wiki/Shoulders_of_giants; last accessed May 21, 2012.

W.F. Shughart II (✉)
Jon M. Huntsman School of Business, Utah State University,
3565 Old Main Hill, Logan, UT 84322-3565, USA
e-mail: william.shughart@usu.edu; wshughart@comcast.net

D.R. Lee (ed.), *Public Choice, Past and Present: The Legacy of James M. Buchanan and Gordon Tullock*, Studies in Public Choice 28, DOI 10.1007/978-1-4614-5909-5_8,

still in print 50 years later – stands unchallenged as the founding document of the field now known as public choice or as "rational choice" in political science circles.

I was privileged to be a member of the faculties of the Department of Economics and the Center for Study of Public Choice at George Mason University in the fall of 1986, when news of the awarding of the Nobel Prize in Economic Science to James Buchanan was announced to the world. As a matter of fact, it was my own (paperback) copy of *The Calculus* that was filmed for later broadcast on that remarkable day.

That personal experience undoubtedly colors my impressions of that Nobel (and noteworthy) event, but it should not detract from my evaluation of the significance of Buchanan and Tullock's joint and independent contributions to the scholarly literature. I also confess to being biased by my appointment in fall 2005 as senior editor (a.k.a. editor-in-chief) of *Public Choice*,[3] the academic journal founded in 1966 by Gordon Tullock[4] that at the outset was – and continues to be – the primary outlet for research by scholars working at the intersection of the disciplines of economics and political science.[5]

The path-breaking nature of Buchanan and Tullock's *Calculus* was recognized immediately. My own assessment thus merely adds marginally to by now widely accepted opinion, which, as Charles Rowley (2012) has written, was by and large enthusiastically positive soon after the book had appeared in print.

---

[3]I had served previously for a decade as the journal's book review editor, then edited jointly by Gordon Tullock's immediate successors, Charles Rowley and Robert Tollison. After being in that capacity for a few months, Gordon observed that I had not done nearly as bad a job as he had expected of me. Those of us fortunate to know Gordon will interpret his remark as very high praise indeed!

[4]It was then called *Papers in Non-Market Decision-Making*, consistent with the rather unwieldy handle of the Committee on Nonmarket Decision-Making, organized at the University of Virginia in the early 1960s, the precursor to today's Public Choice Society. The change of name to "public choice" apparently was adopted at the suggestion of William C. Mitchell (Simmons 2011, p. xiii). On the journal's early history, see Tullock (1991) and Rowley (1991).

[5]Public choice/rational choice should not be confused with so-called new political economy, which emerged in Western Europe and in the Cambridge, Mass., fragment of the "Eastern Bloc" over the past decade or so, and which is exemplified in the works of, for example, Persson and Tabellini (2002, 2005) and Acemoglu and Robinson (2005, 2012). Although the self-styled new political economists plow much the same ground plowed already by the two founders of the "Virginia School" of public choice and of the many scholars who followed their lead, they rarely acknowledge their predecessors' contributions. For instance, a reference to Buchanan and Tullock (1962) appears just once – in a footnote – in Persson and Tabellini (2005); there is no mention at all of either Buchanan or Tullock in the indexes to Acemoglu and Robinson's (2005, 2012) two latest books. One of the key defects in the new political economy is the idea that elected and appointed public officials have incentives, stronger or weaker, to cater to society's welfare, however, that may be defined. That mindset echoes the "prevailing view of political scientists ...," prior to the public choice revolution, "that government is generally benevolent, often benign, and seldom dangerous" (Simmons 2011: 2).

Nobel laureates seem to come and go – often forgotten as quickly as last year's winners of Oscars for best picture, best actor, and best actress. Nobel laureates in economics should not fall from memory so quickly, with the exceptions perhaps of throwaway recipients of that award, such as Gunnar Myrdal and Paul Krugman, who apparently were selected more for the compatibility of their public policy opinions with Swedish political correctness[6] than for the value added by their scientific contributions, or Richard Stone, who by all accounts was chosen in a last-minute compromise between the factions supporting other candidates into which the selection committee had divided that year. Duncan Black, call your office!

As the foundation on which the discipline of public choice has been built, *The Calculus* will hold center stage in what follows if, for no reason other than that one short essay cannot possibly do justice to the vast, wide-ranging and humbling (to their students) body of scholarship produced jointly and independently by the field's two leading lights.[7] The collected works of James Buchanan (1999–2000), edited by Geoffrey Brennan, Hartmut Kliemt, and Robert Tollison, and the "selected works" of Gordon Tullock (2004–2006), edited by Charles Rowley, both published by the Liberty Fund, fill much more linear space than can be housed on one library bookshelf. The areas of study encompassed by these two eminent scholars range from their contributions to the literatures of, inter alia, Austrian economics (Buchanan [1969] 1978) and political philosophy (Buchanan 1975) to the law and legal procedure (Tullock 1980b), rent-seeking (Tullock 1967, 1980a, 1989; Buchanan 1980), autocracies (Tullock 1987, 2001), bio-economics (Tullock 1994), public budget deficits and debt (Buchanan [1958] 1999, [1964] 1982), and, quoting "Buzz Lightyear," infinity and beyond.

So, I begin with *The Calculus* and then follow with idiosyncratic summaries of the works of James Buchanan and Gordon Tullock that have had the greatest influences on my own thinking.

The Costs (and Possible Benefits) of Collective Decision-Making

Although it has now become somewhat commonplace (albeit not universally so) to acknowledge the potential and actual defects in democratic decision-making, *The Calculus* was the first sustained effort to analyze systematically the consequences of recognizing that groups do not take decisions monolithically but rather that political decisions are made only by individuals, given their own preferences,

---

[6]President Barack Obama's Nobel Peace Prize, awarded in 2009 "for his extraordinary efforts to strengthen international diplomacy and cooperation between peoples," easily could be added to the list.

[7]This statement is by no means intended to downplay the contributions of the field's other acknowledged "founding fathers," which in addition to those scholars identified in the first paragraph are William Riker (1962), Mancur Olson (1965), William Niskanen (1971, 1975, 2001), and William Mitchell (1967, 2001).

objective functions, and constraints on behavior (see Olson 1965 for an elaboration of that theme). Because groups are not organic actors, there is therefore no such thing as the romantic notion of a Rousseauian "general will" or anything approximating "society's" (or the "public's") interest (Munger 2001).

If only individuals, having diverse preferences and objective functions, are capable rationally of taking decisions that impact their own wealth and welfare, then the fundamental problem of collective choice is one of aggregating those individual preferences in a way that is consistent with their respective rankings of alternatives. Unfortunately, though, Arrow ([1951] 1963) already had proven that such an aggregation is impossible, except in the case of dictatorship, which obviously is inimical to common notions of "democracy." Individual preferences do not scale up to group preferences. Hence, the outcome of any collective decision-making process depends on the precise rule (e.g., plurality, simple majority, supermajority, or unanimous consent) under which individual choices are tabulated and a "winner" is declared.

The problems inherent in simple majority rule, adumbrated in the works, cited above, of the Marquis de Condorcet, Lewis Carroll, and Duncan Black, who produced examples of "cycling" or indecisiveness in decisions taken in that way when voters are faced by choices over three or more alternatives, be they candidates for political office or policy options, supplied some of the intellectual backdrop for *The Calculus*.

To me, one of the key contributions of Buchanan and Tullock (1962: 63–84), in a chapter titled "A Generalized Economic Theory of Constitutions," based on a working paper by the last-named author and then fleshed out in the next two chapters, is the distinction between two costs of collective decision-making. One of these comprises the costs of decision-making itself, namely, the time and trouble of reaching agreement among a diverse group of individuals, each of whom votes based on his or her own parochial interests. Collective decision-making costs of another kind – external costs – relate to the impact on the minority (i.e., those not belonging to the decisive group) of collective decisions that reduce their own personal welfare (and which they predictably oppose), but with which, owing to government's monopoly of the use of force (its police powers), they can be compelled to comply.

Decision-making costs are at a minimum with dictatorship, in which one person chooses for all. Those same costs are at their maximum if collective decisions are taken under a rule of unanimity, since one person can block an option that everyone else supports. For that same reason, however, a rule of unanimous consent means that no one person can be made worse off by any collective choice and, hence, that external costs cannot be imposed by anyone on anyone else. Under such a rule, no individual is excluded from the majority's will; there is no minority. The decisions of the group therefore must be welfare enhancing in a Paretian sense: many, perhaps most, individuals are made better off by a collective decision to which all agree, and no one is made worse off by it.

External costs plainly are highest with dictatorship, since a dictator consults only his or her own preferences. Those costs decline as the number of people required to agree before a collective action can be taken rises because, obviously, the number of people in the excluded minority shrinks.

Given these tradeoffs, the optimal majority – the fraction of the population enfranchised to decide for all – occurs in Buchanan and Tullock's framework at the point where the (vertical) sum of decision-making costs and external costs is minimized.

Three consequences of Buchanan and Tullock's analysis have been underappreciated – in my view – and are somewhat shocking to my students. First is its implication that there is nothing special about simple majority rule – there is no reason for concluding that the optimal set of decision-makers comprises 50% plus one of the voters who turn out on election day. Second, and what is more important, there is no reason for adopting the same voting rule for all collective decisions. Third, the total costs of collective decision-making fall as the polity is reduced in size and scope.

As a matter of fact, Buchanan and Tullock's model of collective decision-making implies that plurality rule, requiring the agreement of less than half of the members of the relevant group, will tend to be optimal, minimizing the sum of decision-making costs and external costs, when the former are large and the latter are small. On the other hand, a more inclusive majority of, say, two-thirds or three-quarters will be more appropriate when the external costs of collective choices are high relative to the costs of decision-making.

Simple majority rule thus is an expedient, with nothing further to recommend it. But while that rule is used widely, it is also true that more inclusive voting rules have been adopted for certain decisions. "Supermajorities" of some US state legislatures must approve proposals to raise taxes, bond issues by many local governments likewise require the approval of more than half of the voters, and amendments to the US Constitution must be agreed to by two-thirds of the US Congress and by (simple majorities of) the legislatures of three-fourths of the 50 states.[8]

Something approaching unanimous consent is demanded by the First Amendment to the US Constitution, which protects freedoms of religion, of the press, and of peaceable assembly and begins with the phrase, "Congress shall make no law" abridging those freedoms.[9] History has shown, however, that even those freedoms are not always safeguarded during times of war, always guaranteed to candidates for political office in connection with the sources and uses of their campaign war-chests,

---

[8]To be precise, Article V of the US Constitution states in part that:

> The Congress, whenever two thirds of both Houses shall deem it necessary, shall propose Amendments to this Constitution, or, on the Application of the Legislatures of two thirds of the several States, shall call a Convention for proposing Amendments, which, in either Case, shall be valid to all Intents and Purposes, as part of this Constitution, when ratified by the Legislatures of three fourths of the several States, or by Conventions in three fourths thereof, as the one or the other Mode of Ratification may be proposed by the Congress....

[9]The First Amendment states that:

> Congress shall make no law respecting an establishment of religion, or prohibiting the free exercise thereof; or abridging the freedom of speech, or of the press; or the right of the people peaceably to assemble, and to petition the Government for a redress of grievances.

In the course of introducing Professor Buchanan ahead of his Robert M. Hearin Foundation-sponsored public lecture at the University of Mississippi more than a decade ago, I said that it was not true that he would have favored ending the First Amendment with a period immediately after its opening phrase. I, myself, from time to time have wished that that were so.

or honored by the US Supreme Court, which, among other things, apparently has forgotten the unambiguous definition of an "established religion."

A third implication of the analysis is that the two costs of collective decision-making promise to be lower; the more finely gained is the polity within which those decisions are taken. Decisions voted on at the national level carry with them both higher decision-making costs and higher external costs than similar decisions taken at subnational levels of governance. Polices affecting the "reproductive rights" of women (e.g., the conditions, if any, under which abortions are available legally) are cases in point. Decisions approved by a majority at the federal level impact all of a nation's citizens, some of whom may favor "abortion on demand" and others who implacably oppose it. If those same decisions were delegated to state or local levels of a federal system, both costs would be lower and anyone who objected to the chosen policy would be afforded an opportunity to relocate to some other jurisdiction wherein the policy was more closely aligned with their own preferences (Tiebout 1956).

Buchanan and Tullock's analysis of the costs of collective decision-making is set within an approach to that problem fully consistent with a Madisonian perspective. James Madison and many of the founders of the American constitutional republic, who met at Philadelphia in 1787, feared above all a "tyranny of the majority" to which they thought a democracy inevitably would fall prey. That is why they framed a federal system of sovereign state governments, overlain by a national government to which the states delegated clearly enumerated powers and which introduced, in the language of *Federalist No. 51* (Madison 1788), "auxiliary precautions" in the forms of a bicameral legislature, one chamber representing "the people" (the House of Representatives) and the other representing the states (the Senate), along with separate and countervailing branches of executive and judicial power.[10]

It turns out, as we shall see in the next section, that the founders should have worried more about the "tyranny of the minority."[11]

---

[10] In one of the most famous passages ever composed in political philosophy, James Madison (1788) declared further in *Federalist No. 51* that:

> Ambition must be made to counteract ambition.... It may be a reflection on human nature, that such devices should be necessary to control the abuses of government. But what is government itself, but the greatest of all reflections of human nature? If men were angels, no government would be necessary. If angels were to govern men, neither external nor internal controls on government would be necessary. In framing a government which is to be administered by men over men, the great difficulty lies in this: you must first enable the government to control the governed; and in the next place to oblige it to control itself. A dependence on the people is, no doubt, the primary control on the government; but experience has taught mankind the necessity of auxiliary precautions.

[11] According to political scientist Robert Dahl (1956: 80), the democratic process is not "a majestic march of median-voter majorities, but rather the steady appeasement of minorities." The median voter theorem (MVT), as formalized by Downs (1957), predicts that, if voters are distributed continuously and normally along a left-right policy spectrum and voters' ideal points are single-peaked, candidates for political office in two-person races must adopt positions that cater to the preferences of the electorally decisive median voter.

Rent-Seeking and Rent Extraction

Gordon Tullock's article, eventually published in the 1967 volume of the *Western Economic Journal* (now *Economic Inquiry*), is a contribution to the literature of public choice and beyond for which arguably he should have been awarded the Nobel Prize, perhaps jointly with the author of a later contribution by Anne Krueger (1974), who apparently was unaware of Gordon's preeminence, but which gave to his original idea its "rent-seeking" moniker.

The extensive literature that has extended and embellished the theory of rent-seeking, especially as later formalized by him (Tullock 1980a), has been surveyed extensively by, first, Robert Tollison (1982), by him and Roger Congleton (Tollison and Congleton 1995) and, more recently in, among others, Congleton et al. (2008), and Hillman (2012).

An economic "rent" is simply the difference between the return earned by the owner of a resource and that resource's value in its next-best alternative use. The profit of a monopolist, which exceeds the "normal" rate of return earned by the owner of a firm in a hypothetically perfectly competitive industry, is an example of a rent. So, too, are most of the incomes of superstar professional athletes and entertainers. Owing to NCAA rules that limit the compensation of "student-athletes" to tuition, books, and incidental expenses, college football and basketball coaches also collect substantial economic rents.

Tullock's important contribution recognized that the existence of rents supplies incentives for individuals and firms to invest resources in the rivalry to gain access to them. That competition, moreover, is socially wasteful. As James Buchanan (1980) argued later, the pursuit of profits by the owners of private firms generates social benefits: output expands, prices fall, and profits are driven to normal levels. Rent-seeking in the pursuit of artificially created returns in excess of normal generates no social benefits. Because such rivalry determines only the identity of the successful rent-seeker, it consequently has no effect on output or on final product price. The allocative inefficiency (deadweight loss) associated with a contrived output restriction is unrelieved by the competitive forces unleashed by rent-seeking. Production remains below the competitive level, and price remains above it.

A key implication of Tullock's model is that any time, effort, and monies invested in rent-seeking represent complete wastes of society's scarce resources. Lawyers who are hired to promote a particular rent-seeker's point of view plausibly could have been employed more productively in writing contracts. Lobbyists could have found socially more valuable occupations, perhaps in the marketing department of a private business enterprise, assuming that marketing is a worthwhile line of work.

One related theoretical question raised by the theory of rent-seeking is the extent to which the available rents are dissipated by the value of the resources invested in it. As is typical of economic models, the answer to that question is "it depends." Different assumptions as to the structure of the game, including the number of contestants who participate, their risk preferences, the information available to them, the conditions of entry into the contest, and so on, have been shown to determine the relation between the total value of the available rent and the aggregate amount invested by the rent-seekers. Given differences in the assumptions adopted, theoretical results consistent with under-, over- and exact dissipation of the available rents have been reported in the literature.

Tullock's rent-seeking insight helps explain why, since the early 1960s, the budgets of most western democratic governments, especially those of the United States, have run more often than not in the "red," with public spending far outpacing the revenues collected in taxes and tariffs, "user fees," and leases or sales of public assets, such as offshore drilling rights or the ownership of frequencies on the broadcast spectrum. Democracies chronically have been in deficit (Buchanan and Wagner [1977] 2000) once the Keynesian revolution displaced the balanced public budget norm.

Rent-seeking contributes to excessive governmental spending because existing institutions encourage individuals and groups to treat the public budget as a common pool resource to which everyone potentially has access, but in the course of registering their demands for budget shares, no one individual or group has an incentive to take into account the reduction in funds accessible to other demanders. As a matter of fact, owing to the availability of the fiscal option of financing current spending programs by borrowing (deficit finance) instead of by raising taxes, national governments face a "soft" budget constraint rather than a "hard" one. Opposition to spending proposals that would trigger tax increases on the beneficiaries themselves or on income-earning voters in general can be muted if spending is financed by issuing debt, thus shifting the responsibility of paying for it onto the shoulders of future, perhaps yet unborn, taxpayers.

The tragedy of the budgetary commons is exacerbated in a geographically based system of national political representation, such as the one that emerged from the Constitutional Convention in 1787. As time passed, the US Congress grew to 535 souls, comprising 100 senators, two from each of the 50 states, plus 435 members of the House of Representatives, elected to legislative districts within states, with seats being reapportioned every 10 years based on populations determined by the decennial US Census.[12]

The length of the legislative service of every member of the US Senate and House depends not on his or her individual skills, abilities, and predilections for advancing the national or "public" interest but rather on securing the electoral support of a (simple) majority of the constituents he or she represents. Given the prime directive of reelection to legislative office, every member of the House and of the Senate has a strong incentive to support programs and policies that benefit the voters in his or her district or state selectively at the expense of taxpayers in general, vast numbers of which reside and, hence, vote in other congressional jurisdictions. Pork-barrel

[12]Every state is guaranteed at least one seat in the US House of Representatives, regardless of population. According to a "Congressional Apportionment" briefing paper published by the US Census Bureau in November 2011, the State of Wyoming has one representative (representing 532,688 people); California currently has the most (53), each of whom represents 693,522 people. Source: http://www.census.gov/prod/cen2010/briefs/c2010br-08.pdf; last accessed May 20, 2012.

spending programs, with benefits that are concentrated on particular districts, states, or geographic regions, but whose costs are diffused widely, thus are the predictable consequences of public choice theories of governmental behavior.

Such narrowly tailored programs are able to achieve a legislative majority through a series of logrolling deals (Tullock 1959, 1961, 1970), struck pair by legislative pair, in which one legislator exchanges his or her vote in favor of a colleague's pet project in return for that colleague's vote in favor of his or her own. Alternatively, a collection of such narrowly tailored budget items can be bundled together into an "omnibus" spending bill for which every affected member must vote "yea" if funding for one line item of special interest to his or her constituents is to be approved, despite the fact that each element of the package would be defeated soundly if voted on separately, because its total public benefits fall short of its total costs. But a majority vote nevertheless is assured if legislators are driven by the imperative of maximizing the probability of reelection at home. A defense spending bill financing the production of a weapons system that includes funds for subcontractors dispersed nationwide is a case in point. Concentrated benefits and diffuse costs are the hallmarks of a winning electoral strategy for politicians animated by the vote motive.[13]

Rent-seeking comes into play as a result of the constellation of special interests that coalesce around the national budgetary commons. Individuals and groups know that their political representatives in the House and Senate are driven by the vote motive, anxious to secure enough support to be returned to office by a voting majority on the next election day, an end of term that is at most either 2 or 6 years hence. Achieving that objective requires amassing a war chest sizable enough to defeat any prospective challenger by mounting an advertising campaign that extols the incumbent's virtues and disparages those of his or her opponent; supplies funds to supporters to "get out the vote" on election day, including supplying transportation to the polls and "walking around money" to preachers, labor union officials, and other political operatives who can deliver a candidate's supporters to their polling precincts; or secures the endorsements of influential local newspaper editors and other opinion leaders.[14]

In a majoritarian democracy, by definition, virtually every public policy creates winners and losers. It is the parochial interest of the prospective winners to invest real resources in striving to capture the gains (rents) from a policy that redounds to their benefit and of the prospective losers to invest real resources in attempting to prevent their wealth from being expropriated.

[13] As Simmons (2011: 64) puts it, "If a politician has a choice of dividing a million dollars equally among a million citizens or equally among a thousand people she will rationally choose the latter option.... Conversely, if the same politician has to choose between taxing a million people a dollar apiece and taxing a thousand taxpayers a thousand dollars each she will under most circumstances choose the former option."

[14] Prior to election day in the State of Mississippi, retail liquor stores add to their normal stocks of half-pints of whiskey for this very political purpose.

McChesney (1997) subsequently extended Tullock's model by introducing explicitly the interests of the holders of elective legislative office into the analysis and, in doing so, coined the term "rent extraction" to complement in an important way the rent-seeking idea. McChesney's contribution to the literature recognized that the members of Congress and other legislative bodies (e.g., city councils) are not passive actors in the rent-seeking game who simply respond to the competing demands for rents and award them to the individuals or groups that offer the highest political returns net of costs. Given that, through the laws the majority enacts, legislators stand to benefit personally from campaign contributions and other means of political support, well-organized special-interest groups have incentives to 'buy' public policies favoring them at the expense of consumers, taxpayers, and other unorganized or "latent" interests (Olson 1965). McChesney argued, with the support of empirical evidence, that elected politicians rationally would exploit opportunities to threaten to terminate existing rent streams or to expropriate wealth from some other identifiable group. Such threats are made in McChesney's theory of rent extraction and political extortion in the form of so-called milker bills (a familiar characterization on Capitol Hill) so that representatives and senators can be paid for forbearing the proposed action.[15]

Although the model of rent-seeking applies in a wide variety of contexts, the public choice literature has focused on the activities of individuals, groups, and business firms that aim at positioning themselves to capture rents created artificially by governmental policies which, ostensibly to achieve broader social goals, regulate markets and redistribute incomes. Rents can be earned by the owners of firms that are able to secure the many and varied protections on public offer against the (beneficial to consumers) unforgiving forces of unfettered competition. One option is to plead, under the guises of protecting jobs or the health and welfare of ordinary consumers, for government to intervene by erecting barriers to entry in the forms of tariffs and quotas on imported goods, exclusive franchises (the local provider of cable television programming is a good example), and professional licensing requirements for, for example, health-care professionals, including medical doctors and chiropractors, lawyers, certified public accountants, the employees of hair salons, and taxicab operators, to name a few. Regulatory regimes supposedly designed to safeguard the environment, to ensure workplace safety and broad access

[15] Simmons (2011: 74) supplies additional evidence that the Tax Equity and Fiscal Responsibility Act of 1986, which reduced marginal personal income tax rates dramatically and closed many existing "loopholes" in the US income tax code, was triggered primarily by the incentives of members of Congress to "clear the decks," affording opportunities once again to "auction" off [new] tax exemptions and other privileges." Simmons (ibid.) writes further that, "What we have seen since those tax cuts is an annual reenactment of tax exemptions and political rewards in the form of increased campaign monies for compliant Congressmen. In fact, that began immediately after the passage of [TEFRA] with the addition of countless so-called 'transition rules' to protect those interest groups essential to the reelection of important members of the Senate Finance and House Ways and Means Committees."

to health-care services, to protect minorities from discriminatory hiring practices, and to see that consumers are not injured by defective products and are fully informed about credit terms prior to purchase and that automobiles achieve minimum fuel economy standards also are sources of potential rents. The list of rent-seeking opportunities is nearly endless and becomes ever longer as government expands in size and scope.

I have profited personally from applying Tullock's rent-seeking model and the more general interest-group theory of government (Stigler 1971; Peltzman 1976; McCormick and Tollison 1981) to help explain the origins and effects of many previously incompletely understood public policy initiatives. Nowhere is that influence more obvious than in the area of the US antitrust laws and their enforcement by the Department of Justice's Antitrust Division and the Federal Trade Commission. That work began when I was employed by the FTC during the early 1980s as a Special Assistant to Robert Tollison, then the Director of the FTC's Bureau of Economics, and has continued ever since (see, e.g., Shughart and Tollison 1985; Shughart 1990; McChesney and Shughart 1995; and, more recently, McChesney et al. forthcoming). Those contributions treat the antitrust laws as just another form of economic regulation, whose enforcement is susceptible to political influence by the special interests having important stakes in the outcomes of specific cases, namely, plaintiffs, both public and private; defendants; local, state (including attorneys general), and national politicians; judges; and the lawyers and economists who lead or are employed by the agencies themselves.[16]

The Public-Sector Bureaucracy

If well-organized special-interest groups are to achieve their parochial goals of rent capture, they must, in the first place, "buy" simple majorities of the votes cast in the bicameral legislatures that are found in most western democracies.[17] (McCormick

[16] Based on the conclusions of Easterbrook (1984) that many antitrust decrees are regulatory in nature, Shughart and Thomas (2012) develop arguments from observing the shift toward "behavioral" or "conduct" remedies and away from structural remedies in merger law (Clayton Act §7) enforcement under the Obama administration, suggesting that entrepreneurial antitrust bureaucrats see opportunities to "fill gaps" by regulating industries or business practices where Congress has "failed" to impose more formal regulatory regimes.

[17] In the United States, the State of Nebraska is exceptional insofar as it has adopted a unicameral legislature, whose members are elected on non-partisan ballots. That institutional uniqueness has caused many headaches to public choice scholars, almost always resulting in the state's exclusion from empirical research on legislative processes. That exclusion is a clarion call for scholars to explain Nebraska's uniqueness, which dates to the Progressive Era. Answers to that public choice question are nearly as important as explaining why President Abraham Lincoln chose war to prevent the Confederate States of America from seceding from the Union, but welcomed with open arms West Virginia's secession from the State of Virginia.

and Tollison 1981, trailing and formalizing the analysis of Buchanan and Tullock 1962: 233–248, show that, other things being the same, it typically is cheaper for interest groups to secure favorable majority votes in a bicameral legislature when the two chambers are more equal in size.)

In any case, once a regulatory regime is in place or changes to it are enacted, legislatures delegate to the agency they have created authority to promulgate the specific rules that will give effect to the legislature's mandate. For this reason, the heads of regulatory bureaucracies have considerable discretion in crafting the overarching objectives and the day-to-day operating instructions that their underlings are charged with implementing.

The first serious modern student of public-sector bureaucracies, Max Weber ([1922] 1978), characterized such agencies as formal hierarchical organizations, staffed by publicly paid civil servants, holding lifetime appointments, and tasked with supplying public goods and services to the citizenry on an evenhanded basis and at zero prices. That description echoed the aims of the intellectuals of the Progressive Era, who for many years had sought to replace the corruption endemic to the prevailing "spoils system" of the late nineteenth and early twentieth centuries, under which state governors and US presidents distributed influential positions in the bureaucracies of the executive branches of government to their cronies, campaign contributors, and other key political operatives, with a professional, expert, and apolitical set of agency managers who mechanically would implement the laws enacted by public-spirited legislative bodies. As President Woodrow Wilson, one of the leaders of the movement that promoted civil service reform, wrote well before his first electoral victory in 1914:

> The field of [public] administration is a field of business. It is removed from the hurry and strife of politics; it at most points stands apart even from the debatable ground of constitutional study. It is a part of political life only as the methods of the counting-house are a part of society; only as machinery is part of the manufactured product. (Woodrow 1887: 209–210)

How inordinately naïve! The notion of a public bureaucracy, staffed by technocrats appointed to positions of public trust and animated only by the goal of carrying out clear legislative policy mandates in the most efficient manner possible, was exploded by contributors to the public choice literature, beginning with Gordon Tullock (1965) and, two years later, by Anthony Downs (1967).

Tullock's foray into the economic theory of bureaucracy was criticized sharply by William Niskanen as being too casual, heavily influenced as it was by that scholar's own experiences as a US State Department official posted to China. Tullock (1965: 177) offered an explanation for why an "overexpanded bureaucracy," driven by the goal of commanding an ever-larger organizational structure, may lead to a vicious cycle of inefficiency, breeding further expansion, and more inefficiency. Informal as Tullock's analysis had been, subsequent discussions between him and Niskanen crystallized the latter's thinking about the motives of public-sector bureaucrats, with which he had had personal contact as an official of the Ford Motor Company, responsible for dealing with the regulatory process as it affected the US automobile industry in general and Ford in particular.[18]

Niskanen asked what bureaucrats maximize. In his early work, he (Niskanen 1968, 1971, 1975) concluded that their chief goal was budget maximization, since larger budgets meant more agency employees; more vertical layers of organizational hierarchy and, hence, more opportunities for promotion; bigger office buildings; more visible public profiles for top agency officials within the government as a whole; and so on. That budget-maximizing objective could be achieved, in Niskanen's view, because the experience gained in managing day-to-day bureau operations endowed upper-level bureaucrats with informational advantages over less-well-informed members of key congressional committees who voted to approve and appropriate funds to finance bureau activities. That informational asymmetry between the bureaucracy and Congress enabled bureaucrats to make take-it-or-leave-it budget offers that, lacking detailed knowledge of agency operations and having no price or profit signals by which to evaluate bureaucratic efficiency, Congress would be obliged to accept.

Later on, Niskanen (2001) modified his fundamental assumption in arguing that, rather than being motivated by the goal of maximizing the total agency budget, bureaucrats instead were more concerned with the size of their agency's "discretionary budget." Niskanen's change of focus recognized that in addition to being beholden to policy-relevant congressional budget and oversight committees, each agency has a fairly well-defined clientele to whose demands it also must cater. (The US Department of Agriculture administers farm programs; the Department of Housing and Urban Development builds, manages, and subsidizes low-income housing; the Department of Veterans Affairs oversees health-care, rehabilitation, and other programs for veterans of the US armed forces, and so on.) These various legislatively authorized programs must be carried out and the targeted beneficiaries served at some threshold level, if only to minimize complaints of bureaucratic nonperformance, ineptitude, and inefficiency that generate headlines and cause agency officials to be summoned before a congressional hearing to account for their bureau's bad press.[19]

So, in Niskanen's revised way of thinking, bureaucrats want two things, namely, a baseline budget that allows them to fulfill the agency's programmatic responsibilities in ways that minimally satisfy its clients plus a discretionary budget above

---

[18] Niskanen had resigned from Ford as a result of a dispute with top company executives following his principled refusal to support governmental imposition of import restrictions on foreign automobile manufacturers.

[19] Bureaucratic failures can – and often do – lead to pleas for bigger budgets. On the other hand, as Fiorina (1977) observes, bureaucratic sluggishness, the "red tape" associated with formal, one-size-fits-all rules and procedures, and outright ineptitude supply the members of Congress with a convenient scapegoat when their constituents complain.

and beyond the threshold that can be spent to advance their personal interests in promotion, perks, visibility, and other on-the-job benefits they consume themselves. In any case, bureaucrats have incentives to spend their annual budgets in full, regardless of the consequences of that behavior for notions of "efficiency." A bureau that does not do so faces the threat of a reduction in funding in the next budget cycle. That threat is credible even for agencies, such as the National Park Service, that generate income from user fees; revenues from charging fees for service or fining violators of bureaucratic regulations must be turned over to the US Treasury.[20]

No matter what bureaucrats maximize,[21] though, the subsequent public choice literature sees them as operating in a multi-principal/multi-agent setting that imposes constraints established by their clienteles, their congressional "sponsors" (budget and oversight committees), and their external political environments comprising individuals and groups having important stakes in the outcomes of bureaucratic activities. Moreover, both theory and evidence now recognize that members of Congress are not as uninformed as previously assumed about the general directions taken by bureaucratic agencies or of the operating rules they adopt to carry out their legislative marching orders. After all, the congressional committee system institutionalizes a specialization and division of legislative labor and, in doing so, supplies opportunities for individual representatives and senators to "self-select" onto committees that oversee the areas of public policy that are crucial to their own personal goals of reelection to legislative office.

It is thus a no-brainer to explain why the members of congressional delegations from farm states seek appointment to seats on the agricultural committees of the House or Senate or why the representatives and senators from New York City and other financial centers want to occupy seats on congressional banking committees.[22] We therefore should expect bureaucrats to be responsive to the wishes of the members of the specialized committees of Congress that exercise proximate control of their budgets and, if necessary, can embarrass them by holding newsworthy public hearings. So, too, should the bureaucracy be sensitive to the demands of special interest groups that can mobilize political support (campaign contributions, favorable advertising messages, and votes) – or withhold it – within the districts and states those members represent. Indeed, the bureaucrats themselves have strong incentives to behave in ways that promote the reelection prospects of the

[20] The Federal Reserve System is an important exception to that rule (Shughart and Tollison 1983).

[21] Chang et al. (2001) situate the bureaucracy within a more general rational choice model that takes into account public agencies' myriad internal organizations and their interactions with Congress, the president and the courts. For a less technical, highly readable analysis of bureaucracy, see Wilson ([1989] 2000).

[22] US presidents and members of Congress, it should come as no surprise, also monitor and bend to their wills the activities of that most hated of all government bureaus, the Internal Revenue Service. See Young et al. (2001) for evidence of political influences on the IRS.

members of Congress who vote reliably in favor of their agency's budget requests.

Substantial evidence exists of congressional influence on antitrust law enforcement, one of my own areas of scholarly research, lending empirical support to models that recognize the constellation of special interests that coalesce to influence the behavior of the Department of Justice's Antitrust Division and the Federal Trade Commission, which, despite popular opinion to the contrary, are garden-variety bureaucratic agencies. In one of the first contributions to that literature, Weingast and Moran (1983) examined FTC policymaking during the 1970s in the area of consumer protection (see, also, Higgins and McChesney 1986). Early in that decade, the Commission had been excoriated in the press as a bureaucracy seemingly "out of control." The critics focused, in particular, on the FTC's proposal to regulate the content of television advertising aimed at children, earning it the tag of "national nanny." Weingast and Moran's evidence, however, supported the conclusion that, far from being out of control, the FTC was in fact responding to the wishes of the majority of its oversight committee members, who then were in the consumer activist camp. When the membership of the oversight committees shifted later in the decade to a less activist policy stance, the FTC drew in its consumer protection horns and abandoned the "kid-vid" rulemaking initiative.

Similar evidence is reported in analyses of the FTC's enforcement of the law prohibiting mergers deemed to be anticompetitive. Faith, Leavens, and Tollison (1982) find that challenges to mergers evaluated by the FTC were more likely to be dismissed when one of the companies involved was headquartered in a district or state represented by a member of the committee having oversight responsibilities for that agency. Later research shows that FTC merger challenges are more likely, among other things, the more public attention is devoted to the merger (as measured by column inches in the trade press) and the more often FTC officials were called to testify before Congress prior to the commission's law enforcement decision (Coate et al. 1990; Coate and McChesney 1992). Other analyses suggest that the antitrust authorities frequently challenge mergers that fall short of the bureaucratic standards promulgated supposedly to provide guidance to the private sector (Harty 2010).

In short, the naïve Progressive Era idea was that a corrupt and inefficient public bureaucracy, staffed by the political cronies of powerful chief executives, appointed by and beholden to them for their well-paid sinecures, often allowing them to keep at least some of the revenue collected from their clients,[23] could be reformed by replacing the spoils system with a technocratic, apolitical, and professional civil

[23] It was for that reason that the post of customs collector for the Port of New York was for many years very highly valued. Likely as a result of his earlier experiences in that position, including removal from the job by President Rutherford Hayes, President Chester A. Arthur became a staunch advocate of civil service reform, ultimately signing the Pendleton Act in 1883, which required appointments to federal jobs to be based on merit. Source: http://www.history.com/topics/chester-a-arthur; last accessed May 20, 2012.

service, selected by competitive, merit-based procedures, granted tenure for life, and compensated according to a predetermined pay scale. The image of robotic bureaucrats fulfilling administrative mandates handed down by public-interest-driven legislators was undermined utterly by Gordon Tullock, Anthony Downs, William Niskanen, and the many public choice scholars who followed the intellectual trails they blazed. "Civil servants" in those models are not in any meaningful senses different from the stylized rational actors of neoclassical economic theory. They, like all human beings, are motivated primarily by their own objectives for present and future income, promotion in place, status, and other personal rewards.

Many bureaucrats undoubtedly work long hours, are patriotic and want to pursue their personal conceptions of the "public interest." But when push comes to shove, the public choice model points in a different direction. No matter how well-intentioned individual bureaucrats may be, they must serve many masters, including their agency's clientele, the members of relevant congressional oversight committees, who are driven by their own vote motives, and of other special interests, including at times that most unorganized interest group, the taxpayers. It should therefore be no surprise that the ideals of the Progressive Era's reformers have largely gone unfulfilled.

Public Budget Deficits and the Public Debt

Public spending can be financed in one of three ways: by levying taxes on the private sector, by printing money, or by borrowing (selling government bonds to willing investors). In the United States and much of the industrialized world, the last of these tools of public finance was used sparingly prior to roughly 1960. Only wars and other national emergencies prompted governments to resort to the bond market; the public sector otherwise operated on a balanced-budget, pay-as-you-go basis. Furthermore, the issuance of public debt to finance wartime spending was simply an unavoidable expedient.[24] Once the hostilities had ended, the accumulated debt customarily was retired, often by establishing a "sinking fund," into which revenues earmarked specifically for that purpose would be deposited. At most times and in most places, peace brought a return to public budget balance. The normative principle that, except for periods of hard necessity, government should live within its means was rarely questioned and widely practiced.

That pattern was broken beginning in the last third of the twentieth century. Chronic budget deficits became the peacetime norm in the United States until 1998, when, owing to dramatic cuts in defense spending and to the robust economic expansion of the 1990s, the federal government's receipts exceeded its outlays for

[24] "An immediate and great expence must be incurred in that moment of immediate danger, which will not wait for the gradual and slow returns of the new taxes. In this exigency government can have no other resource but in borrowing" (Smith [1776] 1976: 909).

the first time since 1969 (Alesina 2000). The proximate cause of this period of persistent budget imbalance was massive growth in so-called entitlement programs, including Medicare and Medicaid, established to help pay the health-care bills of elderly and poor Americans, both of which were enacted in response to President Lyndon Johnson's call for a "War on Poverty." Such programs, which are open-ended in the sense of providing benefits to everyone who meets predetermined eligibility criteria, ensure that spending will rise continuously as the populations of qualified recipients expand, even with no changes in benefit levels or eligibility requirements. And, indeed, if the future liabilities of these programs are added to those of the social security system, the ostensible budget surpluses of the late twentieth century quickly sink in a sea of red ink.

Why did budget deficits appear suddenly in the 1960s and why have they persisted ever since? "Ideas matter" is one answer to that question. The norm of governmental fiscal responsibility was grounded for roughly two centuries on the intellectual foundations laid by the classical economists, who for the most part saw public debt as being inimical to economic growth.

The classical analysis of budget deficits and public debt was swept away by the Keynesian revolution. In imparting intellectual respectability to debt-financed spending, Keynes (1936) destroyed the norm of public budget balance (Buchanan and Wagner [1977] 2000). Indeed, the relationship between public revenues and expenditures became an unimportant byproduct of government's Keynesian responsibility for actively countering the peaks and troughs of the business cycle so as to maintain the economy at full employment. These ideas were taken to their logical extreme by Keynes's disciple, Abba Lerner (1943), who rejected totally the classical orthodoxy in favor of a doctrine of "functional finance," which judged fiscal policy, not by its impact on budget balance, but by its impact on the economy.

Analyzing the public debt problem from the perspective of public choice, that is, taking into account the interests of the individual economic actors who, as citizens of a democratic polity, collectively must choose methods of financing the expenditures of government, James Buchanan ([1958] 1999: 26–37, [1964] 1982) observed that the decision to borrow involves a tradeoff between present and future taxes. The fact that the national debt must be serviced and eventually retired implies a future tax liability. Accordingly, it is future taxpayers who shoulder the burden when government borrows to finance current spending.

The tradeoff Buchanan identified triggered a lively debate following Robert Barro's (1974) reformulation of what has since erroneously been called the doctrine of "Ricardian equivalence" (O'Driscoll 1977). Barro's theoretical model starts with the assumption that the members of each generation care about the welfare of the next (more precisely, that the utility attained by one generation depends partly on its own consumption and partly on the utility attainable by that generation's immediate descendants). If, in addition, there exists a "chain of operative intergenerational transfers" (private bequests) that connects the current generation to future generations, individuals will behave as if they live forever. Under these assumptions, the issuance or retirement of public debt has no differential impact (relative to the tax alternative) on personal wealth, on aggregate demand, or on capital formation because current taxpayers will alter their bequests to offset the implied change in future tax liabilities. Private bequests will be increased to compensate future generations fully for the heavier tax burden otherwise imposed on them by additions to public indebtedness, and when debt is retired, bequests will be lowered by the full amount of the reduction in the future tax burden. Changes in future tax liabilities, in other words, are fully capitalized in intergenerational wealth transfers, thereby neutralizing completely the effects of changes in the government's budget balance. Debt and taxes therefore are equivalent tools of public finance.

Buchanan (1976) replied that such equivalence is illusory because rational taxpayers predictably will respond to an increase in the public debt, which implies a corresponding increase in future tax liabilities, by shifting income from the future to the present. The attempt on the part of current taxpayers to lower their future tax bills by reallocating their incomes inter-temporally means that individuals will save less under deficit finance than they would under the revenue-equivalent current period tax, thereby impairing private capital formation. It also means that, at prevailing tax rates, future tax collections will not be adequate for meeting debt service and amortization obligations.

Buchanan's broader point was that, even if future tax obligations are fully anticipated, taxpayers are placed in a prisoners' dilemma situation with respect to public debt issues. In particular, future tax liabilities in the Barro model are contingent because each individual is required to make spending plans for himself (and for his immediate descendants) under the assumption that everyone else will likewise plan to discharge his pro rata share of the community's deferred tax liabilities. However, if any one taxpayer fails to do so, the other members of the community will find their future tax bills to be larger than expected even though they themselves acted responsibly. Moreover, if one taxpayer has an incentive opportunistically to shift some (or all) of his future tax burden to others, everyone does.

In any case, the historical record of the past 50 years, a period distinguished in much of the West by persistent government spending in excess of current revenues and ever-growing public debt, is inconsistent with Keynesian orthodoxy, which calls for budget balance over the business cycle. One explanation for the theory's failure to fit the facts is that the political institutions governing fiscal policy choices and the political actors who formulate and implement those policies are missing from the analysis.

The gap between Keynesian theory and political reality is filled by public choice, which brings government within the ambit of macroeconomic policy. Recognizing that the configuration of costs and benefits facing individuals differs as between choices taken collectively and those made privately, public choice helps explain why democratic political processes produce a bias toward deficit spending, a bias that is reinforced by the electorally foreshortened time horizons of politicians and by the "fiscal illusion" of rationally ignorant voters, who underestimate their future tax liabilities.

Simple majority voting rules afford opportunities for taxpayers (and their elected political representatives), who benefit disproportionately from public spending programs in the present period, to shift the burden of financing those benefits to others. Public spending accordingly grows more rapidly than would be the case if financed by taxes on a pay-as-you-go basis.[25]

Government debt issue has sustained the West's welfare states and fueled rapid growth in them in the period since the end of the Second World War. Greece and Spain, as of this writing, are bankrupt; unless rescued by Germany or by the expulsions of some of its most profligate members, the Euro zone is in danger of collapse; and financial market "contagion" threatens the economies of many other nations, including the United States, which has been far from behindhand in spending beyond its means, piling up tens of trillions of dollars worth of public debt as well as unfunded future liabilities in its own social welfare programs. "Austerity" is the order of the day in Europe, but proposals to cut taxpayer-financed entitlements triggered the election of a socialist candidate for the presidency of France and caused the failure of Greece's political parties to form a new coalition government. These events suggest that the beneficiaries of debt-financed public spending will resist public budget cuts to the bitter end.

Concluding Remarks

This year (2012) marks the 50th anniversary of the publication of *The Calculus of Consent*. Next year (2013) is the 50th anniversary of the founding of the Public Choice Society. The 50th anniversary of the academic journal founded by Gordon Tullock, *Public Choice*, will be celebrated in due course (2016). Triple reasons for festivities, indeed!

Founded on the then-remarkable postulate of "methodological individualism," namely, that only individuals, not groups, can choose among alternatives, the field of public choice revolutionized the analysis of decisions taken collectively in committees and all branches of government, including city councils, state and national legislatures, bureaucracies, and the judiciary, wherein the preferences of individuals must be aggregated somehow.

This chapter has summarized a small slice of the vast scholarly research program adopting public choice reasoning to evaluate decision-making at the ballot box, to explore some of the implications of Gordon Tullock's rent-seeking insight, to outline the older and newer analyses of the behavior of public-sector bureaucracies, and to review some of James Buchanan's important contributions to the theory and practice of public finance, especially so in the context of deficits and debt. I empha-

[25] For deeper and more wide-ranging introductions to the public choice literature on deficit finance and the public debt (see, e.g., Buchanan et al. 1986; Rowley et al. 2002; Shughart 2003).

sized along the way the influences of James Buchanan and Gordon Tullock on my own contributions to the literature, primarily in the area of the causes and consequences of antitrust law enforcement, animated by my personal interactions with Professor Tullock and Professor Buchanan's student, Robert Tollison. To the extent of my capabilities, I have strived to pass on those lessons to my own students, especially Jim Couch, Gökhan Karahan, Atin Basuchoudhary, Burak Dolar, and Michael Reksulak.

As I wrote at the outset, I am humbled by my appointment in 2005 as the editor in chief of *Public Choice*. Many years ago, I had two goals in my academic career: eventually to become the editor of that journal and to be elected (on an uncontested Soviet-style ballot) to the presidency of the Southern Economic Association. I have now achieved both goals, thanks to the shoulders of the giants on which I have stood.

Acknowledgments I benefited from the comments and suggestions of Michael Reksulak, Charles Rowley, Diana Thomas, and Robert Tollison on earlier drafts of this chapter. I hereby absolve them of any and all remaining errors, for which I accept full responsibility.

References

Acemoglu D, Robinson J (2005) Economic origins of dictatorship and democracy. MIT Press, Cambridge

Acemoglu D, Robinson J (2012) Why nations fail: the origins of power, prosperity, and poverty. Crown Publishers, New York

Alesina A (2000) The political economy of the budget surplus in the United States. J Econ Perspect 14:3–19

Arrow KJ ([1951] 1963) Social choice and individual values, 2nd edn. Wiley, New York

Barro RJ (1974) Are government bonds net wealth? J Polit Econ 82:1095–1117

Black D (1948a) On the rationale of group decision making. J Polit Econ 56:23–34

Black D (1948b) The decisions of a committee using a special majority. Econometrica 16:245–261

Black D (1948c) The elasticity of committee decision with an altering size of majority. Econometrica 16:261–272

Black D (1958) The theory of committees and elections. Cambridge University Press, Cambridge

Buchanan JM ([1958] 1999) Public principles of public debt: a defense and restatement. In: Brennan HG, Kliemt H, Tollison RD (eds) The collected works of James M. Buchanan, vol 2. Liberty Fund, Indianapolis

Buchanan JM ([1964] 1982) Public debt, cost theory and fiscal illusion. In: Ferguson JM (ed) Public debt and future generations. Greenwood Press, Westport, pp 150–163

Buchanan JM ([1969] 1978) Cost and choice: an inquiry in economic theory. University of Chicago Press, Chicago

Buchanan JM (1975) The limits of liberty: between anarchy and leviathan. University of Chicago Press, Chicago

Buchanan JM (1976) Barro on the Ricardian equivalence theorem. J Polit Econ 84:337–342

Buchanan JM (1980) Rent seeking and profit seeking. In: Buchanan JM, Tollison RD, Tullock G (eds) Toward a theory of the rent seeking society. Texas A&M University Press, College Station, pp 3–15

Buchanan JM (1999–2000) Collected works of James M. Buchanan. In: Brennan HG, Kliemt H, Tollison RD (eds). Liberty Fund, Indianapolis

Buchanan JM, Rowley CK, Tollison RD (eds) (1986) Deficits. Basil Blackwell, Oxford
Buchanan JM, Tullock G (1962) The calculus of consent: logical foundations of constitutional democracy. University of Michigan Press, Ann Arbor
Buchanan JM, Wagner RE ([1977] 2000) Democracy in deficit: the political legacy of Lord Keynes. In: Brennan HG, Kliemt H, Tollison RD (eds) The collected works of James M. Buchanan, vol 8. Liberty Fund, Indianapolis
Chang KH, de Figueiredo RJP Jr, Weingast BR (2001) Rational choice theories of bureaucratic control and performance. In: Shughart WF II, Razzolini L (eds) The Elgar companion to public choice. Edward Elf=gar, Cheltenham/Northampton, pp 271–292
Coate MB, McChesney FS (1992) Empirical evidence on FTC enforcement of the merger guidelines. Econ Inq 30(2):277–293
Coate MB, Higgins RS, McChesney FS (1990) Bureaucracy and politics in FTC merger challenges. J Law Econ 33(2):463–482
Condorcet, Jean-Antoine-Nicolas de Caritat, Marquis de (1785) Essai sur l'application de l'analyse à la probabilité des décisions rendues à la pluralité des voix. Paris
Congleton RD, Hillman AL, Konrad KA (2008) Forty years of research on rent seeking: an overview. In: Congleton RD, Hillman AL, Konrad KA (eds) Forty years of research on rent seeking, vol 1 and 2. Springer, Heidelberg, pp 1–42
Dahl RA (1956) A preface to democratic theory. University of Chicago Press, Chicago
Downs A (1957) An economic theory of democracy. Harper & Row, New York
Downs A (1967) Inside bureaucracy. Little Brown, Boston
Dodgson CL ("Lewis Carroll") ([1884] 2010) The principles of parliamentary representation. Kessinger Publishing, the work was published in 1884 by "Harrison and Sons, London"; the 2010 reprint is by "Kessinger Publishing, Whitefish, MT, USA"
Easterbrook F (1984) The limits of antitrust. Texas Law Rev 63:1–40
Faith RL, Leavens DR, Tollison RD (1982) Antitrust pork barrel. J Law Econ 25(2):329–342
Fiorina MP (1977) Congress: keystone of the Washington establishment. Yale University Press, New Haven
Harty RP (2010) Federal antitrust enforcement priorities under the Obama administration. J Eur Compet Law Pract 1(1):52–61
Higgins RS, McChesney FS (1986) Truth and consequences: the Federal Trade Commission's Ad substantiation program. Int Rev Law Econ 6(2):151–168
Hillman AL (2012) Rent seeking. In: Reksulak M, Razzolini L , Shughart WF II (eds) The Elgar companion to public choice, 2nd ed. Edward Elgar, Cheltenham/Northampton (forthcoming)
Keynes JM (1936) The general theory of employment, interest, and money. Harcourt, Brace & World, New York
Krueger AO (1974) The political economy of the rent-seeking society. Am Econ Rev 64:291–303
Lerner AP (1943) Functional finance and the Federal Debt. Social Res 10:38–51
Madison J ([1788] 2001) No. 51. In: Hamilton A, Madison J, Jay J The federalist. The Gideon edn., ed. by Cary, GW, McClellan, J Liberty Fund, Indianapolis, pp 267–272
McChesney FS (1997) Money for nothing: politicians, rent extraction, and political extortion. Harvard University Press, Cambridge
McChesney FS, Shughart WF II (eds) (1995) The causes and consequences of antitrust: the public-choice perspective. University of Chicago Press, Chicago
McChesney FS, Reksulak R, Shughart WF II Competition policy in public choice perspective. In: Blair RD, Sokol DD (eds) Handbook of international antitrust. Oxford University Press, Oxford/New York (forthcoming)
McCormick RE, Tollison RD (1981) Politicians, legislation, and the economy: an inquiry into the interest-group theory of government. Martinus Nijhoff, Boston
Mitchell WC (1967) The shape of political theory to come: from political sociology to political economy. Am Behav Sci 11(2):8–37
Mitchell WC (2001) The old and new public choice: Chicago vs. Virginia. In: Razzolini L, Shughart WF II (eds) The Elgar companion to public choice. Edward Elgar, Cheltenham/Northampton, pp 3–32

Munger MC (2001) Voting. In: Razzolini L, Shughart WL II (eds) The Elgar companion to public choice. Edward Elgar, Cheltenham/Northampton, pp 197–239
Niskanen WA (1968) Nonmarket decision making: the peculiar economics of bureaucracy. Am Econ Rev 58(2):293–305
Niskanen WA (1971) Bureaucracy and representative government. Aldine-Atherton, Chicago
Niskanen WA (1975) Bureaucrats and politicians. J Law Econ 18:617–644
Niskanen WA (2001) Bureaucracy. In: Shughart WF II, Razzolini L (eds) The Elgar companion to public choice. Edward Elgar, Cheltenham/Northampton, pp 258–270
O'Driscoll GP Jr (1977) The Ricardian nonequivalence theorem. J Polit Econ 87:940–971
Olson M (1965) The logic of collective action: public goods and the theory of groups. Harvard University Press, Cambridge
Peltzman S (1976) Toward a more general theory of regulation. J Law Econ 23:209–240
Persson T, Tabellini G (2002) Political economics: explaining economic policy. MIT Press, Cambridge
Persson T, Tabellini G (2005) The economic effects of constitutions. MIT Press, Cambridge
Riker WH (1962) The theory of political coalitions. Yale University Press, New Haven
Rowley CK (1991) Gordon Tullock: entrepreneur of public choice. Public Choice 71(3):149–169
Rowley CK (2012) Public choice: the origins and development of a research program. In: Reksulak M, Razzolini L, Shughart WF II (eds) The Elgar companion to public choice, 2nd ed. Edward Elgar, Cheltenham/Northampton (forthcoming)
Rowley CK, Shughart WF II, Tollison RD (2002) The economics of budget deficits. In: Mark B (ed) The international library of critical writings in economics, vol 2, 153rd edn. Edward Elgar, Cheltenham/Northampton
Shughart WF II (1990) Antitrust policy and interest-group politics. Quorum Books, New York
Shughart WF II (2003) Budget deficits. In: Rowley CK, Schneider F (eds) The encyclopedia of public choice, vol II. Kluwer, Dordrecht/Boston, pp 49–53
Shughart WF II, Thomas D (2012) Hope and change in the Obama administration's antitrust policies. Unpublished working paper, Utah State University
Shughart WF II, Tollison RD (1983) Preliminary evidence on the use of inputs by the Federal Reserve System. Am Econ Rev 73:291–304
Shughart WF II, Tollison RD (1985) The positive economics of antitrust policy: a survey article. Int Rev Law Econ 5(1):39–57
Simmons RT (2011) Beyond politics: the roots of government failure, rev. and updated. The Independent Institute, Oakland
Smith A ([1776] 1976) An inquiry into the nature and causes of the wealth of nations. In: Campbell RH, Skinner AS, Todd WB (eds) The Glasgow edition of the works and correspondence of Adam Smith, vol II. Oxford University Press, Oxford
Stigler GJ (1971) The theory of economic regulation. Bell J Econ Manage Sci 2(1):3–21
Tiebout CM (1956) A pure theory of local government expenditures. J Polit Econ 64:416–424
Tollison RD (1982) Rent seeking: a survey. Kyklos 35:575–602
Tollison RD, Congleton RD (1995) The economic analysis of rent seeking. Edward Elgar, Aldershot
Tullock G (1959) Problems of majority voting. J Polit Econ 67(6):571–579
Tullock G (1961) Problems of majority voting: reply to a traditionalist. J Polit Econ 69(2):200–203
Tullock G (1965) The politics of bureaucracy. Public Affairs Press, Washington, DC
Tullock G (1967) The welfare costs of tariffs, monopolies, and theft. West Econ J 5:224–232
Tullock G (1970) A simple algebraic logrolling model. Am Econ Rev 60(3):419–426
Tullock G (1980a) Efficient rent seeking. In: Buchanan JM, Tollison RD, Tullock G (eds) Towards a theory of the rent-seeking society. Texas A&M University Press, College Station, pp 97–112
Tullock G (1980b) Trials on trial: the pure theory of legal procedure. Columbia University Press, New York

Tullock G (1989) The economics of special privilege and rent seeking. Kluwer, Boston/Dordrecht
Tullock G (1987) Autocracy. Martinus Nijhoff, Dordrecht
Tullock G (1991) Recollections of an editor. Public Choice 71(3):129–139
Tullock G (1994) The economics of non-human societies. Pallas Press, Tucson
Tullock G (2001) Monarchies, hereditary and non-hereditary. In: Shughart WF II, Razzolini L (eds) The Elgar companion to public choice. Edward Elgar, Cheltenham/Northampton, pp 140–156
Tullock G (2004–2006) In: Rowley CK (ed) The selected works of Gordon Tullock: in ten volumes. Liberty Fund, Indianapolis
Weber M ([1922] 1978) Economy and society, 2 vols. University of California Press, Berkeley
Weingast BR, Moran MJ (1983) Bureaucratic discretion or congressional control? Regulatory policymaking by the Federal Trade Commission. J Polit Econ 91(5):765–800
Wicksell K ([1896] 1967) A new principle of just taxation, Finanztheoretische Untersuchungen. Jena, reprinted. In: Musgrave RA, Peacock AT (eds) Classics in the theory of public finance. St. Martin's Press, New York, pp 72–118
Wilson JQ ([1989] 2000) Bureaucracy: what government agencies do and why they do it. Basic Books, New York
Woodrow W (1887) The study of administration. Polit Sci Quart 2(2):197–222
Young M, Reksulak M, Shughart WF II (2001) The political economy of the IRS. Econ Polit 13:201–220

Chapter 9
The Politics of Medicine

John C. Goodman

In 1948, Britain nationalized health care and made it free to patients at the point of delivery. For the past 64 years, therefore, the allocation of health-care resources has been almost completely determined by the political system rather than by consumer choice and competition in the marketplace. What difference has that made?

An extensive analysis of the British National Health Service (NHS) shows that all its major features can be explained in terms of public choice theory.[1] Far from being the consequence of the preferences of politicians (who could be replaced by different politicians with different preferences in the next election), the major features of national health insurance follow inevitably from the fact that politicians have the authority to allocate health care resources, and from that fact alone.

This analysis is based on the path-breaking insights of James Buchanan and Gordon Tulloch. It applies the general theory of public choice, which they developed, to the field of health policy.

This approach runs counter to the conventional wisdom. A great many British health policy analysts who support national health insurance are quick to concede that the British NHS has defects. But these defects, in their view, merely represent a failure of political will. The ultimate goal, they hold, is to retain the system of socialized medicine and make it work better.

By contrast, I will argue that the defects of national health insurance systems are inevitable consequences of placing the market for health under the control of politicians. It is not true that British health-care policy just happens to be as it is. Enoch Powell, a former minister of health who ran the British NHS, seems to have appreciated

[1] John C. Goodman, *National Health Care in Great Britain: Lessons for the U.S.A.*, Chap. 10.

J.C. Goodman (✉)
National Center for Policy Analysis, 12770 Coit Rd.,
Suite 800, Dallas, TX 75251-1339, USA
e-mail: john.goodman@ncpa.org

D.R. Lee (ed.), *Public Choice, Past and Present: The Legacy of James M. Buchanan and Gordon Tullock*, Studies in Public Choice 28, DOI 10.1007/978-1-4614-5909-5_9,

this insight. Powell wrote that "whatever is entrusted to politicians becomes political even if it is not political anyhow."[2] He went on to say that:

> The phenomena of Medicine and Politics... result automatically and necessarily from the nationalization of medical care and its provision gratis at the point of consumption...These phenomena are implicit in such an organization and are not the accidental or incidental results of blemishes which can be "reformed" away while leaving the system as such intact.[3]

The following is a brief summary.

The Amount of Spending on Health Services

One argument used to justify national health insurance is that, left to their own devices, individuals will spend too little on their health care. This was a major reason why many middle- and upper-middle class British citizens supported the creation of national health insurance for the working class in 1948.[4] Many expected that, under nationalized medical care, more total dollars would be spent on health care than would otherwise have been the case.

Yet, it is not clear that the NHS has increased overall spending on health care. It may even have had the opposite result. This was the contention of Dennis Lees, professor of economics at the University of Nottingham, who wrote that "the British people, left free to do so, would almost certainly have chosen to spend more on health services themselves than governments have chosen to spend on their behalf."[5] The same may be true of national health insurance in other countries.

To see why this is true, let us first imagine a situation in which a politician is trying to win over a single voter. Suppose the politician has £100 to spend on the voter's behalf. To maximize his chance of winning, the politician should spend the £100 precisely as the voter wants it spent. If the voter's choice is £50 on medical care, £30 on a retirement pension, and £20 on a rent subsidy, that should also be the choice of the vote-maximizing politician. If the politician does not choose to spend the £100 in this way, he risks losing this voter to a clever opponent.

Now, it might seem that if the voter wants £50 spent on medical care, we can conclude that he would have spent the £50 on medical care himself if he were spending £50 of his own money. But this is not quite true. State-provided medical care has one feature that is generally missing from a private medical market where patients are spending their own money—non-price rationing. This form of rationing imposes heavy costs on patients (the cost of waiting and other inconveniences), leads to

[2]Powell E (1976) Medicine and politics, 1975 and after. Pitman, New York, p 5.

[3]Powell, *Medicine and Politics*, p. 67.

[4]Lees D (1963) An economist considers other alternatives. In: Schoeck H (ed) Financing medical care: an appraisal of foreign programs. Caxton Printers, Caldwell, p 80.

[5]Lees D (1976) Economics and non-economics of health services. Three Banks Rev no 110 (June) :9.

deterioration in the quality of services rendered, and creates various forms of waste and inefficiency.

Thus, other things being equal, £50 of spending on government health care will be less valuable to the average voter than £50 of spending in a private medical marketplace. It also means that, under nationalized medicine, spending for health care will be less attractive to voters relative to spending programs that do not involve non-price rationing.

Using public choice theory, we can predict that the average voter will desire less spending on health care, relative to other goods and services, when health care is rationed by nonmarket devices. Moreover, the greater the rationing problems, the less attractive health care spending will be. We would also expect even less spending on health care in a completely "free" service like the NHS than in a health service that charges user fees.

Inequalities in Health Care

A major argument in favor of national health insurance is that private medical care allows inequalities in levels of provision.

Aneurin Bevan, father of the NHS, declared that "everyone should be treated alike in the matter of medical care."[6] The Beveridge Report, a blueprint for the NHS, promised "a health service providing full preventive and curative treatment of every kind for every citizen without exceptions."[7] The *British Medical Journal* predicted that the NHS would be "a 100% service for 100% of the population." The goal of the NHS founders was to eliminate inequities in health care based on age, sex, occupation, geographical location, and—most importantly—income and social class.[8] As Beveridge put it, "the essence of a satisfactory health service is that rich and poor are treated alike, that poverty is not a disability and wealth is not advantaged."[9] Similar statements have been made by politicians in virtually every country that has established a national health insurance program.

Yet, levels of provision in Britain, Canada, and New Zealand today may be even more unequal as they would have been in the absence of national health insurance. More than 30 years after the NHS founding, an official task force found little evidence that the creation of the NHS had equalized health-care access.[10] Another study 50 years after the NHS founding concluded that access had become more

[6]Quoted in Economic Models Ltd. (1976) The British health care system. American Medical Association, Chicago, p. 33.

[7]Quoted in Harry Swartz (1977) The infirmity of British medicine. In: Tyrrell E Jr (ed) The future that doesn't work: social democracy's failure in Britain. Doubleday, New York, p. 24.

[8]*British Medical Journal*, 12 Dec 1942, p. 700.

[9]Bevan A (1952) In place of fear. Heinemann, London, p. 76.

[10]Townsend P, Davidson N (1982) Inequities in health care, black report. Penguin, Harmondsworth.

unequal in the years between the two studies.[11] Other scholarly reports have come to similar conclusions.[12]

The problem of unequal access is so well known in Britain that the press refers to the NHS as a "postcode lottery" in which a person's chances for timely, high-quality treatment depend on the neighborhood or "postcode" in which he or she lives.[13] "Generally speaking, the poorer you are and the more socially deprived your area, the worse your care and access is likely to be," says *The Guardian*, a staunch defender of socialized medicine.[14] Scholarly studies of the issue have come to similar conclusions. For example, a study by the Joseph Rowntree Research Trust published in 2000 found discrepancies between geographical locations for all causes of death[15]:

- Nonelderly Britons living in areas with the worst-performing hospitals were 42% more likely to die on any given day than the average for Britain as a whole.
- The nonelderly population living in regions with the best-performing hospitals was 24% less likely to die than the average for Britain as a whole.
- Overall, the study found that if health-care inequality were merely decreased to 1983 levels, some 7,500 premature deaths among people younger than age 65 could be avoided each year.

Other research reinforces these conclusions:

- One study found that if the proportion of cancer-related illnesses and deaths were the same in Britain's lowest socioeconomic groups as in the most affluent, there would be 16,600 fewer deaths from cancer each year.[16]
- The British Heart Foundation (BHF) found that the premature death rate for working-class men is 58% higher than nonworking-class men.[17]

[11] Independent inquiries into inequity and health: the Acheson report. Stationary Office, London, 1998.

[12] Mitchell R, Shaw M (2000) Reducing health inequities in Britain. Joseph Rowntree Foundation, York.

[13] See, for example, "Postcode Lottery in Social Services," *BBC News*, 13 Oct 2000, http://news.bbc.co.uk/2/hi/health/969110.stm; Sophie Borland, "Laid Bare, Scandal of the Postcode Lottery for Dementia Care," *Mail Online*, 13 Dec 2011, http://www.dailymail.co.uk/health/article-2073393/Laid-bare-scandal-postcode-lottery-dementia-care.html; and John-Paul Ford Rojas, "Study Reveals Postcode Lottery," *The Telegraph*, 10 Dec 2011, http://www.telegraph.co.uk/health/8947415/Study-reveals-postcode-lottery.html.

[14] Patrick Butler (2000) Q&A: postcode lottery. The Guardian (Manchester), 9 Nov 2000, http://www.guardian.co.uk/society/2000/nov/09/NHS.

[15] Dr. Mitchell R, Dr. Shaw M (2000) Reducing health inequalities in Britain. Joseph Rowntree Foundation.

[16] Cancer trends in England and Wales, 1950–1999. Health Stat Quart no 8 (Winter 2000):18.

[17] British Heart Foundation, Statistics Database (1998) Coronary heart disease statistics.

- The BHF estimates that more than 5,000 working-class men under the age of 65 die of coronary heart disease each year in Britain because of variations in health-care access for different socioeconomic groups.[18]

The British results are not unique. In most countries with waiting lists for care, the poor wait longer than the wealthy and powerful. For example, a survey of Ontario, Canada, physicians found that more than 80% of physicians, including 90% of cardiac surgeons, 81% of internists, and 60% of family physicians, had been personally involved in managing a patient who had received preferential access on the basis of factors other than medical need. When asked about those patients most likely to receive preferential treatment, physicians reported that 93% had personal ties to the treating physician, 85% were high-profile public figures, and 83% were politicians.[19]

Other studies have reached similar conclusions. One study found that the wealthy and powerful in Canada have significantly greater access to medical specialists than the less well-connected poor.[20] A University of Toronto study found that high-profile patients enjoy more frequent services, shorter waiting times, and greater choice in specialists.[21]

These results are well known in health policy circles, but the conventional view is that they are aberrations that demonstrate a lack of diligence in pursuing an important social goal. In fact, they are the expected result of substituting non-price rationing for the marketplace.

In theory, creating regional equality is a relatively simple task. All governments have to do is spend more in areas that are relatively deprived and less in areas that are relatively well endowed. But most governments have not done this. Why? Public choice theory supplies a possible answer.

Policy makers must make two choices about spending in a particular area or region. First, they must decide how many total dollars are to be spent there. Second, they must decide how to allocate those dollars. In a democracy, there is no particular reason why per capita spending will be the same in all areas.

Per capita spending may differ across voting districts for numerous reasons. Voter turnout may be higher in some districts than in others, which suggests that those districts are willing to "pay" more (in terms of votes) for political largesse. Voters in some districts may be more aware of, and more sensitive to, changes in per capita spending than voters in other districts.

---

[18] Sir Charles George, "Coronary Heart Disease Statistics," British Heart Foundation, 1999.

[19] Basinski AS, Naylor CD (1998) A survey of provider experiences and perceptions of preferential access to cardiovascular care in Ontario, Canada. Ann Intern Med 129(7).

[20] Alter DA et al. (1999) Effects of socioeconomic status on access to invasive cardiac procedures and on mortality after acute myocardial infarction. New Eng J Med 341:(18):1359–1367, 28 Oct 1999.

[21] Dunlop S, Coyte PC, McIsaac W (2000) Socio-economic status and the utilisation of physicians' services: results from the Canadian National Population Health Survey. Soc Sci Med 51(1):1–11.

Given that a certain amount of money is going to be spent in a certain area or region, competition for votes dictates that the money be allocated in accordance with the preference of the voters in that area or region. To return to the hypothetical example in the previous section, let us suppose that £100 is going to be spent in the region of Merseyside, England. If a majority of residents want £20 spent on health services and £80 spent on other programs, political competition will tend to produce that result. Yet, if the residents of some other city want £80 spent on health services and £20 spent on other programs, political competition will also tend to produce that result.

Prior to the establishment of national health insurance, in most developed countries, geographical inequalities reflected community preferences. In general, the citizens of wealthier and more densely populated areas chose to spend a larger fraction of their income on medical care. There is no reason to suppose that their preferences were radically altered by national health insurance, and thus, no reason to suppose that in allocating public spending, vote-maximizing politicians are doing anything other than responding to voter preferences.

The Time Price Versus the Money Price of Care

In Britain, it is relatively easy to see a primary care physician. However, the British wait twice as long as Americans.[22] In fact, the wait to see a specialist is sometimes more than 1 year. In the United States, only 8% of patients wait more than 4 months for surgery, compared with more than one in three patients in Canada and 41% in Britain.

At any one time, hundreds of thousands of patients relying on the British National Health Service are waiting months for hospital surgery. Overall, 2.5 million people are waiting for some type of treatment.[23] Many are waiting in pain. Many are risking their lives by waiting. The cost of such waiting for many of them is undoubtedly greater than the cost (to the government) of their medical care.[24]

An investigation by a British newspaper, *The Observer*, finds that delays in Britain for colon cancer treatment are so long that 20% of the cases considered curable at time of diagnosis are incurable by the time of treatment.[25] A study of cancer

[22] Nick Triggle (2011) Vulnerable patients face ‘painful waits in the NHS. BBC News, 7 Aug 2011, http://www.bbc.co.uk/news/health-14407753.

[23] “Referral to Treatment Waiting Times Statistics,” UK Department of Health, March 2012, http://www.dh.gov.uk/prod_consum_dh/groups/dh_digitalassets/@dh/@en/@ps/@sta/@perf/documents/digitalasset/dh_134123.xls.

[24] “Hospital Waiting Times/List Statistics,” Department of Health, United Kingdom, 2nd Quarter, 2008/2009, http://www.performance.doh.gov.uk/waitingtimes/index.htm.

[25] Anthony Browne, “Cash-Strapped NHS Hospitals Chase Private Patient ‘Bonanza’,” *The Observer*, 16 Dec 2001. Also see Browne, “Deadly Rise in Wait for Cancer Care,” *The Observer*, 3 Mar 2002; and Browne, “How Thousands of Cancer Patients and Doctors Have Been Betrayed,” *The Observer*, 3 Mar 2002.

patients in Glasgow, Scotland, finds the same is true of lung cancer patients.[26] Twenty-five percent of British cardiac patients die while waiting their turn to receive treatment.[27]

According to government reports, one in six people on NHS waiting lists for elective surgery is removed without ever being treated.[28]

While Britain may be one of the worst cases of rationing by waiting, throughout the developed world, people primarily pay for care with time, not with money. That is true even in the United States—both with private and public insurance. But why is that?

Economists are generally scornful of rationing by waiting as a mechanism for allocating resources. Consider people who go to a safety net hospital emergency room for what is essentially "free" primary care and suppose that the market price of the doctor's time would ordinarily by £100. If the services are free, however, a much larger group of patients will try to take advantage of them, including patients who value doctor visits at only £5 or £10. Since demand greatly exceeds supply at a price of zero, the doctor's time is available in this example only to those who are willing to wait the longest. How long will people wait, on the average? Someone who values a doctor visit at £100 will be willing to spend £100 worth of time. (Consider a patient who values his time at his wage rate. If he is paid £20 an hour, he will wait 5 h; if he is paid £25 an hour, he will wait 4 h; and so on.)

Just as price rationing produces a market-clearing *money price of care*, rationing by waiting time produces a market-clearing *time price of care*. In this example, the market will clear at £100 worth of time for the marginal patient. But remember, other people (probably taxpayers) have to pay the doctor £100 in money. That means that the *care is being paid for twice: once with time and again with money*. Non-price rationing, in this example, effectively doubles the social cost of medical care.

One common misconception is that making care free at the point of delivery will make health care more accessible for low-income patients. After all, we all have the same number of hours in a day—even if we do not have the same amount of money in our pocketbooks. Does not a system of paying for care with time create a level playing field across social classes? Although that idea may have theoretical appeal, in reality, it turns out to be wrong.

---

[26]Similar results are likely true of other cancers as well. See Noelle O'Rourke and R. Edwards, "Lung Cancer Treatment Waiting Times and Tumour Growth," *Clinical Oncology* (Royal College of Radiologists) 12, no. 3 (June 2000): 141–44, cited in Kirsty Scott, "Treatment Delays Are Killing Cancer Patients," *The Guardian*, 1 July 2000.

[27]Anthony Browne and Matthew Young, "NHS reform: Towards Consensus?" A Partnership for Better Health Report, Adam Smith Institute, 2002. Approximately 130,000 people in England die of heart disease each year. However, the NHS estimates that only 500 cardiac patients die annually while waiting for care. See Linda Beecham, "Health Secretary Will Target Heart Disease," *British Medical Journal* (23 Oct 1999); "500 Heart Patients Die on Waiting Lists," BBC News, 3 June 1999.

[28]Audit Commission (2003) Waiting for elective admission: review of national findings. Health: Acute Hospital Portfolio, Audit Commission, London.

As we have seen, higher-income, better-educated British patients get more care and better care, especially in relation to their need for care. Furthermore, it is easier for higher-income patients to pay out-of-pocket for care (or even private health insurance) when the need arises.

What is true for Britain appears to be also true in other countries where health-care resources are allocated politically. In Canada, the wealthy and powerful have significantly greater access to medical specialists than less well-connected poor.[29] High-profile patients enjoy more frequent services, shorter waiting times, and greater choice of specialists.[30] Moreover, among the nonelderly white population, low-income Canadians are 22% more likely to be in poor health than their US counterparts.[31]

For OECD countries generally, among people with similar health conditions, "higher-income people use the system more intensively and use more costly services than do lower-income people."[32] It seems likely that the same personal characteristics that ensure success in a market economy also enhance success in bureaucratic systems.[33]

Bottom line: The system works reasonably well for those who are in the best position to change it.

Spending Priorities: Caring Versus Curing

Even as hundreds of thousands of patients languish on waiting lists, the NHS surprisingly provides about nine million nonurgent ambulance rides annually.[34] Overall, the NHS provides nonmedical care services to more than one million people.[35] For

[29]Alter DA et al. (1999) Effects of socioeconomic status on access to invasive cardiac procedures and on mortality after acute myocardial infarction. New Eng J Med 341(18):1359–1367.

[30]Dunlop S, Coyte PC, McIsaac W (2000) Socio-economic status and the utilisation of physicians' services: results from the Canadian national population health survey. Soc Sci Med 51(1):123–133.

[31]O'Neill JE, O'Neill DM (2007) Health status, health care and inequality: Canada versus The U.S. NBER working paper no. 13429. National Bureau of Economic Research, Cambridge, MA.

[32]Glied SA (2008) Health care financing, efficiency, and equity. NBER working paper no. 13881. National Bureau of Economic Research, Cambridge, MA.

[33]Goodman JC, Musgrave GL, Herrick DM (2004) Lives at risk: single-payer national health insurance around the world. Rowman & Littlefield, Lanham, Chap. 21.

[34]"Ambulance Services England 2010–2011," UK National Health Service, 23 June 2011, http://www.ic.nhs.uk/webfiles/publications/Audits%20and%20Performance/Ambulance/Ambulance%20Service%202010_11/Ambulance_Services_England_2010_11.pdf.

[35]"Community Care Statistics 2010–2011: Social Services Activity Report, England," U.K. Department of Health, 28 Mar 2012, http://www.ic.nhs.uk/webfiles/publications/009_Social_Care/Community_Care_Statistics_201011/Community_Care_Statistics_201011_Social_Services_Activity_Report_England.pdf.

example, services such as home care, day care, and meals were provided to 1.34 million people, including:

- 543,000 received home care services.
- 466,000 received equipment or home alterations.
- 372,000 received social workers or occupational therapy.
- 179,000 received day care services.
- 81,000 users received meals on wheels.

There can be no doubt that Britain's choices are the result of conscious political decisions. American economist Mary-Ann Rozbicki asked a number of British health planners the following question: "If you suddenly enjoyed a sharp increase in available resources, how would you allocate it?" The response was invariably the same. They would put the additional resources into services for the aged, the chronically ill, and the mentally handicapped.[36] Commenting on this response, Rozbicki writes[37]:

> It is difficult for an American observer to comprehend that view. He has been impressed by the support services already afforded the non-acute patient (and the well consumer) — the doctor, nurse and social worker attendance at homes, clinics and hospitals for the purpose of improving the comfort and well-being of the recipients involved. He has also been impressed (and sometimes shocked) by the relative lack of capability to diagnose, cure and/or treat life-threatening conditions. The U.S. patient, while having forgone the home ministrations of the family doctor and learned to endure the antiseptic quality of the hospital, also confidently expects immediate delivery of all that medical science has to offer if life or health is under immediate threat.

What political pressures lead decision makers to prefer caring over curing? Rozbicki believes it is a matter of numbers: numbers of votes. Money spent on caring affects far more people than money spent on curing. Rozbicki writes[38]:

> In weighing the choice between a more comfortable life for the millions of aged or early detection and treatment of the far fewer victims of dread[ed] diseases, [the British health authorities] have favored the former. In choosing between a fully equipped hospital therapy and rehabilitation center or nuclear medicine technology, they have favored the former. The sheer numbers involved on each side of the equation would tend to dictate these choices by government officials in a democratic society.

In a typical health insurance pool in the United States, about 5% of enrollees will spend 50% of the money. About 10% will spend nearly two-thirds.[39] The numbers differ a bit from group to group, but in any given year, a small number of people spend most of our health-care dollars.

---

[36] Mary-Ann Rozbicki (1978) Rationing British health care: the cost/benefit approach. Executive seminar in national and international affairs. US Department of State, 17 Apr 1978.

[37] Rozbicki, "Rationing British Health Care."

[38] Rozbicki, "Rationing British Health Care," 18 (emphasis added).

[39] Stanton MW (2006) The high concentration of US healthcare expenditures. Agency for Healthcare Research and Quality, *Research in Action* 19, http://www.ahrq.gov/research/ria19/expendria.pdf.

Now suppose you are a minister of health. Can you afford to spend half of all health-care dollars on 5% of the voters? Even if they survive to the next election, they may be too sick to get to the polls and vote for your party.

From a political point of view, the answer is clearly "no." The inevitable political pressure is to skimp on care for the sick to spend on benefits for the healthy. Put differently, the politics of medicine pushes decision makers to underprovide to the sick so they can overprovide to the healthy.

That is why it is easier to see a primary care physician in Britain than it is in the United States but harder to see a specialist and much harder to access expensive technology. In the 1970s, the British invented the CAT scanner and for a while supplied half the world's usage (probably with government subsidies). But the National Health Service bought very few CAT scanners for use by British patients. The British (along with the United States) also invented renal dialysis, but today Britain has one of the lowest dialysis rates in all of Europe.[40]

Similar observations apply to Canada, where services for the relatively healthy are ubiquitous and expensive technology is scarce. PET scanners, for example, can detect metabolic cancer about a year earlier than an MRI scanner. At last count, the United States had more than 1,000 PET scanners, while the Canadian Medicare system (with one-fifth our population) had only 24.[41]

This explanation is persuasive, as far as it goes. But it is not complete. It is true that the number of potential beneficiaries of home visits far exceeds those of radiation therapy. But all Britons are potentially ill. So, all have an interest in acute care, even if they do not currently need it. To understand these priorities, we must understand why the average citizen would approve of them.

In contrast to America, most Britons are relatively uninformed about the latest medical technology. This ignorance, moreover, is quite "rational." Information is costly. Even in the age of the Internet, it requires an investment of time. The rational person has an incentive to expand his knowledge about any subject only to the point at which the cost of an additional bit of information is equal to its benefit. This is the economic explanation for the commonly observed fact that the average person does not become an expert in medical science.

In Britain, however, the average citizen has much less incentive to become knowledgeable about medicine than his or her counterpart in the United States. Precisely because the US medical market is largely private, a better-informed person can become a better consumer.

But within the NHS, medical services are not "purchased." Suppose a British citizen invests time and money to learn more about medical matters and discovers

---

[40]Goodman JC, Musgrave GL, Herrick DM (2004) Lives at risk: single-payer national health insurance around the world. Rowman & Littlefield Publishers, Lanham, p 62.

[41]Canadian Agency for Drugs and Technology in Health, "Publicly Funded PET Scanners and Cyclotrons in Canada," undated, http://www.cadth.ca/media/healthupdate/Issue8/pet.pdf; and Society for Nuclear Medicine, "Referring Physicians: Positron Emission Tomography (PET) Scan," Center for Molecular Imagining Innovation and Translation, undated. http://www.molecularimagingcenter.org/index.cfm?PageID=7608.

that the NHS is not offering the kinds of services it should. This knowledge is of almost no value unless the citizen can inform millions of other voters, persuade them to "throw the rascals out," and achieve a change of policy. Such a campaign would be enormously expensive, costing the citizen far more than he could expect to recover from any potential personal benefit.

Nationalized medicine affects the level of knowledge that patients have in yet another way. In a free market for medical care, suppliers of medical services have an incentive to inform potential customers about new developments. Such information increases the demand for new services and, thus, promises to enhance the income of those who supply them. In the NHS, the suppliers have no such incentives. Doctors, nurses, and hospital administrators increase their income chiefly by persuading the government to pay them more. They increase their comfort, leisure time, and other forms of satisfaction by encouraging patients to demand not more, but less.

Public choice theory, then, would predict that under a socialized medical system, people will acquire less knowledge about medical care than they would have acquired in a private system. The evidence confirms this prediction. More than three decades ago, Rozbicki wrote that "the British populace appears much less sophisticated in its medical demands than the American populace."[42] Through the years, other commentators have made the same observation and the generalization still appears to be true.

The comparative ignorance about medical science that prevails among British voters has a profound impact on NHS policies. With other things equal, people will always place a higher value on those services with which they are familiar and on benefits about which they are certain. The known is preferred to the unknown and certainty to uncertainty. The average British voter is familiar with and fairly certain about the personal value of the non-acute services provided by the NHS. He or she is probably unfamiliar with and uncertain about the personal value of advanced services for acute ailments.

Another reason why voters will tend to prefer caring to curing services stems from a characteristic of non-price rationing. All of the services of the NHS require rationing. But in some sectors, the rationing problems are far greater than in others because quality can sometimes be sacrificed to quantity. In comparison with American doctors, British general practitioners spend less time with each patient and presumably render fewer services. Nonetheless, this type of adjustment allows the typical patient to actually visit his or her GP within 2 or 3 days of making an appointment. The quality of treatment may be inferior to what US patients receive, but patients are at least certain that they will receive some treatment. Presumably, given the overall rationing problem, patients prefer this type of adjustment.

Such adjustments cannot be made with most acute services. It is less feasible to sacrifice quality for quantity with respect to CT scans, organ transplants, and renal

---

[42] Rozbicki, "Rationing British Health Care," 17.

dialysis. Patients tend to either receive full treatment or no treatment. Very few patient-pleasing adjustments can be made.

These characteristics of health-care rationing have an important effect on the preferences of potential patients, even those who are knowledgeable about medicine. The existence of non-price rationing tends to make all health-care services less valuable than those services would be in a free market. But because non-acute services can be adjusted to increase the certainty of some treatment, whereas acute services generally cannot, the former tend to gain value relative to the latter. Thus, the priority given to non-acute treatment seems rational.

Administrative Controls

One of the most remarkable features of national health insurance is the enormous amount of decision-making power left in the hands of doctors. By and large, the medical communities in Britain, Canada, and New Zealand have escaped the disciplines of both the free market and government regulation. In the view of Michael Cooper,[43] Anthony Culyer,[44] and many other British health economists, this discretion is the principal reason for many of the gross inefficiencies found in the British NHS.

In addition to the power of GPs and consultants, other producer interest groups have gained power and influence. Within the NHS, these include hospital administrators, junior doctors, and nonmedical hospital staff. The complaint made again and again is that the NHS is primarily organized and administered to benefit such special interest groups rather than patients. As Dennis Lees puts it,[45]

> the British health industry exists for its own sake, in the interest of the producer groups that make it up. The welfare of patients is a random byproduct, depending on how conflicts between the groups and between them and government happen to shake down at any particular time.

Government production of goods and services always tends to be less efficient than private production. Nonetheless, the NHS could be run more efficiently. Its administrators could adopt well-defined goals and assert more control over the various sectors to ensure that the goals are pursued. They could create incentives for NHS employees to provide better, more efficient patient care.

That these things are not done is hardly surprising. More than 200 years ago, Adam Smith observed that government regulation in the marketplace inevitably seemed to benefit producer interest groups at the expense of consumers. Things have changed very little with the passage of time. Economic studies of most major

[43]Cooper M (1975) Rationing health care. Croom Helm, London, p 73.

[44]Culyer A (1975) Health: the social cost of doctors' discretion. New Society, 27 Feb 1975.

[45]Lees, "Economics and Non-Economics of Health Services," p. 12.

regulatory commissions in the United States have come to the same conclusion: The welfare of producers is regularly favored over the welfare of consumers.[46] We should not expect the NHS to be different.

Are these phenomena consistent with public choice theory? At first glance, it may seem that they are not. Since consumers outnumber producers, it might seem that, with democratic voting, consumers would always have the upper hand. If sheer voting power were the only factor, this might be so. But two additional factors put consumers at a disadvantage: the cost of information and the cost of political organization.

To achieve any fundamental change of policy, voters must be informed about what kinds of changes they specifically seek. They also must be organized—at least to the extent that they can communicate to politicians their willingness to withhold electoral support unless their desires are satisfied. But as we have seen, information is costly. Organizing a political coalition is also costly. And the incentives for any single individual to bear these costs are extremely weak.

Producers are in a different position. Since they are working in the industry, they already possess a great deal of information about which policies are consistent with their self-interest and which are not. Their costs of political organizing also are much lower because they are relatively few in number and share common interests. In addition, because the personal stake of each producer in regulatory issues is far greater than that of a representative consumer, each producer has a much greater personal incentive to contribute to political efforts that protect the interests of producers as a group.

Producer interest groups, then, ordinarily have enormous advantages over consumer groups in issues involving government regulation of their industry. These advantages appear to be more than sufficient to overcome their relative vulnerability in terms of sheer voting power. This insight was provided by Professor Milton Friedman 40 years ago[47]:

> Each of us is a producer and also a consumer. However, we are much more specialized and devote a much larger fraction of our attention to our activity as a producer than as a consumer. We consume literally thousands if not millions of items. The result is that people in the same trade, like barbers or physicians, all have an intense interest in the specific problems of this trade and are willing to devote considerable energy to doing something about them. On the other hand, those of us who use barbers at all get barbered infrequently and spend only a minor fraction of our income in barber shops. Our interest is casual. Hardly any of us are willing to devote much time going to the legislature in order to testify against the inequity of restricting the practice of barbering. The same point holds for tariffs. The groups that think they have a special interest in particular tariffs are concentrated groups to whom the issue makes a great deal of difference. The public interest is widely dispersed. In consequence, in the absence of any general arrangements to offset the pressure of special interests, producer groups will invariably have a much stronger influence on legislative action and the powers that be than will the diverse, widely spread consumer interest.

Public choice theory, then, predicts that administrative inefficiencies caused by producer interest groups within health-care bureaucracies will continue to be a

---

[46]See MacAvoy PW (ed) (1970) Crisis of the regulatory commissions. Norton, New York.

[47]Friedman M (1962) Capitalism and freedom. University of Chicago Press, Chicago, p 143.

permanent feature of socialized medicine. There is no reason to believe that this defect can be "reformed" away.

Why Has Not the NHS Been Privatized?

In 1978, an article appeared in Medical Economics with the heading, "If Britain's Health Care Is So Bad, Why Do Patients Like It?"[48] That British patients do like the NHS had been confirmed repeatedly by public opinion polls, although its popularity has been declining.[49] And although the popularity of Medicare has also been declining in Canada, Canadians show little interest in moving to a US-type health-care system.[50]

The principle of national health insurance is accepted in other countries for three reasons. First, the wealthy, powerful, and sophisticated—those most skilled at articulating their complaints—find ways to maneuver to the front of the rationing lines. In this sense, national health insurance "works" in other countries because those who could change the system are best served by it. If a member of the British Parliament, the CEO of a large British company, or the head of a major British trade union had no greater access to renal dialysis than any other British citizen, the British NHS would not last a week.

Second, those pushed to the end of the waiting lines are generally unaware of medical technologies they are being denied, at least in comparison to American patients. And, as we have seen, doctors and health authorities have little incentive to increase their level of awareness. As a result, patients in other countries frequently do not know what they are not getting.

Third, patients pushed to the rear of the waiting lines in other countries are often not very insistent about getting their needs met. A number of comparisons of British and American patients through the years have concluded that British patients are more docile.[51] Conditioned for decades by a culture of rationing, British patients put up with inadequacies that most Americans would not tolerate.

---

[48]Fisher JJ (1978) If Britain's health care is so bad, why do patients like it? Med Econ, 21 Aug 1978.

[49]In a poll, the portion of people who were "fairly dissatisfied" or "very dissatisfied" rose to 28% in 1998. People reporting they were "very satisfied" fell to 13%, while the portion who were "fairly satisfied" fell to 45%. Fully 90% of those surveyed thought the NHS needs improvement. See Annabel Ferriman, "Public's Satisfaction with the NHS Declines," *British Medical Journal* 321(7275):1488, 16 Dec 2000.

[50]Between 1987 and 1997, the proportion of Canadians who were satisfied with their health care system dropped from 56% to 20%. Commonwealth Fund 1998 International Health Policy Survey, cited in Karen Donelan et al., "The Cost of Health System Change: Public Discontent in Five Nations," *Health Affairs* (May/June 1999): Exhibit 6.

[51]For a comparison of how patient attitudes and treatments vary by culture, see Lynn Payer (1996) Medicine and culture. Henry Holt, New York.

Comparing British and American patients, one doctor wrote that British patients "have fewer expectations" and are "more ready to cooperate unhesitatingly with the authoritarian figure of the doctor or nurse."[52] An American economist noted with surprise that British hospital patients, "far from complaining about specialists' inattention, a lack of laboratory tests, or the ineffectiveness of medical treatment, more often than not display an attitude of gratefulness for whatever is done."[53] Another doctor summarized the difference in British and American attitudes this way[54]:

> The British people—whether as a result of different life philosophy or generally lower level of affluence—have a much lower level of expectation from medical intervention in general. In fact they verge on the stoical as compared with the American patient, and, of course, this fact makes them, purely from a physician's point of view, the most pleasant patients. The resulting service has evolved over the years into a service that would in my opinion be all but totally unacceptable to any American not depending on welfare for medical services.

In general, the British public has little idea of how much they are paying for health care. Since the NHS is financed through hidden taxes, the perception that it costs little is widespread. Just how the perception of getting something for nothing affects British attitudes toward what most Americans would regard as intolerable defects in the health service was vividly illustrated by the experience of an American congressman on a trip with a group to examine the NHS first hand. He met a young woman with substantial facial scars received in an accident. Although the woman wanted plastic surgery for her face, she said, "I've been waiting 8 years for treatment, but they tell me I'm going to be able to have surgery within a year." Yet when the congressman asked her what she thought of the NHS, her reply was, "Oh, it's a wonderful system we have in Britain. You know, our medical care is all free."[55]

It might seem that an enterprising politician or political party could win a British election by offering the British public a better deal. Why not tell voters what the NHS really costs them, then offer to return their tax dollars so they could purchase private health insurance and health services?

The average British voter would undoubtedly be better off as a result, but that doesn't mean that most would approve of the plan. For one thing, even if voters knew what the NHS really costs, they might not be convinced that the private marketplace could offer a better deal. For years, British politicians have told voters that the NHS is the "envy of the world," and the public has been deluged with stories in

---

[52] Robinson D (1977) Primary medical practice in the United Kingdom and the United States. New Eng J Med 297(4):189, 28 July 1977.

[53] Rozbicki, "Rationing British Health Care," p. 18.

Goodman JC, Musgrave GL, Herrick DM (2004) Lives at risk: single-payer national health insurance around the world. Rowman & Littlefield Publishers, Lanham, p 62.

[54] Quoted in Harry Swartz (1977) The infirmity of British medicine. In: Tyrrell E Jr (ed) The future that doesn't work: social democracy's failures in Britain. Doubleday, New York, p 31.

[55] Quoted by Lew Rockwell in *World Research INC*, March 1979, p 5.

the socialist press indicating that only the rich get good medical care in the United States.[56]

For another thing, defenders of the NHS—including trade unions, thousands of NHS employees, and many British doctors—would play on existing fears and suspicions. Surprising as it may seem, the sagging morale and continual frustrations of NHS doctors have not produced enormous numbers of converts to free enterprise medicine. Perhaps many prefer the "protection" of a government bureaucracy to the rigors of free market competition. Whatever the reason, most of Britain's medical profession supports the idea of socialized medicine.[57] They not only support it but they also resisted proposals to open it to minimal competition by prime ministers Margaret Thatcher and John Major and more recently by Tony Blair.

In almost every country with national health insurance systems, disinterested, knowledgeable observers agree on the need for substantial reform. Even Sweden is searching for ways to introduce the disciplines of the competitive marketplace into its public system.[58]

But among developed countries, most serious attempts at fundamental reform have been blocked by the politics of medicine. Reforms in public sector health care are likely to come about as people seek private sector alternatives rather than through changes at the ballot box.

Applying the Principles to US Medicare

In the US Medicare program, policy makers achieve through patient cost-sharing what Britain and other countries achieve through the rationing of services: They punish the sick to reward the healthy. For example, although basic Medicare pays for many minor services that most seniors could easily afford to purchase out-of-pocket, it leaves the elderly exposed to thousands of dollars of catastrophic costs. This is exactly the opposite of how insurance is supposed to work.

Medicare's hospital deductible is $1,156. Seniors experiencing an extended stay lasting more than 2 months, however, are required to pay $289 per day in cost-sharing. This increases to $578 per day after 3 months, and Medicare pays nothing in hospital costs for patients who stay more than 5 months.[59]

---

[56]Quoted by Lew Rockwell in *World Research INC*, March 1979, p 6.

[57]Walsh J (1979) Britain's national health service: the Doctors' Dilemmas. Science 201:329, 28 July 1979.

[58]A. Wess Mitchell (2001) Sweden edges toward free-market medicine. National Center for policy analysis, brief analysis no. 369, 31 Aug 2001.

[59]For an explanation of Medicare cost-sharing see "Summary of Medicare Benefits and Cost-Sharing for 2012," California Health Advocates, 15 Nov 2011, http://www.cahealthadvocates.org/basics/benefits-summary.html.

When the federal government began regulating Medigap insurance (which fills the gaps in Medicare), congress forced insurers to follow the same pattern. Medigap must pay small bills, but seniors can still experience thousands of dollars in out-of-pocket costs.[60]

The pattern is repeated in the new Medicare prescription drug program (Part D). A "donut hole" exposes the relatively sick to significant out-of-pocket expenses for no other reason than the political desire to provide first-dollar coverage to the relatively healthy. In 2012, the maximum deductible for a Medicare Part D plan is $320. Once the deductible has been met (not all plans have a deductible), Medicare Part D pays 75% of the next $2,610 in drug spending until total drug expenditure is $2,930. The donut hole reflects drug spending that falls between $2,930 and $4,700. Until 2012, it was the responsibility of the enrollee to pay *all costs* inside the donut hole. The Patient Protection and Affordable Care Act created a new benefit in 2012 that pays for 50% of the costs. After $4,700 in total drug spending, Medicare Part D enrollees pay only a modest co-pay of $2.60 and $6.50 for each prescription. The donut hole is slated to close by 2020, however.[61]

[60] Scanlon WJ (2002) Medigap: current policies contain coverage gaps, undermine cost control incentives. Testimony before the Subcommittee on Health, Committee on Ways and Means, House of Representatives, 14 Mar 2002, http://www.gao.gov/new.items/d02533t.pdf; also see Levey NN (2011) Once politically taboo, proposals to shift more medicare costs to elderly are gaining traction. Los Angeles Times, 15 July 2011.

[61] "2012 Medicare Part D Outlook," Q1Medicare.com, undated, http://www.q1medicare.com/PartD-The-2012-Medicare-Part-D-Outlook.php.

Chapter 10
Tullock, Tideman, and the Origins of the Demand-Revealing Process

Nicolaus Tideman

Introduction

As the founding editor of *Public Choice*, Gordon Tullock created a unique outlet for new ideas. He believed that he could evaluate many papers without consulting referees, so he was able to offer fast turnaround as well as personal taste that ran strongly to interestingly unconventional ideas. He was willing to take chances with new ideas before they were clearly exposited and even before it was completely clear they were correct. These ways of Tullock can be seen in particular in his role in bringing the demand-revealing process to the attention of scholars concerned with the efficient provision of public goods.

When looked at in the right way, the demand-revealing process is really quite simple. It is just marginal-cost pricing applied to participation in decisions. But economists had a hard time seeing that such a thing is possible, because marginal-cost pricing generally does not achieve a balanced budget, and our intuitions told us that a process that disregarded budget balance would not be feasible.

I believe that many economists were also led away from understanding what is possible, as I was, by Paul Samuelson's powerful 1954 statement in "The Pure Theory of Public Expenditure":

> *[N]o decentralized pricing system can serve to determine optimally these levels of collective consumption.* Other kinds of "voting" or "signalling" would have to be tried. But, and this is the point sensed by Wicksell but perhaps not fully appreciated by Lindahl, now it is in the selfish interest of each person to give *false* signals, to pretend to have less interest in a given collective consumption activity than he really has, etc. I must emphasize this: taxing according to a benefit theory of taxation can not at all solve the computational problem in the decentralized manner possible for … "private" goods to which the ordinary market applies and which do not have the "external effects" basic to the very notion of collective

N. Tideman (✉)
Virginia Tech, Blacksburg, VA 24061, USA
e-mail: ntideman@vt.edu

D.R. Lee (ed.), *Public Choice, Past and Present: The Legacy of James M. Buchanan and Gordon Tullock*, Studies in Public Choice 28, DOI 10.1007/978-1-4614-5909-5_10,

> consumption goods. Of course, utopian voting and signalling schemes can be imagined. ("Scandinavian consensus," Kant's "categorical imperative," and other devices meaningful only under conditions of "symmetry," etc.) The failure of market catallactics in no way denies the following truth: given sufficient knowledge the optimal decisions can always be found by scanning over all the attainable states of the world and selecting the one which according to the postulated ethical welfare function is best. The solution "exists"; the problem is how to "find" it.
>
> One could imagine every person in the community being indoctrinated to behave like a "parametric decentralized bureaucrat" who *reveals* his preferences by signalling in response to price parameters or Lagrangean multipliers, to questionnaires, or other devices. But there is still this fundamental technical difference going to the heart of the whole problem of *social* economy: by departing from his indoctrinated rules, any one person can hope to snatch some selfish benefit in a way not possible under the self-policing competitive pricing of private goods; and the "external economies" or "jointness of demand" intrinsic to the very concept of collective goods and governmental activities makes it impossible for the grand ensemble of optimizing equations to have that special pattern of zeros which makes *laissez-faire* competition even *theoretically* possible as an analogue computer.[1]

With this passage firmly planted in my brain, I, like many other economists, could not imagine that it was possible to motivate people to report the intensities of their preferences for public activities truthfully. The record and my own recollection both indicate that the first person who understood that it was possible to motivate people to report the intensities of their preferences for public goods truthfully was Edward H. Clarke.

Clarke's Challenge to My Thinking

In the spring of 1968, Ed Clarke and I were both Ph.D. students in economics at the University of Chicago, both writing our dissertations under the supervision of George Tolley. One day Ed approached me in the hall and told me that he had discovered that it was possible to motivate people to report their preferences for public goods truthfully. He offered to explain to me how this was so, but I put him off. With the above quotation from Samuelson resonating in my brain, I was convinced that Ed had to be deluding himself.

That fall I went off to Harvard, and an appointment as an assistant professor beginning in spring 1969, once I had completed my dissertation. At Harvard I was considered an urban economist (my dissertation was titled *Three Approaches to Improving Urban Land Use*[2]), but my fundamental interest could be described more accurately as mechanism design: How can we design mechanisms that produce efficient outcomes? The demand-revealing process is an archetypical example of work in mechanism design, and I was undertaking my own efforts to devise a solution to the problem that Ed had already solved.

[1] Samuelson PA (1954) The pure theory of public expenditure. Rev Econ Stat 36(4):388–389.

[2] University of Chicago, 1969.

In the fall of 1970, I took a year of leave from Harvard to work in Washington as a senior staff economist at the President's Council of Economic Advisors. In Washington I met Selma Mushkin, who was gathering contributions for the book *Public Prices for Public Products*. Selma had already secured one paper that included me as a coauthor,[3] and at my suggestion she accepted the solely authored paper "Efficient Provision of Public Goods"[4] in which I developed my own idea for identifying efficient levels of spending on public activities.

My idea was to find the efficient level of provision as the limit of a sequence of increasingly accurate approximations. Starting with any estimate of the efficient level of provision of a public good, an economist can calculate a revised estimate that is likely to be better, by asking all those who benefit from the provision of a public good to specify a price at which, at the margin, they would not mind trading either increases or decreases in the level of provision of the public good. If people respond truthfully, then the aggregate of the responses reveals whether efficiency is improved by an increase or by a decrease in the level of provision. Each person will have an incentive to respond truthfully under a requirement to trade in either direction at the price named, provided that the current estimate of the efficient amount of the public activity is believed to be an unbiased estimator of the next estimate. Just before I developed my version of this idea, a very similar idea was presented in two other papers.[5] My contribution was the idea of having an adjustment process that would be a sequence of discrete jumps (based on an estimate of the aggregate elasticity of demand) rather than a continuous process, to maintain the plausibility of the belief that the current estimate was an unbiased estimator of the next estimate. This contribution of mine overcame an objection that the process specified in the earlier papers was subject to being slowed to a glacial pace as people discerned the direction of movement and demanded inordinate compensation for continued movement in that direction. However, the idea as I specified it would still motivate a strategic response from anyone who did not believe that the current estimate of the efficient quantity was an unbiased estimator of the next estimate. The idea received modest attention but never really took off. As of May 26, 2012, Google Scholar shows 216 citations to the Dreze and de la Vallee Poussin paper, 122 to the Malinvaud paper, and 23 citations to my paper.

When I received my copy of *Public Prices for Public Products*, I was surprised to see that the article immediately following mine was by Ed Clarke. I glanced at it but I could not understand it, so I set it aside.

---

[3] Smolensky E, Nichols D, Tideman N (1972) Waiting time as a congestion charge. In: Mushkin S (ed) Public prices for public products. The Urban Institute, pp 95–108.

[4] Tideman N (1972) Efficient provision of public goods. In: Mushkin S (ed) Public prices for public products. The Urban Institute, pp 111–123.

[5] Malinvaud E (1971) A planning approach to the public good problem. Swed J Econ 73/1:96–112; Dreze JH, de la Vallee Poussin D (1971) A tâtonnement process for public goods. Rev Econ Stud 38:133–150.

Even before I received the book, there was another occasion when I might have understood Clarke's ideas but did not. In the spring of 1971, George Tolley invited Ed and me to a double-bill seminar at the University of Chicago. I presented my idea from *Public Prices for Public Products* and Ed presented his. I had no understanding of his presentation.

In December 1972, I learned that I would not be offered a promotion to nontenured associate professor at Harvard and began looking for another position. Various possibilities did not work out, and then in late March or early April of 1973, I received an unexpected phone call from Charles Goetz at Virginia Tech, offering me a 1-year postdoctoral fellowship at the Center for Study of Public Choice there. I accepted.

I decided to use my year at Virginia Tech in a systematic study of ways of making collective decisions, with particular attention to their likely efficiency. When I reported this plan to Gordon Tullock, his response was "Well if you are going to do that, you should certainly include Ed Clarke's idea in your survey."

How had Ed managed to persuade Tullock that his ideas deserved consideration? Ed had submitted a version of his ideas to Tullock as editor of *Public Choice*, for consideration for publication. Tullock explained to me that he was not able to understand Clarke's manuscript, but he believed that if it was right it was important, so he decided to publish it.[6] Tullock believed that it was sensible for him to make many editorial decisions without input from referees. Clarke's paper is now the most widely cited paper ever published in *Public Choice*, with 2,121 Google Scholar citations as of May 26, 2012, nearly twice as many as the next most widely cited paper.

I started my review of ways of making collective decisions but put off dealing with Clarke's ideas. By December 1973, one economics professor at Virginia Tech had retired suddenly for health reasons and another had died in an auto accident, so the department head, Wilson Schmidt, asked me if I would be willing to teach for the rest of that academic year and have a postdoctoral fellowship the next year. Since I had no other plans, I agreed.

Thus, I returned to my review of ways of making collective decisions in the 1974–1975 academic year. Once again, I put off any effort to deal with Clarke's idea. Then in March 1975, I attended the Public Choice meetings in Chicago. There I encountered Martin Bailey. Bailey had been head of the Office of Tax Analysis at the U.S. Treasury when I had worked there as a consultant in the spring and summer of 1973. I told him what I was working on and that I still had to deal with the ideas of someone named Ed Clarke. Bailey's response was, "Ed Clarke is right you know."

You could have knocked me over with a feather. Not only had Bailey heard of Ed Clarke and his ideas, but he was telling me that Ed was right! And Martin Bailey was one of the smartest economists I had ever met. He had read Ed's *Public Choice* paper. Now I had an urgent need to contend with Ed's ideas.

---

[6] Clarke EH (1971) Multipart pricing of public goods. Public Choice 11:17–33.

When I returned to Blacksburg, I got out Ed's *Public Choice* paper, determined to do all I could to understand it. I studied it intensely for 10 min or so, and suddenly I understood it. I ran to Tullock's office to tell him the news. He said that I should immediately explain it to others. We organized an instantaneous, impromptu seminar in the living room of the Public Choice Center, inviting whoever happened to be around. When I was about 5 min into my presentation, Tullock started finishing my sentences. When I finished he said, "No one will ever understand this idea the way Clarke explained it. You and I need to write a version that people will understand."

That is how it happened that Tullock and I collaborated on "A New and Superior Process for Making Social Choices." We wrote the paper fairly quickly and submitted it to George Stigler as editor of the *Journal of Political Economy*. The paper was accepted fairly quickly and was published as the lead article in the December 1976 issue of that journal. It is my most widely cited (though possibly least original) paper, at 305 Google Scholar citations as of May 27, 2012, and it is tied for 11th place in the citation ranking of Tullock's works.

I got in touch with Ed and learned that he had not yet succeeded, and thought he might never succeed, in producing a draft of his dissertation that was acceptable to his committee, which included George Stigler. So Tullock phoned Stigler and said, "You know, there is an outside chance that someday Clarke will get a Nobel Prize for this work. It would be embarrassing if you would not give him a Ph.D. for it."

Stigler replied, "OK. We'll look at it again," and in fairly short order, Clarke had his Ph.D.

The record should show that George Tolley, Clarke's dissertation supervisor, has a different understanding of Clarke's progress toward his Ph.D. Tolley told me that as he saw it, there was never any stalemate between Clarke and his committee. Rather, it was a matter of Clarke making continual progress and receiving the degree when he had produced a satisfactory draft.

I wrote to Paul Samuelson, asking him if he agreed that his 1954 statement had been wrong. He replied that, no, he did not feel that any revision of what he had said was necessary. He had not said that it would be impossible to motivate people to report their preferences honestly.

Related Papers

Meanwhile, Tullock asked me to edit a special issue of *Public Choice*[7] devoted to what Tullock and I had called in our *JPE* article the "demand-revealing process." This led us to learn that a number of other persons had been converging on the same idea.

The one other independent discovery of Clarke's idea of which I am aware is the article "Incentives and Public Inputs," by Theodore Groves and Martin Loeb,

[7] *Public Choice*, 29-2 (1977).

published in the *Journal of Public Economics* in August 1975. By my recollection of what I heard about the origin of this paper, it developed from a suggestion that Loeb made to Groves while Loeb was a student of Groves'.

In 1968, the same year in which Clarke had first tried to explain his idea to me, Groves had completed a dissertation at UC Berkeley that resulted in an article in *Econometrica*.[8] Groves' work shares with Clarke's work the central idea of using marginal-cost pricing to achieve efficiency, while disregarding or otherwise managing the resulting lack of budget balance. The essence of the idea in Groves' dissertation and *Econometrica* article is that, to motivate all members of a team to contribute optimally to the team effort, one should promise the whole product of the team effort to every member of the team. The financial infeasibility of such a plan can be overcome if potential members of the team can be persuaded to pay sufficiently high fees for the opportunity to be on the team and if the organizer of the team has the resources to deal with the resulting financial uncertainty. As I understand it, when Groves presented this idea in a class, Loeb said, "Well if that is true, can't you use the same idea to solve the public goods problem?" And this resulted in the Groves and Loeb article in the *Journal of Public Economics*.

In 1968, there was another doctoral dissertation that suggested an innovative way to achieve efficiency by using marginal-cost pricing and managing the resulting budget imbalance. That was Richard Zeckhauser's dissertation at Harvard. In one essay in his dissertation, Zeckhauser dealt with optimal incentives for avoiding automobile accidents. He suggested that optimal deterrence could be achieved by requiring all parties to an accident to pay the full costs of the accident to the government. In an accident with N parties, the government would compensate all N parties for their individual losses and distribute a profit of the $N-1$ times the total loss equally among all members of the community.[9] This is parallel to Groves' incentives in teams, except that the purpose of "team effort" is to minimize a negative product rather than maximize a positive product.

An interesting precursor of this idea of Zeckhauser's can be found in Ronald Coase's famous 1960 article, "The Problem of Social Cost."[10] In discussing the efficiency of institutions for dealing with smoke from factories, Coase says, "If the factory owner is to be made to pay a tax equal to the damage caused, it would clearly be desirable to institute a double tax system and to make residents of the district pay an amount equal to the additional cost incurred by the factory owner (or the consumers of his products) in order to avoid the damage."[11] This is an exact parallel to what Zeckhauser said.

There is one other article that is often regarded as a precursor to Clarke's solution to the public goods problem, namely, William Vickrey's 1961 article

[8] Incentives in Teams. Econometrica 41(4):617, 1973.

[9] Zeckhauser R (1968) Essay II, group decision and allocation. In: Studies in interdependence, doctoral thesis, Department of Economics, Harvard University, pp 33–34.

[10] Coase RH (1960) J Law Econ 3:1–44.

[11] Coase RH The problem of social cost, p. 41.

"Counterspeculation, Auctions, and Competitive Sealed Tenders" in the *Journal of Finance*. The point for which this article is noted is the efficiency of an auction under the rule that the object being auctioned will be sold to the highest bidder at a price of the second-highest bid. Such an auction motivates each bidder to submit a bid equal to his reservation price and therefore ensures that the object will be purchased by the person for whom it is most valuable. This is an application of the principle of the efficiency of marginal-cost pricing because the marginal social cost of putting ownership of the object in the hands of the person to whom it is most valuable is the value of the object to the person who places the second-highest value on it.

There is one other foundational article that should be mentioned in connection with the origins of the demand-revealing process. That is the 1977 *Econometrica* article, "Optimal Allocation of Public Goods: A Solution to the 'Free Rider' Problem," by Theodore Groves and John Ledyard.[12] The essential purpose of this article was to devise a solution to the public goods problem that motivated the truthful revelation of preferences and did not have a budget imbalance. However, to achieve budget balance, Groves and Ledyard sacrificed the dominant strategy feature of the demand-revealing process (the fact that the response that maximized an individual's utility did not depend on the responses of others) and substituted a Nash-equilibrium solution, where in equilibrium each respondent can do no better as long as no other respondent changes his response. The difficulty with this approach is that the mechanism is subject to manipulation of the form of altering one's response in anticipation of the benefits that one will gain from the changes that will be induced in the responses of others.[13]

The Idea

The way that marginal-cost pricing can be applied to decisions about public goods is most easily explained with reference to a binary choice (a choice between two options), with no public budget consequences. Suppose there is a proposal to change the time when gasoline-powered lawn mowers can first be operated on Saturday morning from 9:00 a.m. to 10:00 a.m. Some people want to get up and mow their lawns; others want to sleep in without being disturbed by the sound of lawn mowers. To determine which time is more efficient, we must in some way aggregate the consequences across persons. It is customary to assume that the aggregation is to be done in terms of money, but if there is some accepted measure of the marginal utility

[12] Econometrica 45(4):783–809, 1977.

[13] For a more complete discussion of why the Groves-Ledyard approach to the problem of public goods is not promising, see Chap. 7, Why Nash Solutions are Not Solutions, of M. Bailey, *Constitution for a Future Country*, Palgrave, 2001.

of money to different persons, then the aggregation can be done in terms of utility.[14] For the sake of simplicity, assume that the aggregation is to be done in terms of money. For each person, the value at stake in the decision is measured by the greatest amount of money that the person would be willing to pay to have the decision made in the way that he wanted. If we know all of these amounts, we can add up the amounts in favor of 9:00 and 10:00 and determine which outcome is more valuable. The motivation for people to report these amounts truthfully is provided by marginal-cost pricing.

What, then, is marginal-cost pricing for a decision about when lawn mowers can be operated? If a person's participation in the decision has no effect on the outcome, then the marginal cost of that person's participation is zero. No one who is on the losing side and no one who is on the winning side but whose report of value is less than the difference between the two totals has any effect on the outcome. All such persons are not required to make any payment under marginal-cost pricing. However, the participation of anyone on the winning side whose report of value is greater than the winning margin is costly, because the decision would have gone the other way if this person had not participated. Call such a person a "pivotal voter." What is the marginal cost of a particular pivotal voter's participation? The gross cost is the aggregate value reported by everyone on the losing side. Denote this aggregate loss by L. But this value is more than offset by the gains to those on the winning side, who get what they want because of the pivotal voter's participation. Denote these gains by G. Subtract from this amount the benefit P that the pivotal voter receives, to obtain the gain to others than the pivotal voter, G – P. The net cost to everyone else of the participation of the pivotal voter, whose presence made a difference, is thus the difference in the two totals without the pivotal voter's participation, L – (G – P). This amount can also be calculated as the gain to the pivotal voter minus the difference in the totals with his participation, that is, P – (G – L). Thus, the pricing rule of the demand-revealing process, when applied to binary decisions, is that every pivotal voter must pay their reported gain minus the winning margin. Nobody else pays anything. Tullock and I gave the name "Clarke tax" to the marginal-cost payments that pivotal voters make for changing the outcome.

The question of what is to be done with money that is collected under the demand-revealing process has been a subject of much discussion. If it is shared among the participants, then individuals will no longer have the incentive to report their preferences honestly. Every person will have an incentive to make the outcome closer to a tie, to increase the amounts that everyone else will need to pay, so that their own receipts from a share of the surplus will be greater. Such strategic behavior creates a risk that dishonest responses will result in an inefficient decision. Therefore, efficient incentives require that something else be done with the collected payments. One possibility for any less-than-global collectivity is to hold an auction prior to the

[14] The way to translate from money to utility was explained in I.J. Good (1977) Justice in voting by demand revelation. Public Choice 29(2):65–70.

decision, where persons not in the collectivity can bid for the right to receive the collected payments, and distribute the proceeds of the auction equally among the participants.

While the demand-revealing process motivates individuals to report their preferences honestly, it is vulnerable to strategic behavior by coalitions. If two or more participants coordinate overstatements of their preferences, they can turn a situation in which they would need to pay for having their choice into one in which they do not have to pay, because the action of the partner or partners creates a situation in which their own vote no longer changes the outcome. While such coalition activity can potentially be individually profitable, it can also potentially create a situation in which the coalition partners wind up paying more for a change than the change is worth to them. Tullock liked to point out that the risk of strategic behavior can be greatly reduced by making it impossible for any participant to learn how any other participant had voted. Then, while actually voting, each participant would have an incentive to ignore any commitment that was made to coalition partners and report his preference truthfully.

When there are three or more possibilities for the collective decision, rather than just two, it is possible that the demand-revealing process will produce a voting cycle. Suppose that the choice of the starting time for lawnmowers can be 9:00 or 9:30 or 10:00, and suppose that the amounts of money that two persons are willing to pay for one outcome instead of another are given by Table 10.1.

The amount of money that a person is willing to pay for 9:00 instead of 10:00 or vise versa is not the sum of the amounts from 9:00 to 9:30 and 9:30 to 10:00, because of income effects. If a person has to pay to get from 9:00 to 9:30, he has less money with which to buy the change to 10:00 than when he starts at 9:30. The possibility of income effects that are different for different people creates the possibility of a situation like that shown in Table 10.1, where the aggregate value of a move from 9:00 to 9:30 is $10, the aggregate value of a move from 9:30 to 10:00 is $10, and the aggregate value of a move from 10:00 to 9:00 is $10. Such a cycle would not occur if we were able to translate willingness to pay into utility units accurately, because in that case the value of a change from 9:00 to 10:00 would always be the same as the sum of the value of a change from 9:00 to 9:30 and a change from 9:30 to 10:00.[15] To employ the demand-revealing process for real choices when there are more than two options, one must either insist that participants report preferences that show no income effects, or one must have a device for cutting through cycles if they appear. If participants are required to report preferences that show no income effects, they may respond that they are not able to report their preferences truthfully. And if they are allowed to report preferences that incorporate income effects, situations can arise in which they will not have incentives to report their preferences truthfully.[16] Still, it seems likely to me that

[15] This is a variation on the point made by Tibor Scitovsky in "A Note on Welfare Propositions of Economics and Interpersonal Comparisons of Utility," *Review of Economic Studies*, 1941.

[16] For a more thorough discussion of this point, see N. Tideman, *Collective Decisions and Voting: The Potential for Public Choice* (Ashgate, 2006): 304–310.

Table 10.1 Willingness to pay for changes in the time for lawn mowing to start

	Person			Person			Person	
	1	2		1	2		1	2
9:00	$300		9:30	$200		9:00	$490	
9:30		$310	10:00		$210	10:00		$480

in practical situations voting cycles would arise sufficiently infrequently that they would not prevent the process from being used productively.

The discussion above illustrates the fact that the main features of the demand-revealing process and the main issues associated with it arise in examples in which there is no need for public revenue to finance a public activity. When the process is applied to activities that do require financing, the process is essentially the same, except that every level of expenditure is associated with a specific allocation of responsibility for financing, so that the objects of choice are fully financed options.

When the possibilities among which a choice is to be made lie on a continuum, as with the level of spending on a public activity, a person's preferences can be reported as a demand curve, although this suppresses income effects. (If people were asked to report their income-compensated demand curves, then they would have an incentive to report untruthfully high income effects.) Treating reported demand curves as ordinary demand curves that have no income effects, the efficient level of the activity is the level where the sum of marginal benefits is equal to marginal cost (a condition that Paul Samuelson provided in his 1954 article), and the Clarke tax on each individual is calculated as the net sum of the losses to all other individuals from not having the level of expenditure that would have been chosen if the person whose Clarke tax is being computed had been indifferent with respect to the level of spending, given his assigned contribution.[17]

Appraisal of the Idea

The demand-revealing process seemed at first to be the answer to economists' dreams for a way of making efficient decisions about public activities. But there has been little if any movement in the direction of using the idea. In my view, the greatest contribution of the idea was in sharpening our thinking about attractive ways of making decisions about public spending. Once economists had the demand-revealing process, they came to understand that they wanted not just efficiency but decisions that were Pareto improvements or nearly Pareto improvements. The demand-revealing process is unsatisfying because it allows a group that is undertaxed compared to their benefits to have

[17] For details, see Nicolaus Tideman and Gordon Tullock (1976) A new and superior process for making social choices. J Pol Econ 84 (Dec):1145–1159.

all of their net benefits taken into account in setting the level of public spending, without any adjustment in the share of costs that they are expected to pay. We have always known that there are winners and losers in the public spending process. But current ways of making spending decisions do not entail compulsory deference to those who are not paying their shares of the costs, the way the demand-revealing process does. It seems to me that the most likely path to more satisfying decisions with respect to the level of public spending is not through the demand-revealing process but rather through decentralization, a Tiebout solution[18] where people move to the places that have public taxing and spending patterns that they like.

What Should We Call It, and Who Should Get the Credit?

While Tullock and I called the idea we wrote about "the demand-revealing process," the economics profession has not reached a consensus on what the idea ought to be called. Google Scholar (as of May 26, 2012) shows the following numbers of articles using the following names that might be used for the idea:

1,860 VCG mechanism
1,730 Pivotal mechanism
1,330 Demand revealing
393 Clarke mechanism

When the name "VCG mechanism" is expanded, it becomes "Vickrey-Clarke-Groves mechanism," giving credit in chronological order to William Vickrey for his 1961 article in *Public Finance*, to Edward Clarke for his 1971 paper in *Public Choice* (and possibly his 1972 paper in Mushkin's *Public Prices for Public Products*), and to Theodore Groves for any of a number of his papers. But the choice of these three names for the mechanism is somewhat hard to understand.

According to Google Scholar, the first published listing of the names Vickrey, Clarke, and Groves in that order occurs in the 1979 paper "Efficient Collective Choice when Compensation is Possible" by Theodore Groves, in the *Review of Economic Studies*. The quotation, from page 234, is:

> **Corollary 1** (Vickrey, Clarke, Groves). *If preferences Ri are quasi-linear, ...*

continuing (with mathematical terminology that is understandable only in the context of the framework that Groves was developing) to explain the conditions for a choice in a collective decision procedure to have a dominant strategy. The context makes it clear that Groves was not naming an idea here but rather sharing credit with Vickrey and Clarke for a mathematical result (one that he expressed with much more mathematical precision than either of them had).

---

[18] Tiebout CM (1956) A pure theory of local expenditures. J Polit Econ 64(5):416–424.

According to Google Scholar, the first use of "Vickrey-Clarke-Groves" as an adjective in a published article occurs in the 1981 paper, "Implementing Just and Efficient Decision-Making," by Hervé Moulin, in the *Journal of Public Economics*. The quotation, from the abstract, is:

> A refinement of this mechanism (so-called auctioning the leadership with differentiated bids) allows us to implement an efficient anonymous and neutral outcome: it achieves egalitarianism above the Vickrey-Clarke-Groves decision.

It is notable that while Moulin cites the 1977 paper by Groves and Ledyard, he does not cite any paper by Groves alone. Thus, it seems that while initially "Vickrey-Clarke-Groves" was used to identify the common feature of dominant strategy mechanisms in the constructs of different authors, the meaning drifted, perhaps through an oral tradition, to where the three names denoted a dominant strategy mechanism for choices about public goods. With respect to Vickrey, this is particularly odd because his contribution was concerned entirely with auctions and not at all with decisions about public goods. With respect to Groves, there is a plethora of contributions regarding decisions about dominant strategy mechanisms for the provision of public goods, but they begin with his 1975 paper with Loeb. Thus, a Clarke-Groves-Loeb name would make more sense than Vickrey-Clarke-Groves for a dominant strategy mechanism for public goods, although the publication 4 years after Clarke's is a bit late to give credit for an independent discovery. Still, a jury might decide that it was so hard to understand what Clarke was saying that credit for an independent discovery should be given.

The term "pivotal mechanism" originated in the November 1976 paper, "Partial Equilibrium Approach to the Free-Rider Problem," by Jerry Green, Elon Kohlberg, and Jean-Jacques Laffont, in the *Journal of Public Economics*. They cite Groves and Loeb but not Clarke. They explain the term "pivotal mechanism" on page 380 by,

> The individuals who pay the tax are those whose stated willingnesses-to-pay are such as to change the sign of the aggregate – these individuals are pivotal in the decision, or pivots.

Thus, this name has a coherent connection to what it describes and was in publication a month before "demand-revealing process."

Tullock and I picked the name "demand-revealing process" to use in our December 1976 paper in the *Journal of Political Economy* because we wanted a phrase that was highly descriptive, and we did not mind being a bit provocative.

The reason why some people should choose to call the concept the "Clarke mechanism" is obvious enough. The first authors to use this term were Green and Laffont, in three articles published between 1977 and 1979.[19]

To my mind, there is reason enough to call the concept the pivotal mechanism, the demand-revealing process, or the Clarke mechanism, but there is not an intellectually

---

[19] Green J, Laffont J-J (1977) Imperfect personal information and the demand-revealing process: a sampling approach. Public Choice 29(Supplement 2):79–94; Green J, Laffont J-J (1978) An incentive compatible planning procedure for public good production. Scand J Econ 80(1):20–33; Green J, Laffont J-J (1979) On coalition incentive compatibility. Rev Econ Stud 46(2):243–254.

adequate reason for calling the concept the VCG mechanism. Vickrey, Clarke, and Groves all worked independently with different versions of the same dominant strategy mechanism. But so did Coase and Zeckhauser. The efficiency of marginal-cost pricing had been a commonplace of economics for decades before any of this work. The insight with which Clarke was clearly first was that it was possible to use a version of marginal-cost pricing to motivate people to report their preferences for public goods honestly. If Clarke should share credit for this with anyone, it should be with Gordon Tullock, for his courageous editorial decision to publish an article before he understood it, an article that has become the most widely cited article ever published in *Public Choice*, because if it was right, it was important.

Chapter 11
Public Choice and Two of Its Founders: An Appreciation

David R. Henderson

Introduction

I have thought of myself as a believer in public choice since the tender age of 20. In early 1971, I was in the middle of a year I had taken off to teach myself economics and was working my way chronologically through past issues of the *Journal of Law and Economics* (JLE). Harold Demsetz, then at the University of Chicago Business School, had suggested I do so, and his advice was some of the best I have ever received.[1]

In a footnote to an article in the JLE, I saw a reference to *The Calculus of Consent* by James Buchanan and Gordon Tullock. From both the content of the footnote and the seductive title, the book sounded interesting. So I went to the University of Winnipeg's library and checked it out. In those days, the price of photocopying was 10 cents per page (over 50 cents in today's dollars), and I found myself wanting to copy a lot of pages. Instead, I bought the book and worked my way through it. Thus was born my interest in public choice and in James Buchanan and Gordon Tullock, an interest that has never left me.

In this chapter, I tell what I think is good and interesting about public choice and about two of its "founding fathers," James Buchanan and Gordon Tullock. I also sketch out a promising path for applying public choice in the area of foreign policy, a path Tullock has trod very little and Buchanan has, as far as I know, never trod.

[1] I tell this story at greater in length in Chap. 2, "Hooked on Economics," in David R. Henderson, *The Joy of Freedom: An Economist's Odyssey*, Upper Saddle River, New Jersey: Financial Times Prentice Hall, 2001.

D.R. Henderson (✉)
Hoover Institution, Stanford University, 944 Forest Ave, Pacific Grove, CA 93950, USA
e-mail: davidrhenderson1950@gmail.com

D.R. Lee (ed.), *Public Choice, Past and Present: The Legacy of James M. Buchanan and Gordon Tullock*, Studies in Public Choice 28, DOI 10.1007/978-1-4614-5909-5_11,

The Essence of Public Choice and Why It Is So Upsetting: For Everyone

Public choice is the idea that participants in politics act on the same kinds of motives they act on in their everyday economic lives. Thus, according to believers in public choice, we will not get far in understanding the behavior of politicians or bureaucrats unless we start by assuming that they are pursuing their own self-interest.

James Buchanan put it even more succinctly: Public choice is "politics without romance." In other words, if you see politicians as always, or even often, acting on noble motives, you will make inaccurate predictions about their behavior. Moreover, you will be disappointed.

This disappointment, I believe, explains why many people, and even many economists, are hostile to public choice. It takes one of their most strongly held views of the world and smashes it to bits. Daniel Klein wrote on this at length in his outstanding article, "The People's Romance."[2] When I first met Gordon Tullock, in October 1971, I asked him why he thought the typical economist seemed unwilling to consider some of the basic insights from public choice: concentrated interests dominating the political process, bureaucracies fighting for bigger budgets, etc. He said that many of them are so used to thinking of government as being basically good that it's hard for them to think otherwise. Tullock explicitly mentioned one man who found this difficult—public-finance economist Richard Musgrave. (I don't know whether Tullock based this on a conversation to that effect or on his observations at a distance.) Tullock's take on Musgrave's thinking still sticks in my mind. He said that for Musgrave to think about a society in which the government is not a benevolent helping hand would be like someone on an airplane who looks out and is sure he will crash because an airplane can't stay aloft when it's heavier than air. So, said Tullock, Musgrave and, presumably, many others needed to think that government was benevolent because the alternative seemed too scary.

The alternative *is* scary. When I first heard about Hitler at about age eight and asked my mother who he was, she told me that 15 years earlier he had used tanks and other weapons to try to take over the world. I pictured a nut with some tanks he had bought coming down our highway and invading our small town in rural Canada. I didn't understand at the time why Hitler was such a threat; I had been raised to believe that the police would protect us. Imagine the shock and sudden surge of overwhelming fear I had when, only a few years later, I learned that Hitler *employed* the police and, indeed, ran a whole *government*. That's when the true terror of Hitler dawned on me. So, there is a good reason for *not* looking at politics romantically. If we look at politics "non-romantically," then we will be more on the lookout for budding Hitlers and will be, all else equal, less likely to come under their spell.

So, public choice was a little upsetting for me too. Who doesn't want to believe that there is a benevolent government looking out for you?

---

[2] Klein, Daniel (2005) The people's romance. Indep Rev X(1):5–37.

When I first read Buchanan and Tullock, I was already a libertarian, but public choice led me to two new conclusions, one good and one frustrating. The good one was that I now had even more basis for my free-market views because one of the bottom lines of Buchanan's and Tullock's work was that the incentives for government officials and voters are usually perverse. So, even if one could find a market failure, that did not mean that government intervention would make it better.

The frustrating conclusion was that it is hard to have freedom because governments will often take it away. My own preferred strategy was, and still is, to persuade people to be critical of government. But I remember as if it were yesterday what I heard Buchanan say at a public event to celebrate the Cato Institute's arrival to Washington from San Francisco. He said that in all their work to try to persuade the public and policymakers, the Cato Institute staff should spend a fair amount of time trying to reform the rules, trying to get constitutional reform; otherwise, new politicians would come in and destroy the bits of policy progress they had made. Or, as I would put it, once you get the lion (government) in the cage, how do you keep it there? I still don't know the answer. Even Buchanan's preferred approach of constitutional rules is highly imperfect. Congress, presidents, and courts can all ignore the US Constitution. And they often do.

Tullock: A Memory and an Appreciation

I never took a class from Gordon Tullock, and I was never his junior colleague, but he was definitely one of my most important teachers.

During my year of independent study, after I read *The Calculus of Consent*, I wanted to read other things by Buchanan and Tullock. So, that same year, I read Tullock's *The Politics of Bureaucracy* and *The Organization of Inquiry*, along with about 10 or so journal articles he had written. What an intellectual feast that was! In fact, Tullock's conversational reminiscences of his time in the State Department, in *The Politics of Bureaucracy*, informed my own style in "A Tour of Washington," a chapter in my book *The Joy of Freedom: An Economist's Odyssey*. And his *Organization of Inquiry* is still the most thoughtful work I have ever read on how to maximize additions to knowledge. When Tullock's suggestions for decentralization and incentives are followed, additions to knowledge usually follow; when centralization takes over, as with Nixon's centralization of cancer research, progress typically slows.

A few months later, I learned that Tullock would be speaking at the University of Western Ontario in October 1971 to give a talk at a weekend-long symposium held by the philosophy department. At the time I was taking a year of advanced undergraduate economics to prepare myself for graduate school. His talk was about political revolutions. In it, he pointed out a simple but powerful insight: Any one person's decision to participate in a revolution does not much affect the probability that the revolution will succeed. Therefore, when each person considers participating in the revolution, the benefits he expects to be generated by the revolution are not much affected by his own decision to participate. This is true, noted Tullock, even for the most visible and influential participants. However, he added, a nasty government can individualize the costs very effectively by heavily punishing those who participate in a revolution. So, anyone contemplating participating in a revolution will be comparing heavy individual costs and small benefits that are simply his pro rata share of the overall benefits. Therefore, argued Tullock, for people to participate, they must expect some benefits that are tied to their own participation, such as a high-level job in the new government. Tullock noted that, in fact, the typical revolution involves many of the people who are actually in the government they are revolting against. This is evidence for his model, he explained, because such people are particularly well situated to replace the incumbent officeholders.

His model was insightful and, like much of public choice, only slightly overstated. Also on the program for the symposium were two discussants, Martin Shubik of the RAND Corporation and David Braybrooke of Dalhousie University. But, said the session chair, Shubik had canceled at the last minute and so had been replaced by Mel Watkins, an economist from the University of Toronto. When the announcement was made, there were a number of titters in the mainly Canadian audience. Virtually every Canadian there knew who Mel Watkins was. He was a well-known socialist economist who was trying to get Canada's New Democratic Party (which had been formed in 1961 from a merger of the old Co-operative Commonwealth Federation, a left-wing party that had come to power in Saskatchewan in the 1930s, and the Canadian Labor Congress, an organization much like the American AFL-CIO) to move further left. He was also known for the so-called Watkins Report, the shorthand name for the federal government's Task Force on Foreign Ownership and the Structure of Canadian Investment, which he had headed. The report, published in 1968, had advocated heavy government restrictions on foreign (read: American) takeovers of Canadian firms and on foreign (read: American) investment in Canada. Only a few years later, incidentally, the Trudeau government, to compete with the left, adopted a modified version of the restrictions Watkins wanted.

Watkins was up first. He sneeringly attacked Tullock's model without ever, as I recall, giving one concrete reason or fact to refute it. (Believe it or not, I still have somewhere in my attic the tape of this whole session.) Watkins' tone—and even some of his language—implied that this imperialist American had a lot of nerve coming to Canada to tell us how things are. When Watkins sat down, only a handful of people in the audience of about 150 broke into applause. I think the vast majority of the people in the audience, whatever their individual views about Tullock and his work, thought Watkins had been both ineffective and downright nasty. Braybrooke, when his turn came, gave a more standard discussion, pointing out that Tullock's model fell apart if you put a conscience cost as an argument into the potential revolutionary's utility function.

When the session chair gave Tullock a chance to reply, he quickly admitted Braybrooke's main argument. He went on to say that listening to Watkins' rant made him nostalgic because he hadn't heard that kind of anti-American rhetoric since the days when the communists were dominant on many American campuses. Although he *said* he felt nostalgic, he looked genuinely hurt.

Afterward, I went up and introduced myself to Tullock, and we set up a time to meet for Sunday lunch the next day. After lunch, we walked around the campus and Tullock answered many of my questions about American politics, the Goldwater campaign of 7 years earlier, and on and on. I had Tullock all to myself for those few hours and I took advantage of it.

On Monday, he gave a talk to the economics faculty and students titled "The Charity of the Uncharitable." In it, he pointed out that most Americans give 1% or 2% of their income to charity and that they don't change stripes and suddenly become much more charitable when they enter the polling place. Therefore, argued Tullock, when people support particular programs that look like charitable handouts to others, it's important to examine the details of such programs. Typically, when one does so, he claimed, one finds that the biggest supporters of the programs are people who stand to gain from them. Among the strongest supporters of welfare, he noted, are people who will get jobs administering or studying the welfare programs. Then, he used a memorable simile: Using government welfare to help poor people, he said, is like trying to feed sparrows by feeding horses. For the next few weeks, my friend Harry Watson and I would quote that line to each other and laugh uproariously.

The other thing I remember about his presentation is how uptight the largely Canadian economics faculty was about Tullock's views. They listened quietly and asked a few questions, but did not engage. I could tell—from facial expressions, tone of voice, and body language—that they didn't like what they heard. But they wouldn't take him on. In the following weeks, when I tried to engage some of the faculty about things Gordon had said, I found him dismissed as a "right-winger." The best I heard from a couple of faculty was that he was "a very smart right-winger." At the time, I thought the reaction was due in large part to the Canadian temperament, which I had grown up with and gotten sick of. The basic rule is that you shouldn't argue about things like charity because good people don't argue about such things. Since moving to America in 1972 and having attended countless presentations, I'm now convinced that I was wrong. Part of it, to be sure, was the Canadian temperament. But I've also attended similar presentations at which no Canadian, other than I, was present, and I've seen the same reaction. When a libertarian or conservative wants to take on this or that government policy by talking about its actual effects, an audience of largely "liberal" economists will often not engage. They'll be studiously quiet, and then some will make ad hominem attacks later behind closed doors. I have found that free-market-oriented economists are simply more fun, more enjoying of the intellectual endeavor, and less stodgy than intervention-oriented economists. For me, back in 1971, Gordon Tullock represented some of the best that the US academic economics had to offer. He still does.

James Buchanan: A Memory and an Appreciation

In September 1971, the month before I met Gordon Tullock, I wrote a letter to James Buchanan. I had picked up a copy of his book *Public Principles of Public Debt* and worked my way through it. I found the tone of discovery in the book exciting, and my letter to him was partly fan mail and partly to ask a question. (I don't remember the question, but I think it was about an item in the appendix on local government debt.)

Within a week, I had an answer. I've forgotten Buchanan's answer to my question, but he suggested that I could update his data on local government debt and possibly get an article published in the *National Tax Journal*. I still regret the fact that I didn't do so.

In my experience up to that point, it was not standard practice for a senior, internationally known scholar to give this kind of nurturing attention to one of his or her own students, let alone to a 20-year-old stranger. I later learned, though, that this was James Buchanan's modus operandi.

Fast-forward to January 1975, when I went to Virginia Polytechnic Institute to interview for a position as assistant professor. When I entered Buchanan's office, I discovered that he had taken the time to read a 3-page note I had written showing that when the government imposes a binding ceiling on oil prices but not on gasoline prices, the price of gasoline is higher than if there are no price controls at all. He saw the point immediately, of course, and thought it clever, relevant, and worth publishing. (Later that day, though, a young assistant professor showed me a page out of C. E. Ferguson's textbook in which Ferguson had shown that result.)

I didn't get an offer from VPI but, instead, went to the University of Rochester's Graduate School of Management. In the summer of 1975, though, I was with Buchanan and many other economists at a Liberty Fund conference at Ohio University in Athens, Ohio. One of the first things he said to me when he saw me was that VPI should have made me an offer.

What I noticed about him throughout those few days at the conference was that he handled the give and take with ease, even with newly minted assistant professors. Buchanan clearly didn't seem to think that he had a monopoly on truth. I also remember his candor about his views and his motives for his views, one in particular.

There were a lot of well-known and up-and-coming people at the conference: Bill Niskanen, who had just found out that he was going to be chief economist at Ford Motor, Colin Campbell of Dartmouth, David Friedman, Karen Vaughn, William H. Hutt, and a number of others. At one point, the discussion turned to the estate tax, and most of the people who weighed in said that there should be no estate tax. Buchanan thought differently and passionately so. He thought, like George McGovern during the 1972 presidential campaign, that there should be a 100% marginal tax rate on all estates over a relatively modest amount. The rest of us argued with him. Someone pointed out that such a tax would reduce the incentive to save and, therefore, would reduce capital accumulation and the real income of workers. Yes, I know, he said. Someone pointed out that it would also give people an incentive to pass on assets to their kids when they're alive and to give them an advantage through better schools, lessons, contacts, etc. Yes, I know, he said. It ended in a draw. I was puzzled. He had admitted all of our arguments, but it was clear from his body language and tone that he had not budged one iota. Something else, I thought, was going on.

So during the next break, I went up to him and said:

> Sometimes, when someone has a view and admits problems with his view but those problems don't budge him from his view, it's because something happened, usually relatively early in his life, that led him to that view. I promise I won't judge your view by whether something happened early in your life. But did something happen that involved someone who was really rich?

Yes, something *had* happened, and he was bursting to tell me. In late 1941, before the US government officially got into World War II, Buchanan, to avoid being drafted into the Army, had joined the Navy and enrolled in midshipmen's school in New York. He and his fellow officer candidates were divided by alphabet. In his group of A's and B's, there was no one with an Ivy League background. So someone from the R's was reassigned to head Buchanan's platoon. His name? Bill Rockefeller.

Buchanan recounts this story in his book *Better than Plowing and Other Personal Essays*.[3] He writes, "The initial appointment of cadet officers 'radicalized' me to such an extent that emotional scars remain, even a half-century later." Indeed. While I do think that he should have not have let this affect his views long term, I admired and still admire his candor in admitting it.

One other thing I've gotten from Buchanan—primarily by hearing it from his past students, and mainly from the most-published ones—is his famous line, "Don't get it right; get it written." Of course, ultimately you *should* get it right, but the big challenge in writing for the vast majority of us is to get it written in the first place. His advice reminds me of the famous line in *Finding Forrester*, the movie in which a reclusive author gives advice to a young black kid from the ghetto who aches to be a writer: "You must write your first draft with your heart. You rewrite with your head. The first key to writing is … to write, not to think!"

I could have used Buchanan's advice about writing much earlier in my career because I earned my Ph.D. at UCLA. Buchanan, who spent academic year 1970–1971 at UCLA, sometimes speaks of what he calls "the UCLA disease": the idea that Ph.D. students picked up from their professors that one must be almost perfect. We were not nurtured and encouraged to write the way Buchanan encouraged his students. In fact, it was pretty much the opposite.

---

[3] Buchanan, James M. (1993) Better than plowing and other personal essays. University of Chicago Press, Chicago, p 49.

Foreign Policy: My Main Criticism of Public Choice

My main constructive criticism of public choice is not of public choice itself but of how little it has been used to look at a major area of government policy—foreign policy. This lack is particularly striking because both Buchanan and Tullock are relatively libertarian and critical of intrusive governments. As Robert Higgs has well documented in *Crisis and Leviathan: Critical Episodes in the Growth of American Government*, much of the growth of government in the United States occurred due to World War I and World War II. Higgs gives evidence for the "ratchet effect": Government authority over the economy grew during both wars and then diminished after the wars, but not nearly back to the prewar level of authority. So one would think that Buchanan and Tullock, and many who have come after them and share their political views, would want to apply public-choice tools to foreign policy.

Tullock *has* written on foreign policy. His 2007 book, *Open Secrets of American Foreign Policy*, is full of fascinating facts, insights, and, occasionally, applications of basic economics. For example, he tells of one huge, negative, unintended consequence of a decision by First Lord of the Admiralty, Winston Churchill, during World War I. Tullock writes:

> When Germans first began using the submarines, they would surface fire a shot across the bow of merchant ships and wait until the crew were in the boats, sometimes even giving the boats a tow to someplace near land.
>
> Whether they would have continued with this practice is dubious, but in any event, Churchill, then with jurisdiction over the matter, ordered merchant ships not to stop and if possible to ram the submarine. This led the submarines to change their policy, although they continued to occasionally offer some protection for the crew.[4]

Tullock does not mention *how* the Germans changed their policy, perhaps because he thinks it obvious: The Germans then began to torpedo boats with no warning, and those actions caused the loss of many lives.

Nevertheless, although Tullock's book contains many such insights, he does not apply public-choice analysis to foreign policy.

Buchanan, from what I can find, has written virtually nothing applying public choice to foreign policy. When I interviewed him in 1996, he told me the fascinating story of working as a young lieutenant under Admiral Chester Nimitz. One thing he talked about was what a publicity hound General Douglas MacArthur was. In his *Better Than Plowing*, Buchanan goes further, calling MacArthur a "near fraud."[5] It was clear to Buchanan, from his observations of MacArthur, that politics *doesn't* stop at the water's edge. His comments on MacArthur and on working in a big Navy bureaucracy at Pearl Harbor led me to ask, "Was this one of the early seeds in your thinking about public choice?" Buchanan's terse answer: No. Indeed, the few times

---

[4] Tullock, Gorden (2007) Open Secrets of American Foreign Policy. World Scientific Publishing, New Jersey, p 96.

[5] Buchanan, James M., *Better than Plowing*, p. 57.

I've heard him discuss foreign policy in which the US government is involved, his view tends to be that the US government is pursuing noble ends. But he would never, in analyzing the actions of a domestic bureaucracy such as, say, the Environmental Protection Agency, start with the assumption that the EPA is full of good people pursuing noble ends.

Yet, the chances to apply public choice to foreign policy are many. Former President Eisenhower, for example, introduced the idea of the military-industrial complex and warned us against it. Is there anything to this? Could one do a public-choice analysis to explain why the US government got into certain wars and avoided certain others? What interest groups lobbied for or against these wars or potential wars?

Buchanan, talking about his students at the University of Virginia in the 1960s, writes:

> And these students were very successful in becoming published economists early, many even while still graduate students. This feat was accomplished, quite simply, because the public choice research program was new and there were many, many applications to be analyzed. We could almost literally say to a student, "Pick any politically organized activity, and proceed to analyze its origins, its support, is operation, with the tools of public choice." Those were, indeed, exciting times.[6]

Times could be equally exciting for those who are willing to take a hard, unromantic view of various countries' foreign policies, including those of the country that currently has the most intrusive foreign policy in the world: the United States.

Consider, for example, the incentives of a president who is thinking of making war on another country. By doing so, he can, and probably will, impose huge costs on people in that other country and on people in his own country. He bears only a tiny fraction of the costs imposed on his own people. So, for example, if the war is fought by an all-volunteer force and paid for by taxes, his increased tax burden is his main cost of the war. On the benefit side, he may go down in history as a great president,[7] as Woodrow Wilson did simply for making war, even if the war had, on net, harmful consequences. It follows that these decision makers are likely to engage in too many wars and in wars that are too long and too costly. That's a simple public-choice insight.[8]

Some have ventured down the public-choice path in foreign policy. One of the earliest people to do so was none other than Adam Smith. In an analysis that Anthony Downs could be proud of, Smith pointed out that the costs and benefits to the British of maintaining control over the 13 colonies were not symmetrically distributed.

---

[6] James M. Buchanan, *Better than Plowing*, p. 100.

[7] See David R. Henderson and Zachary Gochenour, "Wars and Presidential Greatness," at: http://papers.ssrn.com/sol3/papers.cfm?abstract_id=2029774.

[8] That insight is in David R. Henderson, "The Economics of War and Foreign Policy: What's Missing?" *Defense & Security Analysis* 23(1):87–100, March 2007 and earlier in Jeffrey Rogers Hummel, "National Goods Versus Public Goods: Defense, Disarmament, and Free Riders," in *The Review of Austrian Economics*. 4:88–122, 1990.

This, he wrote, was why the British government would not give up its colonies easily. Consider this famous passage from *The Wealth of Nations*:

> To found a great empire for the sole purpose of raising up a people of customers may at first sight appear a project fit only for a nation of shopkeepers. It is, however, a project altogether unfit for a nation of shopkeepers; but extremely fit for a nation whose government is influenced by shopkeepers. Such statesmen, and such statesmen only, are capable of fancying that they will find some advantage in employing the blood and treasure of their fellow-citizens to found and maintain such an empire. Say to a shopkeeper, Buy me a good estate, and I shall always buy my clothes at your shop, even though I should pay somewhat dearer than what I can have them for at other shops; and you will not find him very forward to embrace your proposal. But should any other person buy you such an estate, the shopkeeper would be much obliged to your benefactor if he would enjoin you to buy all your clothes at his shop.[9]

In other words, Smith was saying that the cost to Britain of maintaining colonies in order to maintain a preferential trade arrangement was less than the benefits to Britain—thus his statement that the project is unfit for a nation of shopkeepers. But the cost to the *shopkeepers* was a fraction of the cost to Britain; the costs were dispersed across taxpayers and consumers. The benefits, however, were concentrated on the shopkeepers. One of public-choice economists' biggest insights is why, in a representative democracy, concentrated interest groups often gain at the expense of the dispersed consumers or taxpayers.[10] Smith had that one nailed almost two centuries earlier and on foreign policy to boot.[11]

Although I have not specialized in public-choice economics, I have made a contribution by applying public choice to foreign policy. It is as follows.[12]

Consider the above finding that concentrated interest groups often gain at the expense of dispersed consumers and taxpayers. An example would be the sugar industry, which has successfully lobbied to restrict sugar imports. But why is the protection not complete? Why are any imports allowed at all? It must be because the costs to consumers would then get high enough that many of them would put pressure on the government. In short, a "political equilibrium" comes about because the politicians trade off the support of the industry against the feeble opposition from consumers. They hit their political "sweet spot" (pun not intended) with positive, but restricted, imports.

But now imagine how high tariffs would be if consumers were not allowed to vote. The equilibrium would change. The new sweet spot, from the politicians' viewpoint, would be even smaller import quotas and, possibly, zero imports.

We can apply this insight to foreign policy. Among those who bear large costs of one government's foreign policies are people who live in other countries. So, for

---

[9] Adam Smith, *Wealth of Nations*, Volume 2, Book IV, Chap. 7, Part III, p. 129.

[10] This was first laid out in Anthony Downs, *An Economic Theory of Democracy*, New York: Harper and Brothers, 1957, and has become a staple of public-choice thinking.

[11] Of course, one could argue that this was not analysis of foreign policy because Britain "owned" the 13 colonies. I'm indebted to Chad Seagren for this caveat.

[12] The following draws on Henderson, "Economics of War and Foreign Policy," p. 98. It is not an exact quote.

example, if country A's government kills people in country B, the potentially biggest losers from this policy are people in country B. But people in country B cannot typically vote in country A's elections, and cannot typically give campaign contributions to politicians in country A. Therefore, some of the biggest losers from government A's policy cannot directly influence political outcomes in country A. Thus, some of the opposition to its foreign policies, though potentially strong, cannot legally be brought to bear on the politicians making the decisions. A clear implication is that the politicians will not care as much as otherwise about damage done to foreigners and that, therefore, the equilibrium could involve a lot of damage. Couple that with the fact that citizens in country A will be even less well informed about many of these actions than they are about the government's actions in their own country, and the implication is even more destruction in country B than otherwise.

This is just one implication of the public-choice way of thinking. More insights likely await those who apply the public-choice framework to foreign policy.

Chapter 12
Public Choice in the Big Sky

John Baden

Introduction

Dwight Lee asked me to provide a historical, personal account of how James Buchanan and Gordon Tullock, and public choice generally, contributed to environmental policy analysis. I thought this would be easy; I was there at the creation and use public choice daily; by now it's hard wired in. How naive I was to predict an easy job. This has turned out to be a complex and time-intensive task indeed, but one I enjoyed and shared with my wife Ramona and a few friends.

It brought back good memories of times initially with Gordon, then Jim. It also reminded me of the potentials and pathologies inherent to universities. I reviewed their histories and ours. I saw how public choice contributed to a Bozeman, Montana original, the New Resource Economics (NRE). I feel blessed indeed.

Jim, Gordon, and the Path to the New Resource Economics

Jim Buchanan and Gordon Tullock contributed greatly to the scholarly reputation and intellectual attraction of Bozeman, Montana. Due to their work and their participation in ours, Bozeman is the epicenter of the New Resource Economics, aka,

---

I would like to thank Gordon and Jim for their counsel and friendship; Tom Schelling for his friendship and support; Rick Stroup, my favorite "gear drive" economist; my wife, Ramona, for her counsel and loving support during the occasionally trying and more frequent and glorious times; and Michelle Danforth-Mohr for her research on the history of NRE.

J. Baden (✉)
Foundation for Research on Economics and the Environment,
662 Ferguson Ave, Bozeman, MT 59718, USA
e-mail: jbaden@free-eco.org

D.R. Lee (ed.), *Public Choice, Past and Present: The Legacy of James M. Buchanan and Gordon Tullock*, Studies in Public Choice 28, DOI 10.1007/978-1-4614-5909-5_12,

free-market environmentalism (FME). Interestingly, it all began in Bloomington, Indiana.

The backstory involves the University of Virginia (UVA). It is a harbinger of problems evident in today's politically correct university environment. It shows how faculty ideas of "diversity" exclude philosophical differences; toleration isn't extended to those holding classical liberal ideas. This anti-intellectual position was dominant at UVA in the 1960s, Montana State University (MSU) in Bozeman, in the 1970s and 1980s, and remains largely intact in universities today, perhaps even more strongly. It may take the bursting of the higher education bubble to change this. In the meanwhile, let's identify and celebrate positive consequences that occasionally flow from academic censorship and bias.

The ill-liberal bias of UVA was beneficial for Bozeman via a long circuitous path. Here's how it began. Buchanan and Warren Nutter were graduate students at Chicago and both accepted jobs at UVA. They founded the Thomas Jefferson Center in Political Economy and Social Philosophy in 1957. Nutter knew Gordon Tullock from the debate team at the University of Chicago and introduced him to Jim. Jim was impressed with Gordon's manuscript, *The Politics of Bureaucracy*, a manuscript rejected by 38 publishers. The book was ultimately published by Public Affairs Press in 1965 and rereleased by the University Press of America in 1987. Richard McKenzie, who in our early years participated in several Bozeman-based programs, said this in a review: "The *Politics of Bureaucracy* is an underrated and wrongly ignored classic." He noted, "I was lucky enough to read this book as part of a class taught by Tullock himself." McKenzie concluded that Tullock's book also goes well with *Bureaucracy* by Ludwig von Mises and *The Road to Serfdom* by F.A. Hayek.

Together, these three books hit at the core of the problems with public organizations. Unfortunately, these three books get little attention from economists and even less from political scientists. One can only hope that there will be a resurgence of interest in these great books. Christopher Coyne of George Mason University's Mercatus Center concurred in a recent review: "Gordon Tullock's *The Politics of Bureaucracy* must be considered one of the most important works on bureaucracy ever written."

I found Gordon's book extremely useful in identifying problems in federal resource management agencies. I assigned it when teaching forestry courses at Utah State University and Oregon State University and public policy courses at MSU.

Jim offered Gordon a postdoc position, supported by the Volker Fund of St. Louis. Gordon also became a tenured associate professor in UVA's political science department, ultimately a bad fit. Despite the academic success at UVA, or probably because of it, the University was unappreciative. Buchanan insisted Tullock be given a promotion to full professor in political science to acknowledge his scholarly success and to accompany his position in the Thomas Jefferson Center. Tullock had more publications than the rest of the political science department combined. Yet the department committee deemed him not acceptable for promotion. Here are my thoughts based on information from those involved and on several decades of university experience.

Much of the UVA faculty was embarrassed by the mere presence of public choice scholars; they were antithetical to what good academic liberals, generally Democrats and statists, believed. Public choice adherents tend to like and respect markets, property rights, rule of law, individual responsibility, and entrepreneurship. This was and remains a liability in the academic culture. People who understand public choice are also reflexively skeptical of ambitious governmental programs, today's Green energy mandates, for example. They expect such experiments to generate rent seeking, gross inefficiencies, and corruption. Public choice practitioners reflexively place their hope and expectations in separate baskets, anticipating sorry results from political adventures. Such people are not typical academics, surely not in the social sciences and humanities where the normal bias is for expanded government.

Modern "liberals" dominated UVA and wanted to purge their school of public choice, a black mark on UVA. They'd like Buchanan and Tullock better when gone. They soon were. This leads to Bozeman via Bloomington, Indiana, and to the application of public choice to environmental policy. Here's how Jim and Gordon became linked to Bozeman and how they fostered the creation of NRE. Importantly, I knew and liked them, and in the late 1970s, I introduced Jim and Gordon to my MSU colleagues.

Public Choice at Indiana University

I went to Indiana University (IU) in 1966 to study economic anthropology, a grateful beneficiary of the 1960s experimentations in interdisciplinary studies. What luck! IU was the perfect place for me; I could build an individual Ph. D. program from several departments while on a generous fellowship. I also had time and funds to indulge my interests in conservation, the origin of environmentalism, and occasionally work in the woods. I had no specific or assigned duties and found substantial personal support and generous mentoring from faculty in various departments and centers. I had the immense good fortune to have William J. (Bill) Siffin, a specialist in international development, as my major professor.

Bill had no affection for public choice but spent considerable time in the Third World and appreciated anthropology. He was highly tolerant and supportive of my work and me personally. Gordon's life may have turned out even more positively if he had had such a mentor, someone to constrain his costly enthusiasms and odd sense of humor. Since this probably would have been impossible, it's too bad Gordon didn't have a Bill Siffin to backfill his indiscretions as Professor Siffin did mine.

For instance, one advanced graduate seminar with Prof. Siffin required papers circulated a week in advance for discussion. Students would meet privately with Prof. Siffin for an hour a few days before class. This was for a preview and guidance. When my turn came, Professor Siffin merely chatted pleasantly for some time. After a while, I asked when would we discuss my paper. "Never," he responded. "Why?," I asked. "I burned it," he replied with kindness. "There are topics you shouldn't explore in a public setting. Few will understand your argument and most will think ill of you. The story of that paper would follow you and hinder your career. You are ahead if it doesn't exist."

Professors Elinor (Lin) and Vincent Ostrom had recently come to IU from UCLA. We had several common interests, including working with wood, and soon became friends. Although not a student in their fledging center, I was attracted to them personally and to their philosophies. I house sat for the Ostroms one summer while they vacationed in my mother's cottage on the Manitoulin Island of Ontario. The following year, I helped the Ostroms construct their log summer home on an isolated site, no electricity, on the shore of Lake Huron. To them the term "workshop" had physical as well as intellectual meaning.

Here is how the Ostroms' and Buchannan's and Tullock's public choice consolidated at IU. The Ostroms had met Buchanan at UCLA just after he left UVA. Gordon was at Rice, and both he and Jim wanted to relocate. Jim and Gordon's quite different personalities were more than complementary; they were multipliers. All would benefit if they found a common academic home. The Ostroms were working on problems of managing common property resources when they arrived at IU in 1964. They created a center, a "workshop" focused on public choice and political economy perspectives. They emphasized empirical research and applied policy analysis and were explicit in using theory to derive testable hypotheses. Much of their work involved appropriate institutional arrangements for dealing with common property. Their center became the Workshop in Political Theory and Policy Analysis in 1973. Lin won a Nobel Prize in economics in 2009 for her work on the economics of the commons. (Tom Schelling, another Nobel Prize economist with close ties to Bozeman, was her advocate. Tom was impressed that I had worked with her.)

Jim and Gordon's seminal work, *Calculus of Consent* (1962), was one of the Ostrom's key readings. (Mancur Olson's *Logic of Collective Action* was another. Olson wrote his Harvard economics dissertation under Tom Schelling.) The Ostroms told a few graduate students they wanted to attract Buchanan and Tullock to IU. They invited Tullock to Bloomington for talks and to meet faculty. They also hosted a dinner at their home on Lampkins Ridge Road, with a few faculty and at least one graduate student. After dinner, Tullock made some outrageous comment on how the world works. I don't recall his bizarre claim, but clearly remember taking strong and enthusiastic exception. Gordon advised the dinner guests that only stupidity could account for my argument. I persisted, however, but the dispute wasn't settled.

Here's a much later example of Gordon's attempt at humor. In the late 1980s, I briefly, very briefly indeed, ran the Oil and Gas Institute at Southern Methodist University in Dallas. A law and economics professor, Dick Pierce, held an endowed chair in SMU's law school. They had a senior position open, and I suggested Gordon. Prof. Pierce knew Gordon's work, thought this was a good idea, and invited him to Dallas. I hosted a dinner at the Energy Club to introduce the law faculty to Gordon. They had heard of Gordon, but none knew him. Since I was the host, I welcomed everyone and sketched the reasons for my admiration of Gordon. To initiate a discussion, I began to give an account of something I had read that morning in the *Wall Street Journal*. Gordon interrupted me with: "You read a story in the *Journal?* Congratulations! I always thought you were too dumb to learn to read." No one but

Gordon and I laughed, even though I followed with: "That must be why I'm on your editorial board." Regardless of the merits of our respective positions, Gordon remembered me, and not with malice. Later he contributed personal funds to my institutes in Bozeman. I infer he appreciated my candor, nerve, and enthusiasm. My wife Ramona says that at heart, Gordon really is "a sweetie pie," although one with an underdeveloped sense of propriety.

Back now to IU. In 1966, Ostroms assigned grad students articles from Gordon and Jim's journal, *Papers in Non-Market Economics*. Three issues later, it became *Public Choice,* with Gordon the editor. At that time, the journal featured articles applying economic theory to nonmarket phenomena, especially government and politics. (Alas, last time I looked, *Public Choice* published mainly recreational mathematics.) Gordon published one of my first articles, "Choice, Faith, and Politics: The Political Economy of the Huitterite Communes," in 1972 and coauthored with Richard Stroup. Gordon was quite taken by our application of economics to religious organization. That's when he asked me to serve on the editorial board of *Public Choice*.

I feel exceedingly lucky to have gone to IU for grad school. Had I not, I wouldn't have studied with Vince and Lin, met Gordon and Jim, published a book with ecologist Garrett Hardin, studied the Hutterite Brethren, and received a postdoc in environmental policy. All these led to Bozeman and the creation of the NRE with its foundations in public choice.

The Commons at Bloomington and Bozeman

In 1965, Scott Gordon came to IU as chairman of economics. (He was also a professor in the History and Philosophy of Science Department, one of my examination fields.) His classic *Journal of Political Economy* paper, "The Economic Theory of a Common-Property Resource: The Fishery," complemented the Ostroms' activities. They highly recommended it to graduate students. The article did not, however, have a large influence beyond economics and fisheries managers. I soon learned an important pedagogical lesson from an ecologist.

In 1968, U.C. Santa Barbara ecologist Garrett Hardin, a Chicago Ph.D., published "The Tragedy of The Commons" in *Science*. Totally unaware of Scott Gordon's paper, Hardin developed the same logic explaining common pool overexploitation. His piece was literary with several artful and erudite extensions. Garrett excelled in the craft of writing, creating, and using aphorisms. Here is an example, "The morality of an act is a function of the state of the system at the time it is performed." His "tragedy" was a cultural as well as an analytic article, one that anticipated and helped form the Green zeitgeist.

Comparing Scott Gordon and Garrett Hardin's presentations of the same phenomenon was an anthropological lesson. In brief, empathy, cultural symbolism, and mode of presentation matter when communicating logical arguments. Few people find calculus the most compelling form of communication. Jim and Gordon understand this. Hardin's piece was published prior to the first Earth Day, April 21 (Lenin's birthday) in 1970. It was very widely read and immensely influential among academics interested in environmental policy reform and Green lifestyles. All of my friends in biology were captivated by his logic and writing style, so was I, and I arranged to meet Professor Hardin at the upcoming American Association for the Advancement of Science meeting in Chicago. I had dinner with Garrett and his wife, Jane. My missionary task was to explain to Garrett why, even though he had dismissed Adam Smith in his famous *Science* article, economics could be a useful tool in his policy reform efforts. This wasn't so difficult. In a 1959 book, *Nature and Man's Fate,* he had an extensive discussion of the market process as a coordination device with references to economists ranging from Ricardo to Keynes. Also, he was publically dismissive and critical of New Left silliness, much like Buchanan.

I must have succeeded for we exchanged articles, remained in contact, and I became a houseguest of Garrett and Jane in Santa Barbara. A few years later, we decided to produce a book linking ecology and economics. The result was *Managing the Commons,* published in 1978. *Managing the Commons* included articles by Gordon Tullock, the Ostroms, Terry Anderson and P.J. Hill, Richard Stroup, Bob Bish (another IU Ph. D. who studied with the Ostroms), and Kenneth Boulding. Boulding is not usually regarded as a public choice economist, but much of his work, like that of Tom Schelling, complements it. *Managing the Commons* remained in print for 20 years and was widely adopted, usually in various programs in environmental studies. One of my students, Doug Noonan, (a Chicago Ph. D. in economics from the Harris School) and I subsequently published a second edition with IU Press in 1998.

An Environmental Primer

The theoretical approach pioneered in Bozeman has trumped the Progressive Era, command-and-control, engineering approach to natural resource, and environmental management. Before going on, a consideration of problems inherent to studying environmental matters will help us understand the contributions of public choice to environmental issues. First, all environmental topics are technically and scientifically complex. Second, all carry substantial emotional baggage. High complexity and heavy emotions are a dangerous conjunction, ingredients for error, and acrimony. They also foster opportunistic, hypocritical, dishonest politics, and consider global warming, wolves in the Intermountain West, and spotted owls in the Pacific Northwest.

Academics who apply science and dispassionate economic analysis to environmental problems and their solutions face hard slogs. Their work exposes uncomfortable realities of income and opportunity transfers. They make externalities explicit. Politicians and university administrators beholden to them face strong incentives to discount, ignore, or ultimately purge inconvenient analysis. They apply formal and informal pressures. Further, public choice economists are irritants in America's academic culture. This is especially pronounced among Greens.

I find it useful to divide environmental studies into two categories: sludge and romance. The more important involves stuff that reduces biological productivity or sickens or kills people and other living things. Dioxin, heavy metals, and radioactive waste are examples. We call this sludge. The second category includes forests, prairies, parks, wilderness, and wildlife. This is the stuff featured on calendars and in advertisements. It's the romantic side of environmental studies. Brownfield Superfund sites are rarely as attractive, although some parts of Butte's Superfund site actually are.

Tastes vary, as do opportunities to apply public choice to policy problems. It's no mere accident the public choice scholars in Bozeman focus on romance. If our taste were toward sludge, we'd likely be in Boston and studying Judge Richard Stearns' management and remediation of waste in Boston Harbor. It resembled the mother lode of sludge; Butte's old copper pit still does. Instead, we study our backyard topics, wolves in Greater Yellowstone, for example. The romance side of environmentalism is ideally suited to public choice analysis as formulated in the NRE that emerged from Bozeman. This perspective is leavened with insights from economic anthropology and Austrian economics' emphasis on entrepreneurship. Culture and history as well as institutions matter to the NRE, while public choice provides the fundamental framework.

Public Choice Comes to Bozeman

In 1970, MSU in Bozeman was still a small, land grant agricultural and engineering college. When I arrived, the wastebasket in my office was labeled, "Montana State College." This was an unlikely birthplace for economic ideas that challenged the conventional Progressive Era model of natural resource management. The MSU default for ideal natural resource management was acceptance, often enthusiastic, of Progressive Era and New Deal arrangements. This strongly implied deference to agency management. The undirected private sector and the market process were suspect at best. This is no accident. Given Montana's history of corporate control of the political process, suspicions were well founded. The Anaconda Company, its creature, the Montana Power Company, along with the railroads, had a long and sordid history of political rent seeking resembling a Third World nation. That is the setting we entered in 1970.

There were several reasons why our economic orientation was resisted and resented. Much involves history and culture. Montana was a resource producing state, agriculture, mining, and forestry. Depression hit the agricultural sector just after WW I, a decade before it became the Great Depression prolonged and exacerbated by FDR. For most people, Montana was a very hard and hostile place until wealth and technology advanced in the 1970s. Today, improved technology is applied to communications, transportation (five major airlines serve Bozeman/Yellowstone International Airport), automobiles, SUVs, pickups, housing, clothing, and medicine; Bozeman has become a magnet for people with high human capital. Also, Montana is noticeably warmer and no more arid. It's now much easier and more comfortable to live here. How fortunate we are!

Montana is where the prairie socialists from the upper Midwest overlapped the International Workers of the World, the Wobblies, which became prominent in Montana in the early part of the twentieth century as the result of organizational efforts by miners in Butte and lumberjacks throughout the state. The Wobblies' core philosophy, according to the preamble to the IWW constitution, declares "The working class and the employing class have nothing in common.... Rather than organizing workers by trade, the IWW seeks to unite all workers as a class in order to rise up and take over means of industrial production and eventually overthrowing capitalism and creating a more peaceful society."

Aside from parts of MSU's economics department, this was not a hospitable environment for academics with a public choice orientation. While MSU in the 1970s was relatively "conservative" compared to many universities, it was precociously Green and certainly not hospitable to free-market thinking. The University of Montana, the "dancing school" was even worse. Yet, thanks to the counsel, participation, analytic leverage, and good offices of nationally prominent public choice scholars, we've won the intellectual battle. Here's an introduction of what it is and how it happened. Jim and Gordon contributed far more than they know.

Four academics independently came to Bozeman in the early 1970s. Together, we developed the New Resource Economics (aka free-market environmentalism) at Montana State University throughout the1970s and early 1980s. Rick Stroup and I began the foundations of the NRE 40 years ago. In Rick's words, sent as I was writing this chapter: We "started with (1) a 'Chicago school' approach to micro and markets, (2) the B&T [Buchanan and Tullock] approach to public decision making, (3) an Alchian-Demsetz approach to the importance and functioning of property rights and markets [to] how people acted in seeking gain by exchanging them, all buttressed/tempered by (4) an Austrian economics recognition that both risk and more radical uncertainty about the future environment in which the other three factors are subject to change over time and space."

I added an anthropological perspective on the importance of culture and an emphasis on entrepreneurship. Both of these were widely neglected by economists in the 1970s and beyond. Also, I maintained that economists could learn a great deal from public intellectuals outside economics. Consider Tom Wolfe, the journalist, essayist, and novelist. He has a far better understanding of social organization and stratification than any economist or sociologist I knew. (Wolfe's Yale Ph. D. is in American studies.) I argued his work would definitely help economists understand the world they described, especially status motivations. Wolfe understands and communicates the workings of society without employing statistics or graphs; he is a journalist and literary artist. Wolfe's insights are especially useful when considering the Green movement and it's policy proposals that are at times remarkably naive.

After working independent of any formal center focused on public choice, in 1978 I founded an institute, the Center for Political Economy and Natural Resources at MSU. (Later I chose better, easier to remember names, PERC and then FREE.) My colleagues at the Center were Rick Stroup from the University of Washington and later Terry Anderson, also from the University of Washington, and then P. J. Hill from the University of Chicago. Rick's dissertation applied micro theory to the impact of air pollution on real estate prices. Terry and P.J. worked primarily in economic history. Our Center at MSU was highly productive; first movers have an advantage. We worked in environmental policy, a sexy area, and one overwhelmingly dominated by collectivists and statists of various stripes. My colleagues and I were outliers on multiple dimensions. We shared several characteristics with friends at The Public Choice Center at Virginia Polytechnic Institute and State University—isolation and independence.

The Liberty Fund discovered our work, thanks to Clay LaForce and his colleagues in the economics department at UCLA, particularly Armen Alchian and Harold Demsetz. The Liberty Fund sponsored numerous conferences including a series of weeklong conferences for promising young scholars; nearly all were held at Lone Mountain Ranch at Big Sky, Montana. Jim, Gordon, Bob Tollison, Doug North, Vernon Smith, Richard Epstein, Bill Niskanen, Richard McKenzie, and Dwight Lee were among the speakers.

I began the Center with a $20,000 start-up grant from MSU, one the university administrators came to regret, and took no other government money (or any other obtained by force or fraud). Jim and Gordon's good words helped our fledging Center gain foundation support. Grants from the Liberty Fund, Scaife, Earhart, Carthage, M.J. Murdoch, Olin, and a few others I discovered made our work possible. In 1979, with Stroup's help, I organized a MSU conference at Big Sky, "The Environmental Costs of Bureaucratic Governance." The conference was part of the operating program of the Liberty Fund and was the first of our comprehensive assaults on conventional environmental and natural resource management. The conference papers we commissioned became a book, *Bureaucracy vs. Environment: The Environmental Costs of Bureaucratic Governance,* published by the University of Michigan Press in 1981.

In our introduction, Stroup and I wrote, "The essays in this volume share a theme. Although this theme is important, clear, and compellingly valid in a large and varied set of cases, it is only slowly becoming understood. Specifically, we are increasingly convinced that both the environmental and the economic costs of bureaucratic management of natural resources are excessively and unnecessarily high. These social costs are generated by perverse institutional structures that give authority to those who do not bear responsibility for the consequences of their actions (p. 1)."

In addition to chapters by Stroup and me, two of my students and a few field specialist friends, the conference speakers/chapter writers included Terry Anderson, P. J. Hill, Gary Libecap, and Ron Johnson, names familiar in the public choice community. Several other respected economists including M. Bruce Johnson of the University of California Santa Barbara, then president of the Western Economic Association, and Barney Dowdle of the University of Washington joined us as authors. Although ours was no *Calculus of Consent* or *Logic of Collective Action,* it indeed was a breakout book and one published by a highly respected university press. It remains a benchmark in the natural resource literature. It identified causes of fundamental flaws in the organization of federal agencies managing one third of America's land. We also suggested institutional reforms to promote harmony among values that often compete in environmental policy. These include environmental quality, prosperity, and responsible liberty. We identified by principle and by case situations that these values were harmed by the federal agencies created to protect them. These agencies evolved to provide major funding for western universities.

Federal resource management agencies and universities enjoy symbiotic relations. Sharks and pilot fish offer an analogy. Sharks rarely eat their pilot fish. Pilot fish don't nibble their sharks but rather protect them from parasites. They get along well together. This is why the upper administration at MSU did not celebrate our *Bureaucracy vs. Environment* book. Quite to the contrary, they resented and disparaged it. Jim and Gordon would understand. Of course their reaction was not a surprise. Earlier, the VP for research, a biologist, criticized Stroup and me for publishing an article critical of the US Forest Service, "Property Rights, Externalities, and the Management of the National Forests," in the *Journal of Law and Economics*. Rick sketched the article from his notes taken during a public discussion between Milton Friedman and me. Ronald Coase accepted the piece without revision.

The Predictable (in Hindsight) Demise of MSU's Center

Buchanan and Tullock's experience at the University of Virginia previewed distractions coming to MSU. Like their center at UVA, MSU's public-choice-oriented institute was purged by and through university and governmental politics.

In 1982, the MSU president demanded we invite the governor of Montana to give a dinner address at one of our environmental economics programs for national editorial page editors and associate editors. Representatives from papers including the *WSJ, Wash Post, Forbes, Fortune, L.A. Times*, and a dozen second-tier papers attended. We were also required to have one Montana journalist. One qualified, Frank Adams of the *Great Falls Tribune*. He had recently returned from a Nieman Fellowship at Harvard. He accepted our invitation. So did the governor. There is a Montana description of inebriation, "commode hugging, knee-walking drunk." By the time the governor was to give his after-dinner talk, he approached this condition. His eyes couldn't focus on the politician size *#24 type,* and he couldn't read his talk. "I've read enough God damn speeches this week. If you want it, here it is." The governor tossed the pages across the room. For some of the visiting journalists, this was better than rodeo. This really is the wild West. Whoopee!

Frank Adams, the Great Falls, Montana, journalist was a teetotaling Mormon. He took this all in. It was great fodder for describing a politician whose rent seeking and wholesaling he had outed over the years. A few days later, an article by Adams appeared on the front page of the *Great Falls* . It led with, "In a slurred speech punctuated by profanity, Governor…." Only a few of us were amused.

The governor called the MSU president and said I had set him up. The president told me to go to Helena and apologize. I agreed an apology was due. The president was pleased by my agreement. He misunderstood. I explained that while I agreed an apology was in order, it should come from the governor and be offered to my colleagues and guests. Things got progressively worse.

The president asserted that I "was nothing but a mouthpiece for the Moral Majority." No one with an IQ higher than his body temperature could imagine a libertarian Unitarian in that role. The MSU president surely knew better. However, he faced strong political incentives to discount, condemn, and distance himself from our Center's work. Shades of UVA in the 1960s.

Pressures and accusations mounted. The University claimed overhead rate on the Center's grants went from 10% to 48%. The VP for research, the individual to whom I reported, mobilized faculty opposition in political science, history, biological sciences, and ag economics departments. I asked for a peer review, and the president, looking for outside validation, agreed. The president's surrogate (actually a good guy and a respected ag economist) picked two highly regarded ag economists, Vernon W. Rattan of Minnesota and Emory Castle of Oregon state. I selected two economists: Del Gardner, a Chicago Ph. D., who was distinguished professor of economics with joint appointments at U.C. Davis and Berkeley and M. Bruce Johnson, president of the Western Economics Association and chairman of economics at U.C. Santa Barbara. This was a fine and honorable group. I awaited their report. It was to be sent to the University president's office. I waited. And waited. And waited. And called the president's office several times a week. "It's not available yet," his secretary always reported.

Jim and Gordon may not be surprised the president and his office were simply lying. The review was indeed available. M. Bruce Johnson chaired the peer review committee, knew it was important, and sent it in early. When I finally contacted him, he sent a copy to me. It was a highly positive report. (It's available on FREE's website, FREE-eco.org, under history). This account describes university politics, dishonesty, and cowardice. The University made it quite impossible for any honorable person to continue there. Jim and Gordon would surely understand why.

While extremely difficult for my family and me for some time, the MSU saga has a very happy ending. It led quite directly to the progress of public choice in the natural resource and environmental arenas through the development and success of PERC, and then to FREE. Public choice is central to both. Personally and importantly, this experience permanently immunized me to any trauma inflicted by university politics. When encountering smaller scale replications elsewhere, I knew the script and was prepared. I had learned to keep hopes and expectations in different compartments. I shut down the MSU Center and moved off campus where I established the Political Economy Research Center (PERC) first at our ranch and then in Bozeman. Rick Stroup and Terry Anderson, both working out of state at the time, joined me upon their return. (Terry now runs PERC and recently changed its name to Property and Environment Research Center. Under his leadership, it has become a large and highly active organization with many programs, especially during summers. I regard its work highly indeed. Creating it was one of my better accomplishments.)

It's nearly impossible to plan or anticipate the success and evolution of efforts like those that established our Center at MSU. It is the result of several individuals' visions and intellectual entrepreneurship, something that can only spontaneously develop. Much like Jim and Gordon's original Public Choice Center at UVA, once established, it was impossible to eradicate. In a sense, we initiated criticism of Progressive Era resource management institutions and breached the dam holding back agency criticism. Most of our success comes from the public choice analysis of Jim and Gordon. Their courage in sanding up against transitory fads in academia provided an excellent model, one highly worthy of emulation.

Appendices

Foundations of NRE

The New Resource Economics (aka free-market environmentalism) is the disciplined, analytic approach to conservation and environmental management. The NRE has two main themes and several variations, especially at the international level. First is an emphasis on the importance of entrepreneurship in both the for-profit and nonprofit arenas. Briefly, in the natural resource arena, successful for-profit entrepreneurs improve economic production and coordination. They anticipate or respond to commodity scarcities, for example, by converting scrap from lumber mills into particleboard and other useful products. They create ways to give value to waste. Nonprofit or social entrepreneurs find ways to mobilize good intentions in the production of public goods. Common examples are organizations that protect or generate fish and wildlife habitat. Ducks Unlimited, Rocky Mountain Elk Foundation, and Pheasants Forever are examples. NRE practitioners study both types.

The second theme provides a constructive alternative to the bureaucratic management system developed in America during the Progressive Era. This has international implications for a bureaucratic management system that has been copied around the world in the post WW II decades, normally with the same sorry results. Agencies at the federal level manage nearly one third of America's land. The primary agencies are the US Forest Service (1905) in the Department of Agriculture and the Bureau of Land Management (reconstituted from an amalgam of nineteenth-century agencies in 1946), Bureau of Reclamation (1902), Park Service (1916), and Fish and Wildlife Service (origins in 1896), all in the Department of Interior.

Whether measured in terms of ecology, equity, or economic return, most of America's public lands is managed quite poorly. This is no accident but rather is predictable. Public choice theory expressed through the NRE explains much of its failings. It begins with two simple assumptions. First, decisions are made on the margins and are based on information and incentives. Second, institutions generate information with varying quantity and quality. Also, institutions produce positive and negative incentives to act upon that information. These are the key aspects of public choice theory my MSU colleagues and I applied to environmental and natural resource issues. We explained why resource management doesn't fail. It's not because of the standard gauge, simplistic political corruption we associate with Chicago politics. Stupidity, venality, ignorance, and laziness don't explain the failures. Rather, public choice theory provides analytical leverage for understanding the problems—and why state universities, largely dependent on government funding, have been so hostile to its application. Academic culture exacerbates the problem.

In the early decades, the NRE faced nearly unanimous condemnation. Misunderstanding, dismissal, and dishonest posturing were the norms. This held throughout the political and academic arenas. Conventional Greens in the national environmental organizations, such as the Sierra Club and National Wildlife Federation, and university administrators were especially strident in their denunciations. Rent seeking reinforced collectivist ideologies in powerful ways.

It would be hard to overemphasize the contributions of Jim and Gordon to the early work in NRE. In addition to providing the basic analytic framework, their participation and good offices gave credence and respectability to intellectual outliers at a cow college in the most remote of the contiguous 48 states. I suspect their imprimatur led to a great deal of our foundation funding.

During the first Reagan administration, Stroup served as chief economist in the Department of Interior. Bob Nelson, now at the University of Maryland, was a senior economist under Stroup. In his role as director of the Office of Policy Analysis, Rick saw practical and political implications of applying public choice to natural resource policy. In short, neither Sectary James Watt nor the Department's constituencies were accepting of public choice analysis. I, however, enjoyed frequent visits to Interior and cemented friendships at the Heritage Foundation, The Cato Institute, and the American Enterprise Institute. These were all places that welcomed the NRE. They correctly saw it as an environmentally friendly free-market movement. It was and remains a constructive alternative to socialist and fascist Green movements. Also, knowing that I visited DC with some frequency, someone, I believe Jim Buchanan, invited me to visit Blacksburg, Virginia, and give a talk on NRE.

Sylvan socialism, prairie populism, and kindred political/bureaucratic management schemes never work as advertized. Hayekian problems of dispersed information compounded by scientific complexity, political rent seeking, and culturally induced and reinforced stupidity condemn and convert these planning dreams into nightmares. Public choice theory provided the keys to explain this pathology and predict results of proposed reforms. The NRE prospered. Success came despite opposition by academic and government leaders who feared and opposed applying economic logic to the public sector. Over time, the NRE captured the intellectual high ground. Data and logic are stubborn forces indeed, especially when the political targets, mainly federal agencies, have been so dysfunctional. One hundred plus years of failure convinces all but the most naive, and recipients of rents, of the inevitable failure of bureaucratic management of complex biological, political, and economic systems.

Fortunately, logic and data buttressed by examples and applied to interesting topics are powerful, relentless, attractive forces. It's no accident that NRE programs, first at MSU, then at PERC, and for the past quarter-century at FREE, have brought half a dozen Nobel Prize winning economists and hundreds of America's leading economists, law professors, and federal judges to Bozeman. There is wide agreement that FME is intellectually dominant; no responsible scholar still supports the old command-and-control resource management model of the Progressive Era. Special interest politics and bureaucratic pathology, not incompetence or corruption, generate failure. NRE explains why this is the predictable consequence of sylvan socialism and related bureaucratic schemes.

Jim and Gordon were early mentors and had great influence on Bozeman's intellectual currents. Nobel Prize Winning economists Vernon Smith, Doug North, Lin Ostrom, Gary Becker, and Tom Schelling followed. Most have been with us multiple times, Schelling more than a dozen. Although much of his work complements public choice (and Tom has told me of his respect for Jim), Schelling is not normally considered part of the public choice movement. He considers himself an "errant economist."

Some find it remarkable that so many distinguished economists enjoy visiting Bozeman. It is most unlikely that my colleagues and I would have enjoyed this success had Jim and Gordon not worked with us in our early years. I am indeed grateful that Dwight Lee gave me the opportunity to acknowledge their contributions.

NRE at Mont Pelerin Society Meetings, 1991 and 2004

I assume anyone reading this book is familiar with the history and philosophy of the Mont Pelerin Society. For any who are not, MPS is an organization founded by Friedrich A. Hayek and 38 friends at Mont Pelerin, Switzerland, in 1947. It is widely recognized as the world's most prestigious and significant international association of classical liberals and libertarians. Naturally, both Jim and Gordon are distinguished members. Here is how I became involved with MPS.

I finished my Ph.D. at Indiana University in 1969 and accepted a National Science Foundation postdoctoral fellowship in environmental policy. This was just before the first Earth Day in April of 1970. Following Earth Day, many, perhaps most, colleges and universities created environmental programs. Although there were young academics in the traditional natural resource fields such as forestry and wildlife, there was a paucity of candidates for the more general field of environmental policy. This includes economics, ecology, and ethics. As a result of the imbalance between the new, and expanding, demand for environmental studies professors and the short supply, I naturally received multiple offers from schools across the country. Being on good terms with my dissertation committee, and other senior faculty and administrators, they were quite pleased by my opportunities. All encouraged me to accept an offer from a nationally prominent university. While I respected their advice, I told them I wouldn't take it. My choice was to return to Montana, my refuge from the disruptive chaos of the 1960s that afflicted all major universities.

Having my interests at heart, my academic mentors attempted to change my decision. Most of their arguments were valid. For example, they predicted political interference if I accepted an offer from Montana State University. Fortunately, they were totally wrong in predicting that if I went to Montana I would never again have the luxury of consorting with top scholars. At that time, MSU was an academic backwater, and Montana was the most remote of the contiguous 48 states. This, of course, was before regular jet connections, FedEx, UPS, and the Internet erased the cost of distance. Disinclined to heed the counsel of the wise, I bought a small ranch near Bozeman and began teaching at MSU. Luckily, I maintained friendly and productive contacts made in graduate school and obtained a few modest grants and other discretionary funds. This enabled me to bring Gordon, Jim, and other members of the Mont Pelerin Society to Big Sky Country. They were sufficiently impressed with the work done in Bozeman that I had the opportunity to host a regional Mont Pelerin Society meeting at Big Sky, Montana, in 1991 and then a general MPS meeting in Salt Lake City in 2004.

Interestingly, because the group originally couldn't come to an agreement as to what to call the Society, Mont Pelerin founders used the location of the Swiss resort at which they were meeting as a "place holder" until they found a permanent name. Of course, the name Mont Pelerin Society stuck. The naming decision essentially economized on decision costs, an important public choice insight. Because of Montana's current popularity and destination status, if an organization such as MPS were to emerge today, few people would be amazed if the chosen site were Big Sky, Montana. However, in our early years in Bozeman, this was not the case.

The Society has continued to meet on a regular basis. Members include high-ranking government officials, Nobel Prize recipients, journalists, business leaders, and legal scholars from many nations. They meet regularly to present analysis of ideas, trends, and events. Eight MPS members, including Buchanan, have won Nobel prizes. Five of them have participated in programs I've organized from Montana. I am sure my mentors would be pleasantly surprised at this success. We enjoyed this success by creating a public policy niche and applied it to natural resource issues. My colleagues and I built a reputation in this area, thanks in large part to the public choice Jim and Gordon developed.

FREE has hosted two MPS meetings, a "regional meeting" at Big Sky, Montana, in 1991 and the "general meeting" in Salt Lake City in 2004. I am confident that neither of these would have occurred without the personal and intellectual contributions of Jim and Gordon. I thank the late Lin Ostrom[1] and her husband, Vincent, and the public choice movement at Indiana University for making this introduction.

[1] I was saddened to hear of Lin's death just as I was finishing this paper.

Chapter 13
The Public Choice Revolution and Principles of Economics Texts

James Gwartney

Introduction

The 1960s was an exciting time to begin the study of economics. Economics was becoming both more abstract and more mathematical. In macroeconomics, the Keynesian view was challenged by the monetarists, and this debate eventually elevated monetary policy to an equal billing with fiscal policy. The production function theory of Robert Solow was altering the thinking of economists about economic growth, and this analysis provided the foundation for modern growth theory. The theory of market failure was integrated into public finance, and it was widely perceived to provide a powerful justification for more activist government intervention. It was against this background that James Buchanan and Gordon Tullock authored the *Calculus of Consent* in 1962.

The *Calculus of Consent* focused on how political structures and collective decision-making rules influenced outcomes and the operation of the democratic political process. The book spawned a new body of literature that exerted an impact on a sizeable portion of the economics profession. With time, the development of this literature became known as the "public choice revolution." The work of Buchanan and Tullock was central to this new school of thought, and in 1986, Buchanan was awarded the Nobel Prize in economics primarily for his groundbreaking work in the development of public choice analysis.

J. Gwartney (✉)
Gus A. Stavros Center for Economic Education, Florida State University,
250 South Woodward Avenue, Tallahassee, FL 32306-4220, USA
e-mail: jdgwartney@fsu.edu

D.R. Lee (ed.), *Public Choice, Past and Present: The Legacy of James M. Buchanan and Gordon Tullock*, Studies in Public Choice 28, DOI 10.1007/978-1-4614-5909-5_13,

Public Choice and My Career as an Economist

The public choice literature exerted a major impact on my career and approach to economics. In 1967, while a graduate student at the University of Washington, I took a public finance course from Thomas Borcherding, who had recently been a postdoctoral fellow at the Thomas Jefferson Center at the University of Virginia with Buchanan and Tullock. The course focused on their publications and those of other public choice scholars such as Anthony Downs, Mancur Olson, and William Niskanen. Later that same year, Professor Buchanan visited the University of Washington and gave a special lecture on public choice economics and its implications for the economics profession.

In essence, public choice applies the tools of economics to both the market and political processes. Without having knowledge about the operation of both, one is in a poor position to understand how alternative institutions and policies will affect outcomes. This comparative approach seemed so sensible to me I integrated it into both my thought process and teaching of economics. I fully expected the public choice approach to transform economic analysis and greatly expand its relevance.

Upon completion of my degree, I began my career at Florida State University. In the early 1970s, I integrated public choice analysis into my teaching of large lecture principles classes at FSU. The student response was overwhelmingly positive, but the topic was totally absent from the available principles texts. In addition to the omission of public choice, I was also unhappy with the treatment of monetary policy, the Phillips curve, and general analysis of macro stabilization policy in the principles texts of that era. I set out to correct these deficiencies. I contacted several publishers about the idea and put together a proposal for a new principles of economics text. At the time, I did not realize the enormous commitment involved in the writing of a full-length principles text. Had I been better informed about the size of the task, I might well have decided not to undertake it. I thought I could write the text in about a year. Instead, it took two full years of the most intense work of my life.

The result was *Economics: Private and Public Choice,* a principles text initially published in 1976.[1] Through the years, the assistance of coauthors Richard Stroup, Russell Sobel, and David Macpherson was enlisted. The text is now in the 14th edition.[2]

From the very beginning, *Economics: Private and Public Choice* used the tools of economics to analyze the operation of the market and political process in a symmetric manner. The following passage from the preface of the first edition (1976, page xviii) highlights this point and contrasts the approach with that of other texts:

---

[1] Gwartney J (1976) *Economics: Private and Public Choice*. Academic Press, New York.

[2] Gwartney J, Stroup R, Sobel R, Macpherson D (2012) *Economics: Private and Public Choice*, 14th edn. South-Western Cengage Learning, Cincinnati.

> Most textbooks currently do three things. They tell students how an ideal market economy would work, why real world markets differ from the hypothetical ideal, and how ideal public policy could correct the failures of the market. In addition to these three basic areas of study, this book analyzes what real world public policy is likely to do. This important step drives home both the power and relevance of modern economics. Building on the pioneering work of Kenneth Arrow, Duncan Black, James Buchanan, Anthony Downs, Gordon Tullock, and others, the economic analysis of public, as well as private, choice helps to bring the subject matter alive to the student. Students are often puzzled by the gulf between the ideal theoretical "solutions" of economists and the events of the real world. The economics of public choice explains this gulf. Economic tools can illustrate why "good politics" sometimes conflicts with "good economics" (that is, economic efficiency). It is important that we explain what government can do to promote a more efficient use of our resources. But the tools of economics permit us to do more. They permit us to explain why there is good reason to expect that public sector actions will be counterproductive for certain classes of issues.

Public Choice, Mainstream Economics, and Elite Schools

Even though the book has been successful, I am, nonetheless, disappointed that the public choice approach has exerted so little impact on mainstream economics and the content of principles courses. As the above quotation indicates, when the first edition of *Economics: Private and Public Choice* was published, the mainstream approach modeled government as if it was a corrective device available for the achievement of ideal efficiency conditions if the market should fail to do so. Comparative analysis was lacking, and this absence was my primary motivation to author the text. Nearly four decades later, little has changed. Rather than analyzing how both markets and collective decision-making handle economic problems, mainstream economics continues to model government as if it were an omniscient, benevolent social planner available to impose ideal solutions. The highly successful text of Greg Mankiw illustrates this point. Mankiw introduces his discussion of the role of government and the correction of market deficiencies in the following manner:

> To evaluate market outcomes, we introduce into our analysis a new, hypothetical character called the benevolent social planner. The benevolent social planner is an all- knowing, all-powerful, well- intentioned dictator. The planner wants to maximize the economic well-being of everyone in society.[3]

Mankiw then asks what the benevolent social planner should do and goes on to consider the ideal solutions that might be imposed through the political process.

[3] Mankiw G (2012) *Principles of Economics*, 6th edn. South Western Cengage Learning, p 145. Professor Mankiw's analysis of government intervention is representative of the mainstream perspective. Mankiw was the chairman of the president's Council of Economic Advisers under George W. Bush and is generally viewed as a supporter of a market economy.

The other leading mainstream texts follow this same approach. Implicitly, this methodology treats the political process as if it is a corrective device available to impose ideal social outcomes, something like a pinch hitter that always delivers the game-winning hit. But this is a fantasy. A choice between the real world of markets and the hypothetical ideal of government intervention is not an option. Instead, the choice is always about how markets work compared to the alternatives. Put another way, the relevant choice is always between the real-world operation of markets and the real-world operation of the political process.

As the public choice revolution developed, other authors also sought to integrate the analysis of political decision-making and the comparative approach into principles courses. The most important of these were the texts authored by Richard McKenzie and Gordon Tullock (1978) and Robert Ecklund and Robert Tollison (1986).[4] Subsequently, the latter text has gone through five editions. After Buchanan won the Nobel Prize in 1986, I expected that public choice and the systematic analysis of political decision-making would be incorporated into other texts much like, for example, monetarism and rational expectations were integrated into principles texts during the 1970s and 1980s. But, this happened only to a modest degree. Clearly, the public choice revolution is incomplete; it has not altered what is taught in the typical principles course.

The exclusion of public choice analysis is particularly strong at elite schools like those of the Ivy League and the University of California-Berkeley. Perhaps, this is a reflection of the fact that neither Buchanan nor Tullock has had any significant association with these elite schools. While Buchanan's degree is from the University of Chicago, he has spent most all of his professional career at schools in Virginia: the University of Virginia, Virginia Tech, and George Mason University. Similarly, Tullock has been associated with the same set of Virginia schools, plus an appointment at the University of Arizona. Buchanan is exceptional among American Nobel Prize winners in that he has never held a teaching or research appointment at an elite school.

The underrepresentation of elite schools among public choice economists is readily observable at the annual meeting of the Public Choice Society, the professional organization of public choice scholars. For example, 296 public choice scholars presented papers at the March 2012 international meeting of the Public Choice Society held in Miami. Only five of the presenters were from either an Ivy League school or the University of California, Berkeley. Among the five, only one was a faculty member with an appointment in an economics department.

This underrepresentation reminds me of an incident that occurred just a couple of months after Buchanan won the Nobel Prize in 1986. As a faculty member at Florida State University, I was involved in the interview process of prospective

[4] McKenzie R, Tullock G (1978) *Principles of Modern Political Economy*. McGraw-Hill, New York and Ecklund R, Tollison R (1986) *Economics: Private Markets and Public Choice*. Little, Brown and Company.

candidates for an open position. One of the candidates was a highly recommended student who had just completed his doctoral degree from a prestigious Ivy League school with a specialty in public finance. When asked about his knowledge of Buchanan, Tullock, and the public choice literature, the student admitted that even though he had just completed his doctoral degree with a field in public finance, he had never heard of Buchanan prior to his selection for the Nobel award. The members of the interview committee were shocked by this deficiency, and needless to say, he was not offered the position.

Underrepresentation of public choice in the economics departments of elite schools has been a major deterrent to the dissemination of the analysis. These departments supply a substantial share of the new faculty members at other departments throughout the nation. They also command prestige, and faculties at other schools often follow their lead. Thus, it is quite difficult for a new theory or methodology to exert widespread impact without attracting support from the top tier of schools.

Why Does Public Choice Matter?

Why does the exclusion of public choice analysis from mainstream economics make any difference? The asymmetric treatment of the political process relative to markets diminishes the relevance of economics and leaves students with a romantic, and highly misleading, view of government and the operation of the democratic political process. There are three major reasons why this is the case.

1. *The omission of public choice from mainstream economics creates a central planning mentality.* For the mainstream economist, economics is about deriving ideal solutions under restrictive assumptions. Essential information such as consumer preferences, costs of production, rate of return for alternative investments, and size of spillover effects are generally assumed to be known. For the proponents of this approach, economic analysis involves the derivation of "optimal" levels of taxation, subsidies, distribution of income, budget deficits, government spending, and dozens of other key variables within models containing known information. In this fantasy world, economics is about deriving ideal solutions to multi-equation mathematical models. This approach makes economics look highly sophisticated, and its practitioners appear to be engineering geniuses. No doubt, the sophistication of such models is a contributing factor to their popularity at elite schools.

But, there are numerous problems with this approach. The information incorporated into the models is generally unavailable to any central authority. The supposed "ideal" solutions often alter incentives and generate secondary effects that undermine the validity of the models. Most importantly, as public choice analysis reveals, the real-world political decision makers will be more interested in votes and winning the next election than the adoption of supposed ideal solutions. As a result, there will often be a conflict between "good politics" and economic efficiency.

The bottom line is straightforward: the real world is dynamic and more complicated than the models, and therefore the potential of centralized government planning is far more limited than mainstream analysis implies. Moreover, even when the models are largely correct, the political incentive structure will often undermine the adoption of productive policies. Real-world political decision makers are neither saints nor benevolent omniscient social planners. Instead, they are motivated primarily by the winning of the next election, and when pursuit of this goal conflicts with idealized efficiency, the former will dominate over the latter. Nonetheless, mainstream economics continues to ignore public choice analysis, and therefore it leaves students with a false impression about the political process and its potential to promote the efficient use of resources.

2. *The democratic political process is short sighted, and, if unconstrained, it will lead to excessive debt.* As public choice analysis indicates, there will be a strong incentive for political officials to favor policies that generate highly visible current benefits at the expense of costs that are less visible and observable mostly in the future. This incentive structure explains why politicians will find debt financing and unfunded promises highly attractive. Policies of this type will make it possible for them to provide voters with visible benefits that will enhance their chances of winning the next election, while concealing the cost and pushing its most observable components into the future.

As the dominance of Keynesian economics undermined the balanced budget paradigm during the 1960s and 1970s, James Buchanan and Richard Wagner used the tools of public choice to explain that this would lead to perpetual budget deficits.[5] While politicians have a strong incentive to spend money providing "goodies" to voters, they will be reluctant to levy taxes because this imposes a more visible cost. Borrowing provides politicians with an alternative: it allows them to spend now and push the visible taxes into the future. This is also the case with unfunded promises of future benefits like those of Social Security and Medicare. Like borrowing, unfunded promises of future benefits make it possible for politicians to take credit for the promised benefits now without having to levy the equivalent current taxes.

The historic record is consistent with the Buchanan-Wagner view. During the past 52 years, the federal government of the United States has run 47 budget deficits, but only five surpluses. During fiscal years 2009–2012, nearly 40% of federal expenditures were financed by borrowing. The federal debt has grown to levels not seen since WWII. Unless the incentive structure is changed—for example, by requiring a two-thirds or three-fourths majority to approve spending measures or additional borrowing—the

[5] See Buchanan JM, Wagner R (1977) *Democracy in Deficit: The Political Legacy of Lord Keynes*. Academic Press, New York, for a detailed analysis of the Keynesian Revolution and why acceptance of the Keynesian paradigm will lead to excessive debt and financial troubles.

experience of Greece indicates that politicians are unlikely to bring spending under control until the situation reaches crisis proportions.

Currently, budget deficits are pushing government debt to dangerously high levels in several countries. Public choice analysis explains why this is happening and what might be done about it. In contrast, because it ignores the shortsighted nature of the unconstrained political process, mainstream economics sheds little or no light on the forces underlying budget deficits, growth of government debt, and the presence of unsustainable transfer programs. Hence, the omission of public choice from the mainstream perspective renders it largely irrelevant for the understanding of the major economic issues confronting countries throughout the world.

3. *Like markets, unconstrained political democracy has deficiencies. The special interest effect and rent seeking are particularly important sources of political inefficiency.* Public choice analysis indicates that political officials will have a strong incentive to favor the position of well-organized interest groups receiving concentrated benefits at the expense of costs that are not easily identifiable and spread thinly over the vast majority of voters. Typical voters will have little incentive to invest the time and effort necessary to inform themselves on many issues because they will recognize that their vote will not be decisive. Thus, most will be uninformed on the overwhelming bulk of issues. In contrast, well-organized interest groups will often feel strongly about policies that serve their interests and therefore be willing to provide politicians supportive of their policies with campaign contributions and other political resources. As a result, elected political officials will have a strong incentive to support the position of special interests, acquire political resources from them, and then use the resources to run campaign ads and solicit the support of the largely uninformed electorate. This will be the case even if the programs favored by the special interests are counterproductive. The empirical evidence is highly consistent with this analysis. The popularity of tariffs, quotas, business and agricultural subsidies, ethanol mandates, targeted tax breaks, and bailouts of specific industries and highly unionized firms is largely a reflection of the special interest effect.

Favoritism provides politicians with something they can trade for political support. In turn, businesses and other interest groups will seek to obtain more government favoritism via lobbying, campaign contributions, and other forms of schmoozing political decision makers. Economists use the term "rent seeking" to describe such actions designed to secure the windfall gains and above-normal profits generated by government favoritism.[6] Rent seeking is a natural outgrowth of

[6] Gordon Tullock conducted the pioneering research on rent seeking. In a classic 1967 article, Tullock illustrated that tariffs, quotas, government grants of monopoly, subsidies, and other forms of government favoritism generated rent seeking costs over and above the deadweight losses highlighted by the static neoclassical model. See Gordon Tullock (1967) The Welfare Cost of Tariffs, Monopolies, and Theft. *West Econ J* 5(3):224–232.

government activism. When the government is heavily involved in the granting of contracts, subsidies, tax credits, low-interest loans, regulatory favors, and other forms of government intervention, business firms, labor organizations, and other well-organized interests will compete for the government favors. The result will be a shift of resources away from productive activities and into rent seeking. Economic inefficiency will increase, and growth and prosperity will slow. Rather than the ideal outcomes of the naïve mainstream models, rent seeking, crony capitalism, and political corruption will emerge.

Implications of the Imbalanced Mainstream View

The tools of economics enhance our understanding of both the market and political processes. They indicate that both have various types of shortcomings—that there is both market failure and government failure. Most mainstream principles courses cover market failure in the form of economic instability, monopoly, externalities, and public goods. Potential ideal solutions to market failures are also provided. But, coverage of government failure is absent. Government failures resulting from the shortsightedness effect, the special interest effect, and rent seeking are ignored. Instead, government action is treated as a corrective device. The real world of markets is always compared with idealized government action. In the world of mainstream economics, market failure is a likely possibility, but there is no such thing as government failure. This asymmetric and imbalanced coverage leaves students with an unrealistic and distorted view of how the political process works and the potential of government activism to allocate resources efficiently.

The imbalance of the mainstream approach also deters understanding of the current economic situation. Economics provides considerable insight on the structure of the institutional and policy environment consistent with growth and prosperity. Stable and predictable policies, rule of law, and economic freedom establish the foundation for gains from trade, private investment, and innovation, which are the key sources of the growth process. In contrast, persistent policy changes, temporary tax and spending policies, and discretionary regulatory action generate uncertainty and play into the hands of the rent-seeking special interests. Public choice analysis highlights both of these points. However, because of its omission of public choice, mainstream economics misses the fundamental causal forces underlying the excessive debt, constant policy changes, and crony capitalism that are undermining prosperity throughout the world.

Conclusion: The Need to Complete the Public Choice Revolution

The public choice revolution is incomplete. It has exerted an impact on a segment of the economics profession and provided insight about how the political process works. It explains the forces underlying today's major economic issues: budget deficits, unsustainable growth of government debt, unfunded pension and transfer programs, political favoritism and inefficient special interest spending, and movement of resources away from productive activities into rent seeking. It also provides insight concerning structural changes that would help address these problems. In contrast, mainstream economics provides neither understanding nor direction concerning how to avoid the troubled waters ahead. The bulk of the economics profession continues to ignore public choice analysis, and it is almost totally absent from most principles texts. As a result, the mainstream approach is leaving both current students and the general public with a misleading, false, and romantic view of government and the operation of the democratic political process.

Clearly, public choice analysis and the work of scholars like Buchanan and Tullock are just as relevant today as they were four decades ago. Hopefully, a new generation of economists will grasp this point and complete the public choice revolution. There are a couple of reasons for cautious optimism. First, a set of 20 Voluntary National Content Standards for Economics has been developed by the Council for Economic Education (formerly the National Council on Economic Education), the National Association of Economic Educators, and the Committee on Economic Education of the American Economic Association.[7] These standards are designed to reflect the current status of scholarship in the discipline. They were updated in 2010 and approved by the AEA Committee on Economic Education. The standards cover the role of property rights, entrepreneurship, and dynamic competition, topics that often receive little attention in principles courses. More important from a public choice perspective, the standards cover both market failure (Standard 16) and government failure and special interest politics (Standard 17). This indicates that when economists think seriously about the content of a balanced course in modern principles of economics, they recognize that sound analysis requires examination of the operation of both markets and the political process.

Second, there has been a virtual explosion of literature that is now referred to as the new institutional economics during the past two decades. In contrast with the derivation of optimal conditions under restrictive assumptions that characterizes so much of modern economics, the new institutional approach focuses on comparative analysis. Building on the work of Nobel laureates Friedrich Hayek and Douglass North, the methodology of the new institutional economics examines how alterna-

---

[7] See Council for Economic Education (2010) *Voluntary National Content Standards in Economics*. Council for Economic Education, New York.

tive forms of economic, political, and legal institutions impact the performance of economies. Leading contributors to this literature include Daron Acemoglu of MIT, Robert Barro, Edward Glaeser, James Robinson, Dani Rodrik, and Andrei Shleifer of Harvard, Xavier Sala-i-Martin of Columbia, Oliver Williamson of the University of California, Berkeley, and Barry Weingast of Stanford. Several of the important articles were published in the premier journals of the profession, including the *American Economic Review*, *Quarterly Journal of Economics*, and the *Journal of Economic Literature*. Thus, this literature and its methodology are penetrating the elite schools and journals to a greater extent than has been the case for public choice analysis. Hopefully, the wider professional acceptance of the comparative approach will pave the way for greater integration of public choice into mainstream economics.

Economic analysis is equally applicable to market and political decision-making. It indicates that there is both market failure and government failure. It is long past time that this realism be incorporated into mainstream economics. George Stigler once remarked that a person who considers only market failure is like the judge of a singing contest, who immediately declares the second contestant the winner after hearing the performance of the first.[8] This is precisely what happens when mainstream economics treats government as a corrective device and continues to exclude public choice analysis. It is time for the profession to consider the second singer.

[8] See Tregarthen T, Rittenberg L (2000) *Economics*, 2nd edn. Worth Publishers, New York, p 304.

Chapter 14
The Calculus of Consent, Fifty Years Later: A Personal Tribute to James Buchanan and Gordon Tullock

Richard B. McKenzie

Any celebration of the substantial and esteemed academic careers of James Buchanan and Gordon Tullock must try to cover their scholarship, both together and separately. I use "try to cover" because full coverage is virtually an impossibility, given how voluminous their scholarly records are. However, I am quite confident that other contributors to this volume will make admirable efforts to make a credible coverage, with special attention, of course, given to their groundbreaking classic work, *The Calculus of Consent*, which changed the way so many people around the world assess government policymaking. They changed people's assessments in a very simple way, by breaking with the then entrenched tradition in economics, political science, and law of assuming that people operating in the political sphere were fundamentally different from people operating in their private spheres. When people moved from the private to the public spheres, they changed their motivations in some fundamental way, shifting from serving their *private interests* to serving in much more laudable ways the *public interest*. That was the norm in thinking before Buchanan and Tullock and a handful of other public choice thinkers.

Buchanan and Tullock dared to assume the exact opposite, that the motivations of people inside and outside of government are more or less the same. People in both the political and private spheres are necessarily drawn from the same pool and, as a consequence, must have at some fundamental level much the same elevated and degenerate motivations to improve their own lives and the lives of mankind. With that unifying assumption, Buchanan and Tullock focused their analysis on how the

---

Richard McKenzie is the Walter B. Gerken Professor Emeritus of Enterprise and Society in the Paul Merage School of Business at the University of California, Irvine. He was a Ph.D. student at Virginia Tech from 1969 to 1972.

R.B. McKenzie (✉)
Paul Merage School of Business, University of California,
3 Owen Court, Irvine, CA 92617, USA
e-mail: mckenzie@uci.edu

D.R. Lee (ed.), *Public Choice, Past and Present: The Legacy of James M. Buchanan and Gordon Tullock*, Studies in Public Choice 28, DOI 10.1007/978-1-4614-5909-5_14,

differences in the institutional settings affected decision making in the public and private spheres. Change the features of either institutional setting, public or private, and the efficiency and welfare outcomes could be expected to change with some predictability.

I will leave it to other contributors to this volume to discuss and expand on Buchanan's and Tullock's many scholarly contributions on constitutional constraints, decision rules, organizational structures, and other areas that emerge from this key twist in the founding assumptions about people's unity of motivations. In this chapter, I want to offer a more personal tribute to these two giants of our academic time for what they contributed to my work and to the work of so many others. These contributions may never be known to all those who have only read, and will read far into the future, their scholarly works at a distance from the academic aura that surrounded them jointly and separately and that so many of us were able to bask in and gain from being their students and colleagues.

A Near Miss and a Close Encounter

To understand exactly why I feel such a personal debt to Buchanan and Tullock, you must first grasp the circumstances under which I fell within their orbit. First, you must understand that I was never a good student in economics. I began a teaching career at Radford College in the mid-1960s with only a master's degree, granted somewhat grudgingly to me by the economics department at the University of Maryland, with the faculty at the time dominated by devoted Keynesians. (I say my faculty committee "grudgingly" awarded my degree because they strongly suggested that I *not* apply to their Ph.D. program.)

At Maryland, I remember being drilled in Dudley Dillard's, Charles Schultz's, and Barbara Bergman's classes on John Maynard Keynes' solutions for the ills of the business cycle. Their classes were filled with part-time students who in real life slaved away in the halls of bureaucracies in nearby Washington, DC Their classes were also filled with the then conventional macroeconomic graphs, the so-called Keynesian cross, the liquidity trap, and the Phillips curve. The students were abuzz with how macro-instability was nothing short of a *la grande failure* of the market system. I learned well how the macroeconomy could gravitate toward a less-than-full-employment equilibrium and how added savings could sink the economy further. The "paradox of saving" was revealed truth. I also learned how government could come to the rescue by being the buyer of last resort, which necessarily meant deficit spending that had no limits, at least not in the theory purveyed. After all, I was assured, "We owe the public debt to ourselves." Proof of the efficacy of Keynesian fiscal magic was shown in theory by assuming "multipliers" of 10 and even 20 – really! (Keynes himself assumed a multiplier of 10!) The then widely accepted "balanced-budget norm" was fiscal folly to, I would dare to say, everyone on the faculty, chosen with some care by the chair of the economics department and one of the first Keynesian devotees, Dudley Dillard.

In more advanced classes on comparative economic systems (which focused almost exclusively on central economic planning methods), I learned the various ways by which aggregate demand could be matched with aggregate supply by changing production quotas at the industry level and by altering the income distribution. Nationalization of industries was an accepted mechanism for ensuring the workability of central economic planning. In Allan Gruchy's class on comparative economic systems, the efficacy of planning was never an issue; the only issue worthy of our classroom and scholarly attention was that of which form of planning the United States and other countries should adopt (e.g., the "indicative planning" of France or the more involved and detailed central planning of the Soviet Union). The development of guiding national input/output tables, with an unbelievably elaborate grid filled with input/output coefficients, was seen by Gruchy and others in the department as the highest of intellectual challenges, and of course there was great faith that such a matrix could be made to work, if only the "right" coefficients could be found.

I don't recall anyone ever mentioning the inherent problems of planning, for example, where and how the central planners would get the data they needed to do their jobs or how the coefficients in the input/output table could be adjusted to fit ever-changing technologies. Similarly, I don't recall anyone ever questioning how politics might muck up the best-laid Keynesian yearly fiscal plans or the longer term and more detailed 5- and 10-year central plans. (Mancur Olson was not yet on the Maryland faculty.) Everyone seemed to believe that all problems of macroeconomics and central planning could be reduced to that of educating enough policymakers and economists on the dictates of Keynesian and central planning theory and handing over to the informed and elite policymakers and politicians the power to do their jobs, most notably that of dampening, if not eliminating, the business cycles, which were holding back economic growth through their effects on aggregate investment. Dispensing with the balanced-budget norm could be seen as nothing short of a social good for the times and all future times. The breaking of such a fiscal constraint could only promote growth because it would permit wise men in the seats of fiscal power to stabilize the macroeconomy.

No matter how absurd this course of study now seems (thanks in large measure to Buchanan and Tullock), I bought into the intellectual menu that was dished out at Maryland and went off to teach what I had learned at Radford College, at the time an all-women's state school 18 miles from Virginia Tech in Blacksburg. My heavy teaching load (5 classes a quarter, or 20 a year) at Radford was dominated with courses in macroeconomics and comparative systems.

And yes, I was at the time, the mid- to late 1960s, a disciple for Keynes (and his surrogates at Maryland). My lectures were filled with Keynes' critiques of "classical economics" and with all the graphical tools learned at Maryland. I framed Keynesian theory with multipliers of ten or greater. And would you believe, I also took my Maryland training a step further by developing a course during my second year of teaching around John Kenneth Galbraith's *The New Industrial State*, which was released in 1967. Yes, I was also a devotee of Galbraithism, which is to say that I saw all of the country's economic and social ills emanating from the stranglehold that the country's 500 largest corporations had on the private and public sectors and would continue to have for the indefinite future. How wrong could Galbraith be, and how wrong could I be in buying into, hook, line, and sinker, Galbraith's demagogic view of the economic world?

My lectures were filled with how government policy could be the savior of much that ills mankind. I suspect that Keynesianism became the rage within the economics profession simply because it offered all adherents (me included) a sense of having an elevated role in society, that of leading the masses to the ways of economic salvation. We no longer had to reserve our intellectual firepower for trying to figure how the economy worked or, maybe, just how people went about improving their own lots in life, which as Friedrich Hayek showed was a daunting task at best. We could offer real cures for all others, if only they would listen.

In my third year of teaching, I remember how after lecturing on Keynes' objections to classical economics, I told my students, "Maybe one of these days we will also learn that Keynesian economics is as intellectually bankrupt as Keynes knew classical economics to be." I did not know at the time how prescient, in a few short years, my words would become (or how in contemporary times Keynesianism would be brought back from the dead as the hope for saving the country from the Great Recession).

In the fall of 1969, I joined the newly organized Ph.D. program at Virginia Tech for none of the right reasons and for all of the wrong reasons. After my first 3 years of teaching at Radford, I knew I wanted to make teaching – not researching and writing – my career. I did not need a Ph.D. to gain tenure at the time at Radford – all I needed to do there was to continue breathing for a total of 7 years (and not make overtures to the female students). Radford actively discouraged research on the grounds that it took time away from teaching duties, which, at the time, was just the way I liked it. I went back for my Ph.D. because Radford offered to pay me half salary for each year I was enrolled. With a teaching assistantship at Virginia Tech, I would lose little in the way of income. Having a Ph.D. would also make it a little easier to advance through the professor ranks at Radford. In short, I wanted my union card. Learning additional economics was decidedly secondary. Learning how to think about microeconomic issues was tertiary at best. I did not plan a career of thinking, researching, and writing. I wanted to teach, period.

I did not choose Virginia Tech because Buchanan and Tullock joined the faculty there the year I joined the Ph.D. program. I really didn't care who they were or what they taught. And, really, I did not know of their reputations. I wanted only to specialize in subdisciplines within economics that would be useful back at Radford, which were international economics and monetary economics. I had no interest in public finance or public choice economics that were Buchanan's and Tullock's strong suits, and I did not take their courses in those areas. Their courses were simply not key to my limited career aspiration, at the time, which was to return to Radford and have a "professor chips" career, affecting in some way the professional and personal lives of the students in my classes.

As you might have guessed by now, separately and together, Buchanan and Tullock literally turned my professional life around, abruptly and totally (but in distinctly different ways, as I will explain). How did the turnaround happen? Let me explain Buchanan's and Tullock's separate impacts and, in doing that, draw out the commonalities in their approach to professoring and in their influence, which go beyond their published works.

Professor Buchanan's Impact

My good fortune was that in the fall that I joined the Virginia Tech Ph.D. program, Buchanan was assigned to teach microeconomics, or rather his version of microeconomics. He didn't teach from any required textbook. He expected us to absorb Armen Alchian and William Allen's *University Economics* independent of class assignments and lectures. His main admonition to the class on the first day was for us to learn everything in the Alchian and Allen book. If we did, we would be well prepared for any future preliminary examination in microeconomic, he assured us. He then held up a manuscript copy of Gary Becker's forthcoming book, *Economic Theory*, and said he might be drawing lecture points from that book. I immediately wrote Becker, asking for a copy, which, surprisingly, he sent in short order.

Buchanan's main teaching methods were twofold. First, he would come to class and pose a problem that was central to his writing at the time. As I remember, he spent more than three classes discussing a paper in which he and Charles Goetz were trying to challenge the conventional view of the distorting effects of monopoly. He would use class time to work his way through the problem at hand, asking us, the 25 or so students in the class, to think with him and, if possible, to outthink him or guide his thinking. In the main, he allowed us to see his mind at work on defining the problem at hand and then trying to turn conventional analysis on its head. As he and we students grappled with the problem, we could feel his struggle and came to understand how doing good research required mental dedication and gymnastics, or else the problem at hand might not be worth tackling. He also showed us how he was open to our help (indeed, encouraged our help), which came with the implied message that we could take up the struggle with him and then take up other struggles with problems of our own.

For me, I learned that scholarly work was something of an academic Easter egg hunt. There was some potential pain in the hunt itself, but then there was some obvious delight to be had when "eggs" were found. Ever since his class, I've always seen economics as thinking explorations, which always start with a lot of unknowns and can sometimes end with discoveries of new thoughts that might never have been seen had the struggle never been taken up. I left his class constantly puzzling over so much around me, whether out in the backyard gardening, riding a bike, or standing in line at grocery stores.

Buchanan's second major teaching method was old fashioned, probably adopted from his mentor Frank Knight. Buchanan assigned weekly papers that by and large involved economic puzzles for which he did not always have a ready-made solution. Let me give you two examples of his paper assignments. First, I can remember to this day his first assigned topic, which went something like this: "Robert Mundell starts the preface of his new book, *Man and Economics*, with the claim, 'Economics is a science of choice.' My question to you is simply this, Is it?" The topic blew my mind (as well as the minds of everyone else in the class) – at first. I was even more perplexed because I had started every course I had taught to that point in my career with the conventional claim that scarcity was at the foundation of economics, and the fact of ever-present scarcity meant that choices were unavoidable, which made costs, whether overt or covert, ever present. That meant choices were omnipresent. Of course, I *knew* that economics was a science in that its methods mated hypotheses and empirical evidence. My first thought was to wonder how Mundell could possibly be wrong, but then my second thought was that had the statement been as solidly correct as I had made it out to be in all of my past opening lectures, Buchanan would not have asked us to question it. In my consuming work on that paper during the first week, I couldn't help but take apart the claim, eventually asking, what is meant by "science"? "Choice"? When those questions are posed, the potential inherent internal contradiction in Mundell's claim surfaces. *Real choices*, founded on subjective evaluations of local conditions of individuals, would prove difficult, if not impossible to predict, and if they could be predicted, then presumed choices might not be real choices at all, maybe only the illusion of choices.

While Buchanan had serious reservations about predicting *choices* per se, my second example of Buchanan's paper assignments reveals how Buchanan was convinced that given people's choices in terms of real goods bought or sought, the directional changes in people's behavior could be predicted within limits by a single economic principle, the *law of demand*, that was, more or less, broadly applicable.

That fall, government-mandated and subsidized flood insurance was all the rage in national policy circles. The controversy over what to do was almost as controversial, albeit on a smaller scale, than Obamacare is today. As best I can remember, the critical concern in the media and congressional debate was largely restricted to the fairness of more government subsidies and the impact of the government intrusion on individual liberty. Buchanan asked us to do what would not have occurred at the time to the professors I had at Maryland. He asked that we write one of our weekly papers on the economic consequences of subsidies, before he had said anything in class about moral hazard and adverse selection, concepts which are seen today as crucial to economic thinking on so many issues, but which I had never heard mentioned in my Maryland classes or read in the several introductory textbooks from which I taught.

In effect, Buchanan asked us to discover those concerns and to ferret out their relevance both to the issue of people individually buying flood insurance and to the issue of people in flood-prone areas receiving flood-insurance subsidies. I still remember the joy of stumbling upon the concepts of moral hazard and adverse selection and then being able to see how subsidies affect people's proclivity to build in flood-prone areas and how the subsidized flood-insurance benefits could be capitalized into the value of properties subject to intermittent floods, which means that all gains to the stream of flood-insurance subsidies into the relevant future could be effectively eliminated for all future property owners as those benefits were capitalized into the prices of flood-prone properties.

That fall semester, we didn't so much learn economics as we learned to *think* about economic problems of all sorts. We also learned a critical lesson, at least for me, that conventional wisdom, no matter how entrenched, was subject to challenge. Indeed, searching for ways to challenge conventional wisdom, even turning it on its head, could give life to our work and, by the way, make economics fun. Discovering counterintuitive arguments became for me the Holy Grail of my life's work. To the end of my teaching career, I gave the flood-insurance problem to my students in my microeconomics courses.

I also took from Buchanan's class a lesson he took from his classes with Frank Knight, that is, to hold respect for authority at a distinct distance. Be ready to dispute the simplest of conventional claims. Indeed, widely repeated conventional wisdoms are a gold mine for scholarly papers. Even by the late 1960s, Mundell was a notable economist (he won the Nobel Prize in 1999), but he was not above challenge. Moreover, I learned that semester that economics can be as much about philosophy and methodology as it is about drawing on accepted modeling – no, more so, a lesson that was more deeply embedded in my way of doing economics when I discovered that semester that Buchanan had recently published his *Cost and Choice*, which I digested before the term was over.

In so many prior classes I had had as an undergraduate and graduate student, professors had literally slopped their way through their lectures, droning on as if they had not prepared for class, which was often true. We've all had professors who have expressed pride in not giving a damn about teaching or how they could write more papers if they were derelict in their classroom duties, both in and out of their classes. I was struck that first semester at Virginia Tech at how Buchanan conveyed the opposite message – that professoring was a privilege that came with obligations, a prominent one being to be prepared for class and have an open office door, with the expectation that students would come to class or his office at least somewhat prepared.

How did he convey those messages? First, by coming to class with pages of typed notes. Second, by rarely closing his door. Third, by actually writing comments on our papers, if he did not append one or two pages of typed comments. I was totally taken by his willingness to set aside whatever he was doing when I asked him if he had a moment.

Finally, all of us who have known Jim Buchanan understand that we have had an unheralded secret advantage in our careers over others from other universities: his willingness to read our postgraduation works promptly and always with pages of typed comments appended to his marked up version of our papers that he would place on our desks (while we were still graduate students or, for me, when I returned to Virginia Tech for short teaching stints in the 1970s) or that he put in the mail in short order.

Buchanan was my dissertation director. Most dissertation directors can take weeks, if not months, to return first drafts of their students' dissertations. In my case, I vividly remember placing my first draft, which ran more than 250 manuscript pages, on his desk just before 5 PM one day, only to find Buchanan's marked up version, with an untold number of typed single-spaced pages of comments (on yellow onionskin paper, of course), on my desk in the basement of the Public Choice Center *the very next morning*!

After graduation in 1972, I took an assistant professorship at Appalachian State University. One of the side lessons I learned from being in the Virginia Tech program and from watching Buchanan, Tullock, and other professors in the Public Choice Center was the importance of thinking and writing, revealed in Buchanan's example, which meant that writing a half-dozen, or even a dozen, papers a year, plus a book or two, was not considered unusual and was more or less expected. When I settled in at ASU and started my career of churning out a stream of papers and books, I had an advantage on publication of my papers because I had Buchanan in my corner, giving generously of his time to review and comment on my work and all with unbelievable promptness. I would send Buchanan a paper, and he would have it back to me in no time at all, with pages of comments – long ago when papers and messages travel at the snail's pace of the post office. He was so prompt and predictable on getting papers back, that on any number of occasions, I would put one of my papers in a manila envelope addressed to Buchanan and then go to one of my colleagues and say something to this effect: "Notice that I am putting this paper in the mail to Jim Buchanan today. I am willing to bet you a cup of coffee that I will get this paper back with one or more single-spaced pages of comments a week from today." Without fail, I won the bets and had any number of cups of coffee off Buchanan's tireless generosity with his time and wisdom with a former student.

At one point, when I got back to Tech, I told Buchanan's longtime and revered assistant Betty Tillman how remarkable it was that he would get my papers back so promptly and with obvious attention to detail. I was struck by her reaction, "Honey, I hate to tell you this, but he doesn't just do it for you. He does it for everyone. There's hardly a day that goes by that he doesn't get at least one paper in for review, and he almost always has his comments written by the next morning." I have made my commentary a "personal tribute" because I don't think more than a handful of today's generation of economists have benefited from such ongoing help from their major professors.

I have to add that Buchanan's comments on my papers followed a somewhat predictable format. He would always start by saying something positive about the content, focusing on maybe how well the paper was written (if lost for positive comments on content). Having made me feel good, he would then add his incisive comments, which sometimes forced me to set the paper aside. But there was one time, on a paper of mine on "The Planned Obsolescence of the Constitution," he didn't start with his usual positive remark. He wrote to this effect: "Dear Dick, We all write good papers and bad papers. With some papers we pursue publication; with others, we trash them. In the process of writing any number of papers, we acquire great wisdom in deciding which papers are which. You will acquire great wisdom in deciding what to do with this paper." I didn't need for him to say more, which he didn't. I never tried to revise that paper.

At a conference at East Tennessee University organized in the early 1990s to celebrate Buchanan's Nobel Prize, all the speakers were asked to give papers on some aspect of the economics of education (especially economic education), with some tie to Buchanan's work. The opening line of my paper crystalized the importance of my serendipitously coming within Buchanan's orbit of influence: "When I was in Nobel Laureate James Buchanan's microeconomics class in the fall of 1969, he taught me very little. I say that with pride here in this August setting because Professor Buchanan would be the first among you to understand that I could not offer a higher compliment. He understands, as he got me to see, that the measure of good teaching is not how much you teach, but in how much is learned by students – and then how much can be done with what little is taught and learned. The first principle in economics principles should be economy in the principles covered." So true, so true, but a point about teaching that many professors never get. I've spent a career trying to equal Buchanan in how much my students can do at the end of their classes with me with the handful of principles – most notably, the law of demand – that I cover time and again with different problems I have assigned them.

At some point early in my microeconomics courses, I have started a lecture with a story. I tell my students, "In one of Professor Buchanan's classes, he was lecturing away on some esoteric theory. In the middle of the lecture, I raised my hand to say, 'But, Professor Buchanan, in the real world ...' at which point Professor Buchanan cut me off to say, 'Mr. McKenzie, the real world is a special case and therefore we need not consider it.'" My students usually burst out in laughter after which I try to relate the overarching lesson I learned from Buchanan's class: "It is true that there is humor in Professor Buchanan's comments, but there is also a great deal of wisdom. Today is a special case out there in the real world beyond the walls of this classroom. There will never be another day like it. Things are ever changing. Tomorrow will be another special case, and all following days will each be special cases. What we need to do in this course is to find ways of understanding the special cases that pass us by day by day. Principles of economics are a means for us to see at least some unity in the daily special cases. I'm hoping that we will devise or just cover in this class those relatively few principles that are as relevant to the special cases of your future days as they are to those of today. If all we do is take up a study of the details of the real world as we find it today (or the recent past), we will never finish the coverage of the details, because of the 'great buzzing confusion' of the full complexity of the real world as we find it today. There are simply too many details, almost all of which are irrelevant to what happens today, tomorrow, or the next day. So if you ever think what we do in here is 'unreal,' you are right – by intention. There will be an unreality to what we do in this course, but that is by design – and done in the hope that we will come to a better understanding of the flow of special cases in the real world than we could possibly achieve if we tried to understand the real world in its full complexity." I wish I could say that part of my initial lecture was original, but those few lines capture the essence of what Buchanan got me to see both during and after his class.

From Buchanan's course, I charted a new course for my career, that of becoming, to the best of my abilities, a contrarian economist.

The Dynamic (and Different) Duo

James Buchanan and Gordon Tullock were an odd academic couple, in that they differed so radically in the way they approached their scholarship. When I was in Virginia Tech's graduate program, I came to see Buchanan as the formal scholar, someone who strove to have the arguments and verbiage just right, the logic tight and correct. He was clearly Frank Knight's protégé, both in style and temperament, which still makes him proud. He came to the discipline of economics with hesitancy and reservations about what conventional economics could add to human knowledge, which is to say that he came to the discipline with discipline of thought. He was skeptical of empirical analysis because of the extent to which so much economic *data* was subjective, hardly as objective, and knowable, as the data in the hard sciences. Rocks and chemicals simply have no capacity to evaluate and, therefore, no capacity to make decisions that can change their behavior. Meteorites can't choose to change their courses and can't talk back to their observers.

Although he was an undergraduate math major, Buchanan sometimes would scoff at the then burgeoning hyper-mathematizing of economics and empirical work that seemed to be little more than data mining or, worse, leading to conclusions that were absurd on their faces. I remember that one assistant professor had published in an elite journal a highly mathematical proof that bisexuality was necessarily more efficient than heterosexuality (or homosexuality). Bisexuality offered more chances (maybe double the chances) for dates and, therefore, greater utility from dates. I'll never forget how in a hallway discussion of the paper, Buchanan listened quietly and then tersely destroyed the paper with the quip, "Yes, if we liked to eat rocks, we'd have an abundance of food everywhere."

Buchanan leaned more toward economic philosophy and methodology than he did to modeling (although *The Calculus of Consent* and his other books are filled with modeling) and certainly empiricism, with so much empiricism being a fig leaf for "scientism" (one of Hayek's choice put-downs for empirical work in the social sciences). To him, so much econometrics and, for that matter, mathematical economics proved only that water ran downhill. Buchanan seemed to recognize, as did Knight, that economics could only be a partial view of human behavior and therefore should be approached with some caution, if not skepticism over how much the discipline could contribute to our understanding of human behavior.

Tullock, on the other hand, was decidedly different. He did not come to economics as a trained economist, perhaps to his good fortune. He often boasted about how his formal economics training had been limited to one bad introductory course. But no matter, Buchanan probably accurately described Tullock one afternoon in the foyer of the Public Choice Center when he observed that Tullock was a "natural economist." That is to say, he (Tullock) saw *homo economicus* as more or less an accurate and largely complete description of human behavior (and, for that matter, pigeons, rats, ants, and termites). Cost/benefit analysis was a part of Tullock's DNA and, by extension, the DNAs of practically all species, to 1° or another.

I remember how, when the Public Choice Center was in the small framed white house near the duck pond on the Virginia Tech campus, I dared early in my first semester to interrupt Tullock one afternoon, challenging him on how he could be so cocksure that people could finely and accurately weigh off the costs and benefits in all choice situations and on all margins, only to get a short and sharp (maybe stern and somewhat playful) tutoring session on the economics of making economic cost/benefit calculations and how habits and mistakes had foundations in the cost/benefit calculus. And all readers of this volume are familiar with how Tullock throughout his career employed *homo economicus* to good effect on a host of topics, from voting to information gathering and to rent seeking, bureaucracy, and even to charity. While Buchanan was always the formal theorist, methodologist, and philosopher in search of something approximating Truth (or at least partial Truth in the form of "relatively absolute absolutes") concerning the human predicament and, like Frank Knight, was always on guard for the limits to the application of economic models, Tullock was the ever-pragmatic lawyer who was not so much in search of Truth as he was in search of arguments that would result in favorable verdicts from his peers in the economics profession.

Many who consider Tullock's work have noted how he has always been inclined to "think outside the box." The problem with that characterization for those of us who knew him is that he resisted being seen inside the "box," conventionally defined. He has always been a true economic maverick who has rejoiced in twisting the thinking of those who had found comfort inside professional boxes. And what remains so notable about his work is how seemingly minor twists in conventional economic thinking could have a profound and lasting effect. Consider his groundbreaking work on "rent seeking." His central contribution was to recognize that if there are economic rents to be gathered from government market intrusions or government spending, political entrepreneurs would compete for those rents, causing the dissipation of much, if not all, of the sought-after rents through the waste of real resources on lobbying, if not outright graft.

Consider also government farm subsidies. Conventional wisdom held that the subsidies would benefit those who received them into the indefinite future. In his work on the "transitionary gains trap," Tullock simply noted how the expected stream of subsidies would become capitalized into the price of, say, land, dissipating any net gains to future farmers who bought the land and, in the process, making the elimination of subsidies politically difficult at best. The concepts of rent seeking and transitionary gains traps have become so embedded in conventional economic thinking through mountains of journal articles built around them that many young economists today do not know their source.

Tullock's natural inclination to apply economics to any and all situations never came out more clearly (when I was around) than when one morning I stood in a group of professors and one or two other graduate students in the center hallway just outside Tullock's office, then located in the old president's house. The topic of discussion was the economic rationale for the regulation of automobile safety. Someone made the usual point that regulating the cars' brakes and headlights was consistent with government's fundamental duty to protect citizens from each other. If cars are required to have brakes and headlights, then drivers could avoid accidents and harm to others. Good enough for the assembled group, but not for Tullock who, after hearing the conversation from his desk, put down his Dictaphone to join the group and to observe that the case for regulating the *internal* safety of cars with requirements for, say, padded dashes, collapsible steering wheels, and air bags was far different than the case for the regulation of *external* safety of automobiles in the form of required brakes and headlights. He made a now commonly accepted point, "The regulation of internal car safety would lead to lower cost for reckless, high-speed, drunk driving, which would encourage such behaviors – and have the perverse effect of causing drivers to increase the harm done to each other, a perverse outcome, indeed."

We couldn't help but chuckle, thinking his comments were pure Tullock, but then he went where no other economist at that time would think to go: "I've got the right solution for government reducing the harm drivers do to each other: Have the government require the installation of daggers on steering wheels, positioned two inches from drivers' chests. How reckless would people then drive? Accidents would be reduced and lives would be saved" – end of story, except Nicolas Tiedemann (another "natural economist") was in the group.

Tiedemann paused for a moment and came back with the retort, "Gordon, I'm not so sure lives would be saved. Suppose you are driving along a main road in downtown Blacksburg with the dagger pointed at your chest. Now, suppose a young co-ed walks into the street, what are you going to do, slam on the brakes? Not likely, because of the potential for impelling yourself on the dagger. No, you would speed up so that when you hit the co-ed, you wouldn't jar the car!" Even Tullock had a good laugh on that one. I relate this story mainly because it reveals the extent to which Tullock encouraged venturesome thinking, even when the logic led to impractical deductions.

Tullock truly seemed unconcerned about setting a priori limits to the application of economic models. Rather, he seemed to operate with the view that the limits to economics were like *beauty* – he would know them when the conclusions no longer made sense. Buchanan seemed bounded in what ways or how he would use economics. He was prone to be cautious in the topics he would take up. Again, he convinced me that economics had to be a partial view of human behavior. Tullock seemed unbounded, willing to run headlong after any and every application of cost/benefit analysis. He was willing to work with economic logic only when it could be used to good effect with the professional jury he was addressing and content to leave the empirical work to others (consider his rent-seeking theory), but he was also willing to work with numbers (or have his graduate assistants work the numbers for him) when empirical work seemed needed to convince the "jury" of the rightness of his arguments. He convinced me that there was no topic I could not approach without some hope of obtaining insights via economic methods that I would not otherwise see. I must confess that in many of my writings I have taken on the role of the lawyer before a yet-to-be convinced "jury" (whether in professional or policy circles).

Buchanan and Tullock made for a very good team in the Public Choice Center for each other and, more importantly, for the graduate students who marveled at their individual voluminous contributions to the literature of several disciplines. We saw how Buchanan attempted to check Tullock in his free-wheeling approach to economics and showed us graduate students that issues of methodology and philosophy had important roles in the repertoire of good economists. At the same time, we saw how Tullock persisted in his "economic imperialism" in spite of criticisms and, in the process, showed us how economics could be fun and insightful when we least expected it.

Professor Tullock's Influence

Like Buchanan, Tullock was also alert for going counterculture when you least expected it. One afternoon, I was in the hallway of the Public Choice Center just outside Tullock's office with a handful of professors and graduate students, all taking up the conventional view of *science* and *economic science*, as laid out by, say, Milton Friedman. Theory was absolutely essential for guiding empirical research, so the conventional argument went, and theories that could not be empirically tested were of no value. After a lengthy interaction, Tullock did what he was priceless at doing. He emerged from his office to interrupt with quick comments that at first were baffling: "You have it all wrong. Theories that cannot be empirically verified might be some of the most important theories we can devise. If they provide meaningful insights that cannot be empirically tested (or verified), then there is no other way to come to those insights other than through those theories. Should we always ignore the value in the insights simply because the required data is unavailable or inaccessible?"

Over the years, I've tried Tullock's argument on my hard and soft science colleagues who, in a knee-jerk manner, have dismissed it. But after years of remembering Tullock's insertion into our conversation, I've had to come to a conclusion that I often came to when Tullock seemed to espouse an argument that initially seemed absurd: He's right – but, with Buchanan's influence, I couldn't help being on guard for the limitations of untestable theories.

After all, the before-mentioned theory on the optimality of bisexuality is not empirically testable, to my knowledge (care to divine people's solid data on sexual preferences and happiness?), but the analysis also makes for nonsense cloaked in the garb of first and second derivatives. Also, there is now a good chance the theories in physics that suggest the existence of a "multiverse" (or multiple universes) may never be testable simply because the many (potentially, an infinite number of) universes could be moving away from each other (and from our known universe) at speeds greater than the speed of light, which means there is now no known way of making contact with other universes. However, might not theories of the multiverse expand our understanding of the "world" we live in, even though it doesn't fit with conventional views of *science*? Besides, *evidence* in economics is always shaky at best, as long as the concern of economic theories is subjective evaluations of alternative courses of actions.

What I have found truly ironic about Gordon Tullock has been his insistence on applying the self-serving model of man, optimizing on every margin, without reference to any internal constraints such as morals. Tullock has been so persistent in applying economics everywhere that people might deduce that in his narrow perception of human behavior, he might believe his models, so much so that he models his own behavior with reference to his analytical models. However, I have to insist that Gordon Tullock, the "natural economist," is one of the most moral-bound human beings (set aside economists) I've ever met. His word is his bond, and his sense of morality defines the core of his nature. As evidence, I point to the fact that when he edited *Public Choice*, he paid for six subscriptions from personal funds on the grounds that he didn't want anyone to think he was misusing his editorial position for private benefit. Tullock might slough off his purchase decision as purely economic: The gain from not losing the respect of unknown others was simply greater than the personal cost of the subscriptions. I have to insist that he is wrong, wrong, wrong. He bought the subscriptions because it was the *right* thing to do. He has done too many *right* things by me to think that he models his own behavior after the economic models of man that he has so adeptly used in his analysis. (Gordon, I hear your objections, but you are just wrong on this one, unless you are willing to concede that rational people can be *internally* constrained by first principles, as Adam Smith insisted they are.)

My Divided Career Path and *The New World of Economics*

Readers might now understand why I came away from the Virginia Tech Ph.D. program with a bifurcated career path. On the one hand, I have written several articles and books on strictly methodological issues with the goal of understanding on my own terms what Buchanan understood about the limits of economics as a science and methodology for understanding human behavior. As a consequence of Buchanan's influence, when behavioral economists and psychologists began criticizing economics for its rationality foundations, with one behavioral psychologist writing a book titled *Predictably Irrational*, I had to take up the challenge and understand on my own terms why economists persisted in using rationality when evidence was mounting on "economic anomalies" and irrationalities. The result was my book *Predictably Rational?*, in which I grappled with the limits of behavioral economics and with the behavioral economists' criticisms of conventional economics. I came to understand that the growing body of evidence from behavioral economists that people are prone to irrationalities as validation of a long-held central point of economics, that human behavior is exceedingly complex, people's environments are exceedingly comply – all the more reason for economists to simplify their models by assuming people are, at some level, rational.

When I started work on this book, I took a trip to meet with Buchanan at his cabin home outside of Blacksburg to discuss possible themes in the book, with one of my better turns of words being something to the effect. If people were as rational as economists assume they are, then we would not have to explain rationality to them, or, for that matter, explore all the deductions that derive from the rationality premise." I spent 2 hour with Buchanan over a lunch of egg biscuits and ice tea. Dwight Lee reported later that Buchanan didn't understand why I stayed such a short time. He just didn't understand that, after 2 h, I was exhausted intellectually and physically just trying to keep up with him when he was 90 and the topic was mine, not his! He simply wore me out.

On the other hand, I have made a career out of applying economic models to one policy topic after another, starting with the economics of economic education in the 1970s to the economics of obesity, movie theater popcorn prices, and child welfare in more recent years. Readers might understand why Tullock, not Buchanan, was willing to team up with me to write *The New World of Economics*, which, when it was first published in the mid-1970s, made something of a splash in the college market for readers, for it was truly the first *Freakonomics*. Tullock and I took up the economics of a whole host of topics that, during the 1970s, most economics professors would not have thought came within the purview of their disciplines: the economics of marriage, divorce, riots and panics, dying, walking on the grass, and ants and termites. We even dared to take up the economics of sex – not prostitution, but sexual relationships between normal consenting adults. And in the volume, we tried to make the analysis accessible to the lowest level students and their professors. *The Wall Street Journal* even saw fit to carry a column – not just a book review – on the book on its op-ed page, featuring the graph we included on the supply and demand for normal sex by undergraduate students, as determined by questionnaire, which so happened to have an equilibrium price that, at the time, was close to the price of streetwalkers in Atlanta. (And don't ask how we determined the prices charged by Atlanta streetwalkers.)

Through writing that book with Tullock, I probably came to know how his mind works better than most of his other colleagues, and I certainly learned how to have fun with economics – and with limited effort. We finished the first edition of *The New World* in less than 6 months, mainly because we drew on papers that we had written individually over several years and that had not found a publication "home." The book was adopted the first year in more than 500 colleges and universities in the country, all the way from introductory classes in community colleges to Ph.D. classes in microeconomics at elite northeastern universities. The book went through five editions and was translated into five languages. We'd like to think that it has had at least some influence on the future of introductory economics, especially on the integration of public choice economics into conventional economics courses. And, incidentally, *The New World* was seen as so daring at the time that the acquisition editor at the stogy business and economics publisher Richard D. Irwin hid the book from the founder Richard D. Irwin. Sure enough, when he learned of the book's publication (or so I was told), he stormed into the acquisition editor's office to demand, "What the hell is this?" as he slammed the book down on the editor's desk. The editor quietly went to his files to pull out the adoption and sales reports. Irwin looked it over, smiled, and said quietly, "That's more than fine," after which he turned and left the office.

Because of the considerable success of *The New World*, another publisher asked Tullock and me to write a full-blown economics textbook that would differ substantially from the mold for textbooks laid down by Paul Samuelson in 1948. We were given considerable leeway to infuse the book with public choice theory. Somehow, Tullock and I agreed on what is now a mysterious split on the writing duties. I was to do the microeconomics sections, while (would you believe!) Tullock would do the macroeconomics sections, plus add in international and public choice economics. After waiting for months for his portion of the book manuscript, Tullock one morning flopped down on my desk his half, all 350 manuscript pages. I quickly went through the pages, but there was an obvious problem that I had to bring to Tullock's attention the next day. I went into his office to sheepishly tell him, "Gordon, do you realize that you only have four-and-a-half manuscript pages on Keynesian economics?" Nothing was ever more telling about the tremendous gulf in the graduate program at Maryland and Virginia Tech than Tullock's snarled response, "Agreed, but tell me something important I've left out!" I had to agree, but I also insisted that the book would never be published if the Keynesian section were not expanded, at least somewhat. Knowing his resistance to giving Keynes any more respect, I ultimately expanded the Keynesian sections and did so significantly, drawing on what I had remembered from my Maryland days, not what I had added to my Keynesian repertoire during my Virginia Tech days (which was little to none, other than what was wrong with Keynesianism). However, you must know that the Keynesian analysis was infused with public choice points, not the least of was that even if Keynesianism made for good economics, which we noted was problematic, it could make for terrible politics, given that it broke the "balanced-budget norm," a point that Buchanan and Richard Wagner made in their book published in the mid-1970s, *Democracy and Deficits,* which is one of their more unheralded and prescient fiscal arguments of all times, given the recent failures of so many European economies and the downgrade of the United States' credit ratings for the excessive buildup of public debt. The textbook was released in the late 1970s under the title of *Modern Political Economy*, which enables me to say that I have published far more pages with Gordon Tullock than any other economist, including Jim Buchanan.

Many professors on personnel committees attest that textbooks should not, and do not, count for much more than a cup of coffee in promotion reviews. Yet, *The New World* opened up my career in two major ways. First, I became associated with Tullock, which means that for more than two decades I could bask in the aura of his growing professional prominence and, by association and to a lesser extent, in Buchanan's professional achievements.

Second, it gave me some name recognition that opened my career path to an expanding array of professional opportunities that I would not have had if *The New World* had never been published. Although my colleagues at the University of California, Irvine, would likely deny that *The New World* had any influence on their decision to hire me in 1991, I am totally confident that it did, if not directly, then surely indirectly as it gave me a host of publishing opportunities I would not have had. Perhaps just as importantly, I had Tullock in my corner, always willing to give me more credit for *The New World* than I deserved with everyone who brought up the book with him and to offer prompt reviews on a mountain of papers I wrote and sent him in the 1970s, 1980s, and 1990s.

And *The New World* has once again risen from the ashes. Because of the stunning sales success of *Freakonomics*, a publisher asked us to radically revise and update *The New World* for new generations of economics students. It came out in a sixth edition in 2012. The new edition can't possibly meet with the same market success as the first edition, mainly because the expansive application of economic thinking is no longer the novelty that it was in the 1970s, but we will see. What is remarkable is that *The New World of Economics* has had a "second coming" after a hiatus of more than two decades, a feat that I don't think has been duplicated by any other contemporary book designed for economics classrooms.

By the way, Tullock also had my dissertation back to me with comments within 24 h after I had given it to him. His chief comment was, "Minimal but acceptable," to which I responded, "That's optimal!" He retorted, "Well, you're right there," an open concession he rarely made with graduate students.

Concluding Comments

My experience at Virginia Tech within the intellectual orbit of James Buchanan and Gordon Tullock was truly transformative for my career aspiration and path. Before going there, I just wanted to get by as an obscure but well-intended teacher in an equally obscure teaching-college outpost. Afterward, I felt compelled to set publishing standards that, while sought with due diligence, ultimately were beyond my reach. Nonetheless, the effort was worthwhile, more so than anyone would have thought possible before my graduate stint at Virginia Tech.

But I must confess, my time within the Buchanan/Tullock orbit was a challenge of trying to reconcile their disparate approaches to economics. Being in the graduate program at Virginia Tech was probably what it would have been like for physics students who had an opportunity to be in a think tank organized around Albert Einstein, the founder of general relativity physics, and Niels Bohr, a founder of quantum physics, two views of the physical world that have yet to be reconciled or unified. Both approaches have been very useful for their respective uses but at the same time much at odds. The same can be said of Buchanan's and Tullock's separate approaches to economics. I can only surmise that Buchanan has remained uncomfortable with Tullock's and others' (including my) relentless extensions of economics to areas of human behavior in which trading by distant parties is of little consequence. But yet, he has had to concede that Tullock, in his unchecked intellectual ways with economic models, has had substantial influence through a continuous flow of insights so many other more constrained theorists never noticed.

I must also confess as I close, my experience within the Buchanan/Tullock orbit has been both the boon and bane of my career. The boon part is obvious. I changed my career goals and became an overachiever, due in no small way to the scholarly and professional standards set by Buchanan and Tullock.

The bane part is not so obvious but derived from the same source, the scholarly and professional standards set by Buchanan and Tullock, along with the contributions to the collegial interactions of the faculty in residence at the center. I came to believe that good teaching, as well as good scholarship, was a professional duty and that interacting with and mentoring students was a duty for professors. I grew to assume that professors everywhere would be in their offices most hours of the day and interact on a daily basis as did the professors in the center. I came to assume that colleagues everywhere would at least come close to doing what Buchanan and Tullock did, review papers promptly and add perceptive insights for improvement. I came to believe that writing six or even twelve publishable papers, and a book or two, was the norm. Moreover, I came to believe the critical component of papers was good and interesting *ideas*, which trumped by a large margin the names of the journals where they were published. No doubt about it, the more prestigious the journal, the better for the publication, but we all had a clear understanding that elite journals regularly published papers deficient in good ideas. A transformative idea might have to be released in a low-ranking journal simply because it was transformative and couldn't be reconciled with conventional wisdom that all too often walls out good ideas that are disruptive to conventional wisdom. Tullock's creation of the journal *Public Choice* was an ingenious strategic move to circumvent the walled garden of the then conventional thought in economics, political science, and law.

I consider my chapter a "personal tribute" to Buchanan and Tullock for the enormous work they did to structure an intellectual environment in which so many others, me included, could flourish and do economics outside the walled garden.

The bane part of the Buchanan/Tullock orbit for me, however, comes from the fact that I spent a career trying to find academic environments in which I and others could recapture the interactive and synergetic intellectual environment that was found at the center. I recaptured something of that environment in my short stint in the early to mid-1970s at Appalachian State University, not so much from being around similarly thinking economists but by being able to interact with professors from several disciplines who had disparate views on everything but who were willing to work through and try to understand and appreciate their – or, rather, our –disciplinary differences. I recaptured something of the center environment again for the first half-dozen years of my tenure at Clemson from the late 1970s to the early 1980s, during which department members, led by the spunky Hugh Macaulay and the more reserved Bruce Yandle, who provided the sort of moral leadership Buchanan and Tullock did, had wonderful, exciting, knockdown policy arguments over morning coffee. There, prompt review of colleagues' papers was expected. As a consequence, we all accomplished more in scholarship than should have been expected.

I spent the rest of my career trying to recreate the magical time we had at Virginia Tech, with only limited success. When I expressed my frustrations over not being able to recapture the environment to a former Clemson colleague, he offered wisdom, "Remember, Richard, we had those good times. Many younger faculty members don't really know what they are missing." His comment made me realize my good fortune in having passed for a time through the Buchanan/Tullock orbit at the Center for the Study of Public Choice. They created magic out of hard work and dedication to task, something that all those out there who admire their separate and joint written works from afar cannot fully appreciate.

Chapter 15
James M. Buchanan and Gordon Tullock: A Reflection on Two Disruptive Economists

Bruce Yandle

Introduction

Each of us is shaped in our work and life by powerful people and their ideas as we encounter them in our formative years. As academics, we are sometimes said to stand on the shoulders of those who came before us, suggesting that we might be able to see more and further than those who lifted us up. James M. Buchanan and Gordon Tullock had a powerful influence on my work and life. They affected not just my work but how I attempted to live as a member of the academy. But as to standing on shoulders, I hasten to say that I would never claim to have seen more or to have seen further than either of these two intellectual giants.

Buchanan and Tullock entered my life when I began graduate studies in economics in 1967 at Georgia State University. I was 34 years old when I started my graduate work. I had not been in a classroom for more than a decade. In a few words, I was totally ignorant of what was going on in economics, of who was doing what, what might be considered to be important, and why all this even mattered. I had been in business for 15 years. Such academic concerns never entered my mind during those years. This was obviously not the case with my faculty, and they generously and sometimes painfully introduced me to the wonderful world of economics. Part of that introduction focused on *The Calculus of Consent* 1962, just out in 1962, and other path-breaking work that was emerging from the pens of Buchanan and Tullock. Their joint and individual work became critically important in research and writing that I did as a doctoral student and throughout my career.

On taking a faculty position at Clemson University, I was fortunate to have a senior colleague who pointed the way for me and taught me a lot of applied price theory. Professor Hugh H. Macaulay became my mentor and then coauthor. As good luck would have it, Macaulay was well acquainted with Buchanan and Tullock,

B. Yandle (✉)
Clemson University, 100 Clemson Street, Clemson, SC 29631, USA
e-mail: yandle@bellsouth.net

D.R. Lee (ed.), *Public Choice, Past and Present: The Legacy of James M. Buchanan and Gordon Tullock*, Studies in Public Choice 28, DOI 10.1007/978-1-4614-5909-5_15,

admired their work, and was active in the new budding field of public choice. The association with Hugh reinforced the Buchanan-Tullock imprint already forming on my work and life.

I was fortunate again to take a Washington assignment in 1976–1977 working with James C. Miller III, a University of Virginia Ph.D. and Buchanan-Tullock devotee. Jim Miller had been a member of my Georgia State dissertation committee and was at the time leading a small group of White House economists who were engaged in reviewing federal regulations.

My first Washington opportunity led to a second one in 1982–1984 when I worked with Jim Miller, while he was Chairman of the Federal Trade Commission (FTC). I held the agency's senior management position as executive director and also led a program where the FTC intervened as an advocate for competition in the regulatory proceedings of other agency's rulemaking activities. Mugged by the realities of the FTC and Washington experience and having returned to my Clemson faculty position, I became an even more dedicated Buchanan-Tullock student. I applied lessons from public choice repeatedly in my research and writing. In all cases, there were particular articles and books that were critically important to my work.

Now, some 45 years after first being introduced to the world of James M. Buchanan and Gordon Tullock, I find their ideas to be just as powerful as when I first encountered them, if not more so. Even today, I find myself reviewing their *Calculus*, their work on rent-seeking behavior and other seminal contributions.

My reflections on the Buchanan and Tullock imprint follow the outline of the personal story I just provided. But as I write these thoughts, I find a distinctive common element in the Buchanan/Tullock contribution to economic thought. Their ideas were more than just powerful additions to the economic way of thinking. Indeed, the Buchanan/Tullock contributions were *disruptive* to the orthodox way of thinking. In fact, their ideas were so disruptive that a new subdiscipline—public choice—emerged as a vehicle for carrying their ideas forward, along with the related ideas of their students and compatriots. What may have been a settled approach for thinking about political decision making pre-*Calculus* became obsolete or at least incomplete post-*Calculus*. Where political economy focused primarily on welfare considerations and prescriptions for getting things right, pre-Buchanan/Tullock, political economy became a positive science in the wake of their contributions. These two disruptive economists literally transformed major parts of the discipline.

The next part of this chapter gives more detail on how the Buchanan-Tullock disruption influenced my graduate studies and dissertation. In this section, I highlight two particular books that were important to me then. This section is followed by a discussion of work I did during my first Washington assignment. Here, important work by Buchanan and Tullock recast the way we interpreted regulation and partly transformed regulatory studies from a normative to a positive field of inquiry. This chapter's next major section describes some of my work at Clemson University that followed my first Washington assignment. The story describes my effort to contribute to theories of regulation and explains how the ideas of Buchanan and Tullock inspired those efforts. The next section focuses on my second Washington experience and again relates some of this experience to the Buchanan-Tullock influence. To close this chapter, I offer some final thoughts on James M. Buchanan and Gordon Tullock that go beyond their academic and intellectual contributions and speak to some of their personal characteristics that in my view are well worth recognizing and emulating.

A Graduate Student's Encounter with the Virginia School

In 1967 when I entered Georgia State University's graduate program, I had no idea about schools of thought in economics or even the meaning of schools of thought. Having been a part of the business world for more than a decade, I tended to be more focused on finding solutions to problems and implementing them as opposed to searching for the meaning of problems and the development of different theories for understanding them. In a word, I was application oriented. I had a lot to learn.

Graduate work in economics in the late 1960s and early 1970s was heavily focused on neoclassical price theory and macro- and monetary economics with a heavy helping of mathematical economics and econometrics tossed in for good measure. Then, and of course, and now, doctoral students could go for days in their studies without encountering many words, paragraphs, and simple diagrammatic explanations of how markets emerged and functioned and why economists should be concerned about evolving institutions. In those days, little attention was paid generally to the interaction of economics and politics, to property rights institutions, and no attention was given to the works of Hayek, Mises, and other Austrian school economists. Far more stress was applied to building mathematical models to illustrate and explain first and second order equilibrium conditions. And along with this concern for comparative statics came an emphasis on welfare economics and maximizing social welfare in a constrained economy. Efficiency considerations were stressed in these normative studies. There was little to no discussion of a positive theory of government action, and hardly any work in public sector economics that went beyond taxation, equity considerations, benefit-cost analysis, and the budgeting process.

While struggling to come up to speed in this world, I learned about the Virginia School in the most pleasant way possible. Georgia State had three faculty members who had studied with Buchanan and Tullock at Virginia. Two of these became my professors, and the three of them became key members of my dissertation committee. These were Richard A. Bilas, James C. Miller III, and Richard S. Wallace. As time passed, I became seriously exposed to Buchanan, Tullock, free-market economics and the Virginia School. But that was not before having a most surprising encounter with Professor James Buchanan.

In 1968, we graduate students were informed that Professor James Buchanan would be visiting our campus and delivering a paper. We were also informed that Buchanan was one of the heaviest hitters we would likely ever encounter and that we should push aside all excuses and work and show up for the Buchanan lecture.

Still laboring with bordered Hessians and other abstract expressions of economic reasoning, I had the feeling that I would likely not understand a word this great economist would utter. After all, if he was so great, then surely his models would be more complex than anything I had seen before. I entered the Buchanan seminar room prepared for the worst.

But the worst did not come. Buchanan smiled, expressed a special welcome to the graduate students in the room, something we rarely heard, and then indicated that he was reformulating how he looked at some basic economic relationships; he said that he was not as certain about some theoretical explanations as he had once been. Needless to say, this was both comforting and unsettling to graduate students intent on finding truth. He then said that he would soon celebrate his 50th birthday. Noting this, he told us that Mark Twain had said that anyone under 50 was a fool, which set us back a bit, and that all those over 50 were damn fools. With that, Buchanan won the hearts of every graduate student in the room.

He then proceeded to develop a graphical analysis that involved an individual with a budget constraint in a two-good world. One of the goods in the consumption bundle was strictly private; the other good was strictly public. Buchanan's analysis showed how the individual adjusts to a new equilibrium when an extraneous and uncoordinated party produced additional units of the public good. In the process, we learned lessons about external effects, private and public goods, and multiple equilibria that might emerge when the private/public mix changes. We were, in fact, given a short introduction to Buchanan's *Demand and Supply of Public Goods* (1968). With these ideas racing through my mind, and occasionally getting tangled with bordered Hessians, I wanted to learn more about Buchanan's work. I then encountered *The Calculus of Consent* and in doing so became aware of Gordon Tullock's creative mind.

The Calculus of Consent was not on a reading list in any of my graduate courses. It was in an unknown category like Hayek's *Law, Legislation and Liberty*, a part of the underground reading and conversation that was inspired by our Virginia faculty members. Of course, *The Calculus* was not like any economics I had encountered. Indeed, I wasn't even sure it was economics. But as our bull sessions on the Virginia literature became more intense, those involved became inspired to learn more economics. In short, I found a new reason for buckling down harder in my doctoral studies. Buchanan's and Tullock's work and the recognition they were receiving for that work gave me a new perspective on just how large the world of economics could become.

While struggling to catch up with fellow graduate students who had a fresher economic education than mine, I was encouraged by my Virginia faculty, especially by Richard Bilas, to write a dissertation on property rights solutions to the externality problem. This effort placed me square into the Buchanan-Tullock camp, made *The Demand and Supply of Public Goods* a foundation source for my work, exposed me to Buchanan and Stubblebine's "Externality" (1962), and then, to top it all off, gave me the opportunity to have my key dissertation paper read by Professor Buchanan, who generously encouraged me to stay the course. The green light he offered gave me a marvelous boost of confidence. Few things can be more important to a doctoral student trying to find his way through the woods of academia than words of encouragement from a noted scholar, especially from one as busy and productive as James Buchanan. I would later learn that Professor Buchanan is noted for his quick response to requests for such reviews, particularly when the request involved a student who seemed to be working hard.

Regulation, Rent Seeking, and Public Choice One More Time

In the spring of 1976, after having established myself somewhat as a Clemson faculty member, I joined a small group of economists in a White House unit charged with reviewing and preparing formal regulatory filings on newly proposed regulations. This was a unit of the Council on Wage and Price Stability (COWPS) and was led by James C. Miller III. While one part of the council was attempting to regulate prices, a holdover activity of the Nixon Administration, the Miller unit was working to reduce the burden of regulation, which theoretically could free up the economy to produce more wealth.

Like many other academic economists who arrived in Washington before and after me, I thought I knew the answers to the government's unfortunate regulatory habits. It seemed to me that few Washington bureaucrats and executives understood simple supply and demand economics. Even worse, there seemed to be no awareness of opportunity costs, the wonders of market competition, and how the rule of law could be used to address what some called market imperfections. And surely, no one in Washington seemed to realize that government attempts to make the world a better place could fail. It didn't take me long to learn that the Washington bureaucrats and executives generally knew as much if not more economics than I knew and that I had misspecified the model for understanding Washington's ways. In short, I was mugged by the realities of public choice. I soon learned that there were some elements of political demand and supply that I had not recognized. *The Calculus* had come back to haunt me.

This mugging came in the form of conversations I had with special interest lobbyists who came calling at COWPS and with whom I spoke in the course of reviewing regulation. Much to my surprise, I learned that inevitably there were industry groups who were lobbying for more regulations, provided it was of a certain type, and these lobbyists often sang off the same page as the so-called consumer advocates who also lobbied for regulation.

Into the midst of this, I discovered a powerful Buchanan-Tullock journal article, "Polluters' 'Profit' and Political Response: Direct Control Versu Taxation" (1975). This article disrupted the old way of thinking about regulation that government rules were always forced down the throats of firms and industries that had only free-market economists on their side. The article became another foundation stone in my analytical arsenal. In crystal clear terms expressed through neoclassical price theory, the two authors explained why there was industry demand for certain kinds of pollution control regulation and how a regulatory agency could happily if not unwittingly become a cartel manager while still pursuing its regulatory mandate. The piece explained why industry was (and is) always opposed to emission taxes but at the same time can be strongly supportive of emission standards.

Along with this piece came an explosion of academic work built on the work of Gordon Tullock (1967) and Anne O. Krueger (1974) on rent seeking through government action. Put simply, the study of political behavior was becoming a field of positive analysis, explaining how the world works, in parallel with normative efforts to make politics work more effectively. And of course, this was what *The Calculus* had wrought.

When my COWPS assignment ended in 1977, I returned to Clemson and teaching and research on regulation. In 1980, a powerful collection of papers on rent seeking was published by Texas A&M Press. Edited by Gordon Tullock et al. (1980), the volume became another foundation stone in my research arsenal. The Washington experience and Buchanan/Tullock interaction laid the foundation for a small contribution that I would make to the theory of regulation.

Bootleggers, Baptists, and Rent Seeking

Once again, good fortune smiled on me. Two of my Clemson colleagues were deeply engaged in a research project that was applying financial markets analysis to regulatory questions. Michael T. Maloney and Robert E. McCormick were focusing on regulatory episodes that involved the US Environmental Protection Agency's air quality guidelines for the copper industry and the Occupational Safety and Health Administration's cotton dust standard. They, too, were drawing on Buchanan's and Tullock's work on rent seeking, and they were applying the essence of "polluters' 'profit'" in building their theoretical models. Maloney and McCormick (1982) went on to publish evidence that abnormal positive returns were generated to shareholders of firms in the copper and cotton textile industries in association with final implementation of the regulations they had studied.

As Maloney's work with McCormick was drawing to completion, Maloney and I became involved in a separate project that focused on a public choice explanation of major features of the Clean Air Act of 1970 (CAA). The CAA's distinguishing feature was found in its use of technology-based standards with more severe emission standards applied to new versus existing pollution sources. When illuminated by a rent-seeking spotlight, the legislation was clearly cartel forming. Buchanan and Tullock had explained that standards that restrict pollution also restrict output, which is just what monopolists aspire for. If restrictions can be obtained through government, it is all for the better. As Maloney and I worked together, I was inspired to write a short footnote that compared bootleggers and Baptists, who individually support Sunday closing laws that shut down retail liquor stores, to industry lobbyists and environmentalists, who separately seek stricter environmental standards on newly built industrial plants. The bootlegger/Baptist theory emerged from a dense network of economic thought that had begun with *The Calculus* and had reached a sort of crescendo with the 1980s rent-seeking literature.

With bootleggers and Baptists bouncing in my mind, I headed to Washington in 1982 for a second time. Shortly after arriving, I published my bootlegger/Baptist (1983) paper in *Regulation*. Once again, I had joined Jim Miller's staff, this time as executive director with the US Federal Trade Commission (FTC). At the time, the FTC and every other federal regulatory agency were in a state of painful retrenchment. New regulations had emerged at an almost explosive rate during the Carter Administration. There had been a veritable feeding frenzy as special interest groups lobbied successfully for a host of new regulations. Dedicated to turning things around, the newly elected Reagan Administration pushed for regulatory reform and deregulation.

I played a bit part in this effort in leading an FTC intervention program. This involved identifying regulatory proceedings at other agencies that involved rules that could have an anticompetitive effect on US markets. As advocates for competition, FTC lawyers and economists prepared legal filings for and participated in regulatory proceedings. For example, the FTC was a regular contender before the US International Trade Commission when industry protection was being considered by way of quotas or tariffs. Oddly enough, it seemed, consumer advocates never opposed such protectionist measures. Part of the answer was found in a public choice explanation of demand for regulation. Historically, organized labor and consumer groups had worked hand in glove in favor of regulation of labor markets and the workplace. The combined effort enjoyed political success on that front and then coalesced to support protectionist measures that sheltered organized labor from international competition. Buchanan and Tullock taught us a lot.

A Man's a Man for A′ That

Scottish poet Robert Burns reminds us that for all that brilliant people may accomplish in their lives, we must still realize that they in the end share a common heritage with the rest of us; they are human beings. I have made a personal effort in this chapter to explain how James M. Buchanan and Gordon Tullock disrupted orthodox thinking in economics about private and public action and about how market forces can be interpreted in the broadest possible way to explain richly dense aspects of human action. I have saluted their contributions by reflecting on how those contributions entered my life as an economist and then formed major elements of the toolkit I and others have called on over the course of 45 years. But while pointing to the brilliance of their insights and contributions, I have not paused to explain how these two men influenced the approach I attempted to take in how I worked and how I interacted with students and colleagues. I now close this chapter with those thoughts.

Those who know James Buchanan and Gordon Tullock as individuals know that they are each quite distinct people. In spite of his quick humor, Buchanan can easily be rather formal in his dealings with people and can also display a quick temper when offended or challenged. Gordon Tullock, on the other hand, enjoys catching people off balance with his quick wit and his ability to swap blows in intellectual debate. While Buchanan internalized neoclassical price theory and then used the theory to transform the field of public finance into public choice with Tullock, Tullock embodied the logic of the law along with what seemed to be an almost inherent understanding of price theory. Amazing things transpired when the two of them interacted.

But this is about their brilliance and productivity, not about their behavior as people in the academy. Here, their brilliance came through in another way. They were generous with their ideas, they were generous with their time, and they were generous with their encouragement for students and colleagues who were willing to work hard to learn and apply economic logic to the world's problems. These two scholars always seemed to find the time to read a paper and comment on it, to suggest ways to improve a piece of work, or bluntly to suggest a paper was hopeless in its current form. These two scholars loved the written word, take great pains to write clearly in plain language and eagerly offered recommendations for publishing in journals or elsewhere. They also enjoyed opportunities to host dinners, luncheons, and receptions; they welcomed those occasions when they could interact informally with students and colleagues.

Yet while Buchanan and Tullock did all this and more to encourage scholarly work and the sharing of ideas, they also set the highest standards for integrity, truth telling, and promise keeping in their professional lives. All who have been touched by these two disruptive economic scholars are privileged to know two generous human beings who believe in working hard, sharing what they learn, and standing for the highest standards of integrity.

References

Buchanan JM (1968) The demand and supply of public goods. Rand McNally, Chicago
Buchanan J, Tullock G (1962) The calculus of consent. University of Michigan Press, Ann Arbor
Buchanan JM, Tullock G (1975) Polluters' profits and political response: direct controls versus taxation. Am Econ Rev 65:139–147
Buchanan JM, Stubblebine WC (1962) Externality. Economica 29:371–384
Krueger AO (1974) The political economy of the rent-seeking society. Am Econ Rev 64:291–303
Maloney MT, McCormick RE (1982) A positive theory of environmental quality regulation. J Law Econ 25:99–124
Tullock G (1967) The welfare costs of tariffs, monopolies, and theft. West Econ J 5:224–232
Tullock G, Tollison RE, Buchanan JM (eds) (1980) Toward a theory of the rent-seeking society. Texas A&M Press, College Station
Yandle B (1983) Bootleggers and baptists: the education of a regulatory economist. Regulation May/June:12–16

Chapter 16
Public Choice and Public Life

Randy T. Simmons

In the fall of 1977, I entered the University of Oregon's graduate program in political science. My undergraduate education was in behavioral political science, and I went to graduate school planning to study public opinion polling. But then John Orbell introduced me to James Buchanan's book, *Freedom in Constitutional Contract: Perspectives of a Political Economist*, and Bill Mitchell introduced me to Gordon Tullock's book, *The Social Dilemma: The Economics of War and Revolution*. I did not read *The Calculus of Consent* until later, but these two books began the lessons I learned from the Buchanan and Tullock Virginia public choice enterprise. Buchanan and Tullock made me completely rethink the direction of my graduate education. By the time I defended my dissertation, I had been baptized and confirmed into Virginia public choice.

My political science professors had taught that loving my neighbor is good policy. Buchanan noted that the New Testament does not answer the question of who is my neighbor and explained how rational people will and often must adopt different ethical rules when moving from small to large groups. My undergraduate economics professor had taught that economics was the study of choice within constraints. In "Law and the Invisible Hand," the second chapter of *Freedom in Constitutional Contract* (1977, p. 25), Buchanan explained that studying choice should not be the purpose of economics at all:

> I have often argued that there is only one principle in economics that is worth stressing, and that the economists' didactic function is one of conveying some understanding of this principle to the public at large. Apart from this principle there would be no basis for general public support for economics as a legitimate academic discipline, no place for economics as an appropriate part of a liberal education. I refer, of course, to the principle of the spontaneous order of the market which was the great intellectual discovery of the eighteenth century.

R.T. Simmons (✉)
Jon M. Huntsman School of Business, Utah State University,
694 South 300 East, Providence, UT 84332, USA
e-mail: randy.simmons@usu.edu

D.R. Lee (ed.), *Public Choice, Past and Present: The Legacy of James M. Buchanan and Gordon Tullock*, Studies in Public Choice 28, DOI 10.1007/978-1-4614-5909-5_16,

Notice that I said, "my undergraduate economics professor." There had only been one, as I took only one undergraduate economics course—an introduction to macroeconomics course taught from a Keynesian perspective. I got a "C." As soon as I read some of Buchanan's essays, I realized I needed to understand at least the language of economics and went to the economics department head, who did me a huge favor. Rather than suggest courses, he gave me a copy of Alchian and Allen's *University Economics* and told me to read the chapters and work through the problem sets at the end of each chapter. If I did that, he said I would know more about economics than anyone in his department. I think he was joking, but teaching myself economics through Alchian and Allen allowed me to read Buchanan, which had been my goal.

I had taken an undergraduate two-course sequence on American constitutional law in which we read the text of the constitution and relevant case law. It was descriptive and only analytical in the sense of comparing different interpretations of the constitution. Buchanan began and ended his book discussing the importance of constitutional contract for human freedom. He discussed how different rules produce different outcomes. He asked why majority rule has any moral authority over any other decision rule. He asked how and why different rules emerge, all questions we had not asked in constitutional law.

The overriding issue in my undergraduate political science education was "the public interest." Buchanan and Tullock explained that we can only understand government outcomes if we concentrate on private interests operating within governmental structures. For my professors, government existed to promote the public interest. They had no theory of government failure. Some feared that elites were too powerful and called for elite excesses to be controlled by more politics. There were concerns about corruption and the perennial "waste, fraud, and abuse," but no systematic way for understanding exploitation by government officials. There was some understanding of government as a venue where competing interests reached agreement, but agreements were seen as being achieved through a kind of invisible hand of political competition. If the government was not meeting the values of a particular interest, the reason was usually that the interests were underrepresented in the polity. Solution? Expand the number of competing interests. The prevailing view among political scientists was that government is generally benevolent, often benign, and seldom dangerous. To them, politics is where conflicts of values are resolved, inequalities narrowed, inequities solved, and character developed.

Buchanan and Tullock confronted these beliefs head-on. They echoed Bastiat's claim that government is a form of organized plunder—hence Buchanan's call for constitutional contract. He said, "Individuals can secure and retain freedom in constitutional contract; they cannot do it in any other way" (1997, p. ix). By tying human freedom to constitutional contract, he explicitly rejected anarchy. They adopted a self-interest-based theory of political interaction. Buchanan explained, "Once we so much as acknowledge that the unit of consciousness is the human being (that it is Buchanan and not "society" that writes this sentence), explanation of interaction among separate persons by a model of self-interested motivation necessarily becomes acceptable to a degree" (1977, p. 5). Tullock simply rejected public interest claims and said that all actors, private or public, act out of self-interest. He said that coups, revolution, war, and providing public goods are best understood by identifying private benefits to organizers and joiners.

One part of Buchanan's analysis that appealed to me was his explanation of his project in that book (and more generally in all his work). He had two purposes. First, he wanted "to cause economists" to think about the political nature of economic order—to think about the laws and institutions within which economies function. He wanted to impose what he called "conceptual order on the institutional complexities." He noted that it is easy to derive a logic of order in people's everyday economic lives but that it is immensely more difficult to derive a logic of politics. Second, he wanted to "widen understanding of the fundamental principles of economic order among social scientists and social philosophers generally" (1977, p. 6). Notice that he did not say he wanted to widen understanding about economics. Rather, he said he wanted to cause economists and noneconomists to recognize "fundamental principles of economic order." He and Tullock had laid out some of those principles in *The Calculus of Consent,* but they had certainly not been adopted or even understood by any of the political scientists that I had encountered.

Although he proposed a revolutionary way to understand the reasons for rules, the effects of rules, and ways in which they emerge, Buchanan claimed that he was not revolutionary. "I am modest in my claims," he said. He went on, "If my general explanatory arguments are persuasive, some progress toward extended discussion of constitutional reform should be guaranteed" (1977, p. 8). His modesty seems somewhat false since he also claimed that the economic profession's emphasis on choice was wrongheaded—that economists were practicing a discipline that "did not merit general public support."

Although Buchanan at least pretends to be modest, Tullock is neither modest nor pretends to be. In print as well as in person, he delights in making astonishing statements. He starts the chapter titled "The Paradox of Revolution" with this statement: "It is the purpose of this chapter to demonstrate that the image of revolution that we find in the literature is a false one. I shall also, I hope, demonstrate why this false image is so appealing to intellectuals and historians" (1974, p. 36). He ends the chapter by saying, "Revolution is the subject of an elaborate and voluminous literature and, if I am right, almost all of this literature is wrong" (1974, p. 46). He says that by examining the utility calculus of the participants, we can understand that any public goods produced by the revolution will be byproducts of the pursuit of self-interest.

Tullock taught lessons that I have used in class for years. In discussing the roots of conflict, he lays out one of the most fundamental that government is an inefficient transfer engine. A political decision that costs you \$10 might make me better off by just \$5, or it may make us both worse off, even if one of us wins the competition. I demonstrate this principle in the classroom by selling a dollar bill. Bidding starts at a nickel and goes up in 5-cent increments. The winner gets to purchase the dollar bill, but I get to keep the money from the top two bidders. I have always sold the dollar bill for more than \$1. Bidding always devolves into two students bidding until they reach the dollar, but then keep bidding in hopes of minimizing their loss from losing and still having to pay their most recent bid. The game provides great opportunities for discussing Tullock's point elsewhere that rent seeking often results in the losses of the losers outweighing the gains of the winners, and worse, the gains of the winners are less than the value of the policy they achieve. I have had bidders offer a bribe to the other to stop the bidding, but only after bidding exceeds $1. As Tullock said about the $10 loss and $5 benefit, the outcome could be improved if a bribe of $7.50 were offered, but institutional structures usually make such bribes impossible.

Tullock described such situations as the $10 loss, $5 benefit, and the sell-a-dollar game as "social dilemmas," situations in which conflict is socially inefficient but it is rational for players to enter the game. He explains, "The social dilemma, then, is that we would always be better off collectively if we could avoid playing this negative-sum game, but that individuals may make gains by forcing the game upon the rest of us" (1974, p. 4).

In *The Social Dilemma*, Tullock identified a core problem of politics: very often, person A wants something person B owns. If A and B are in a market, then voluntary transactions can lead to peaceful outcomes. But when A wants what B has and uses politics to get it, each must spend resources that never get recaptured. Coercion becomes the means of accomplishing A's ends, and B must invest in lobbyists or politicians to fend off A's efforts. They are in a form of the sell-a-dollar game in which the total spent (invested) will often be greater than B's property was originally worth.

Tullock reaches out well beyond the confines of mainstream economics to apply the rational choice model to issues of autocracy and war and peace. By downgrading the relevance of romantic, utopian thinking and introducing a much-needed dash of realism, Tullock provides a wake-up call for all individuals who cherish and seek to defend individual liberty.

Besides providing the paradigm that has guided my academic life, Virginia public choice provided some preparation for the 10 years I spent in city government, 6 years as a member of the city council and 4 years as mayor. It gave me models for understanding local politics, as well as cognitive dissonance from being both a public choice theorist and an elected official. Local politics really can be politics without romance and not just because much of what local government does is the unromantic chore of building and maintaining sewers and collecting garbage.

Although I knew about the importance of rules and the dangers of rent seeking, I assumed problems would be relatively minor in the politics of Providence, Utah, a city of just 6,000 people. I assumed that government close to "the people" might be somewhat exempt from some of the politics-without-romance analysis I had learned from the Virginians. I was wrong. Those who assume that local politics is superior to state or national politics should spend more time in local politics before making such a claim. What I learned from my time in city government is that government is government whether large or small and that even local democratic politics is not really government by the people. Instead, it is a (sometimes intense) competition for power among contending interests. Everyone playing the local politics game engages in playacting and mythmaking ritual, suppressing and distorting information, stimulating envy, and promoting excessive hopes. The stakes might not be as high in dollar terms as in national politics, but the effects on citizens' lives are more immediate and personal. Voters are as rationally ignorant and governed by nonsensical ideologies in local as in national elections. Bureaucrats maximize budgets and authority. Most, if not all, of the basic lessons from Virginia public choice apply equally to local as to state and national politics. Politicians, voters, interests, and bureaucrats are all able to act and choose without paying the costs of their actions—that is, they are exonerated from responsibility.

In a training session for members of city councils and planning commissions, an official of the Utah League of Cities and Towns sounded a bit like Tullock when he said, "The Bill of Rights was written to protect citizens from people like you." Although The Bill of Rights was written to protect citizens from the national government, the League of Cities and Towns official captured a useful truth about city government, which is that mayors and city council members are the same kinds of people Tullock wrote about in *The Social Dilemma*. They are often tyrannical and self-serving. They ignore the effects their decisions have on citizens. Sometimes they are just mean. Citizens are no better. They hold naïve views about democratic processes, organize their neighbors to steal property rights from other neighbors, are self-serving, and are mean-spirited. The amazing thing about all this is that elected and appointed officials and the citizens they represent often are well-meaning, conscientious people who are pleased to be in "public service."

I observed behaviors in local politics that were just like those in the Virginia public choice models. One difference between local and national politics is that at the local level, the politics are far more personal. At the local level, you see those your actions might hurt. On the one hand, that means that you see those who might be harmed from your actions and might feel worse than harming faceless others. On the other hand, you see those who might be harmed, and you may *want* to harm them. Personal animosities show up in city council meetings on a regular basis. I have joked that being a small town mayor is somewhat like being a parish priest. In each case, you find out things about your neighbors you wish you did not know. In the priest's case, he encounters people who feel badly about things they have done and are trying to improve. In the mayor's case, he or she encounters people who are trying to use government to take advantage of their neighbors. These people never explain that they are trying to take advantage of others, and most do not believe it of themselves. But, a non-romantic view of local politics demonstrates that they are, in fact, engaged in the politics of theft.

Although the primary business of cities is providing infrastructure—water, sewer, roads—and public health and safety, the primary activity of city councils is making land use decisions. City councils spend most of their time debating what can be built where, how close buildings may be to the street and to property lines on side- and backyards, minimum lot sizes, minimum and maximum building sizes, maximum building heights, whether street trees are required and of what species and size, allowable plantings between curbs and sidewalks, whether curbs and sidewalks are required, whether basketball standards are allowed in the driveway, how many pets a family may have, what animals are considered pets, how many unrelated people living together are considered a family, and on and on. One way to understand these activities of local government is to use Tullock's example of A wanting something owned by B. Lot sizes, planting, building heights, etc. all affect what choices B can make with his property. They are ways of granting A some of B's property rights.

I thought of Tullock when a retiree called me to talk about the home being built next to his. He lived on the hillside on one side of our valley and had an exceptional view of the mountains 20 miles away. He took me out on his deck, showed me the view, and then pointed to the house being built just below his. He explained that the roof on that house was going to block part of his view and that a realtor told him the lost view was worth $80,000. He asked me to stop the builder from building the house so high. I asked if he had made the request to the builder, and he said he did not want to cause problems. The family building the home seemed like nice people, and he did not want to upset them. But, it was apparently fine for me as mayor to upset them. To me, it seemed like the perfect Tullock example of A bribing B, so they each get something they want. I suggested he offer to purchase a view easement that would make it worth their while to reduce the height of their home. I tried a Buchananesque discussion about the importance of rules and process and that the home being built met the city code for height restrictions, that the zoning ordinance did not contain view restrictions, and that his deed did not contain a view easement on his neighbor's property. Rather than negotiate and use market processes, he really wanted me to somehow use my "powers" as mayor and stop them.

At my very first city council meeting as mayor, the council chambers were packed with citizens opposing proposed rezones that would allow a 20-acre field and a ten-acre nonproductive fruit orchard to be subdivided. The 20-acre parcel produced alfalfa and the owners grazed horses on it part of the year. The ten-acre parcel had not been farmed for more than 50 years. The city council chambers were packed with people opposing the proposed rezones. The proposed developments, they argued, would negatively affect the quality of their lives. A neighbor to the 20-acre piece objected to a series of backyards filled with noisy kids fronting his property line rather than the peaceful, green, horse pasture he enjoyed so much. A woman across the street said there would be so many homes and children she would be able to hear mothers yelling at their children "like fishwives." Each of these said they preferred that the property remain in agriculture, but if it had to be developed, it should be at a density of no more than one home per acre, which would reduce the number of available lots from 56 to 16 and the value of the property by about three-quarters.

Both of the proposed developments were consistent with city zoning ordinances and the general plan. The general plan had been in place for about 20 years, and the zoning ordinances followed the general outlines of the plan. A city's general plan might be viewed as a property rights constitution in which the owners contract with the city government to protect or obtain certain development rights to their property. That understanding of property rights is clearly not a Lockean understanding, but is a practical understanding of how government and property rights interact in practice. A general plan and subsequent zoning ordinances are often thought of by property owners as a statement of the owners' rights. They allow owners to anticipate the future and make investment decisions accordingly.

The opponents to the developments had a much more fluid understanding of the nature of property rights. They assumed that they could simply force their view on the owners because they showed up in force to city council meetings. They were not swayed by the city attorney's explanations about what was legal. In *Freedom in Constitutional Contract* (1997, p. 85), Buchanan suggested that such actions are nothing more than people saying that they want something and if the state has the power to make it happen, it ought to happen. Such an approach is certainly not a constitutional one and has great potential to violate individual freedom.

A neighbor to the ten-acre property understood that she was engaging in unethical politics. She said, "Opposing this development may not be very Christian, but when it comes to my money, I have to speak up." She was afraid that the new houses would obstruct her view of the mountains and would take away the privacy she had enjoyed in her backyard.

Others tried to wrap their arguments against development in public interest claims. One citizen, a Ph.D. economist, claimed that the new development would create negative externalities in the form of more traffic and lost open space. She complained about the potential for increased traffic in front of her home on "her" street. I asked if her deed included the city street in front of her home or a clause establishing a maximum number of cars passing per day. I also suggested that Ronald Coase would suggest that externalities were two-way, that if she stopped the development, she was creating an externality for the property owners and potential home owners in the developments. She did not understand. It was clear she was the kind of economist that Buchanan wanted to educate.

I suggested that this could be a perfect example of Coasean bargaining and suggested that the opponents purchase the development rights from the owners. Property rights were clear, and there were not enough people involved to make transaction costs very high. They got angry at the suggestion and accused me of being in the developers' pockets. My attempts to explain that property rights were clear and that the way to accomplish their ends was through the market were, to them, simply more evidence that I favored development over preservation. My further attempts to describe how constitutional contracts worked got nowhere, and telling them they were simply rent-seeking thieves (I used more polite words) further upset them.

Soon after the public hearings on these two developments, the planning and zoning commission members asked me to come to one of their meetings to explain my "vision" for how the city should develop. My inner public choice analyst, who by this time had followed Buchanan's footnotes to Hayek, immediately started raising questions. Why should politicians have visions? Who had sufficient information about people's wants in the present and in the future to know the best uses of parcels of land? Would there be substantial changes in preferences about home and lot sizes as there were shocks to the economy? I went to the planning commission and explained that my vision for the future of my city was for people to be able to plan their own lives. I hoped that neighborhood order would emerge rather than be planned. I certainly did not want a city in which governmental power could be used to force one group's values on other groups. The members of the planning and zoning commission were not amused, as they had sought appointment to the planning and zoning commission precisely because they had their own visions they wanted to impose on the citizens. They tend to say "city" rather than "citizens," perhaps because "the city" is an impersonal target for their ambitions. I cautioned the commissioners that their preferences in many areas were unimportant given the constraints placed on them by state law. State law, at least in Utah, constrains planning commissions to a relatively narrow set of actions they may take. My impression was that our city's planning commissioners were not interested in constraints on them, just in the constraints they could impose on others.

Tullock has often said in informal conversation that he never votes because it is simply irrational. He notes that one's vote is inconsequential in a national election. I have never asked him if that model of voting would predict that an election in a city of just 6,000 people (1,800 registered voters) might be at least somewhat more rational. The chances of being the deciding vote among 1,800 voters are substantially better than the chances of being the deciding vote among millions. In local elections across the United States, and in my city, voting turnout averages only about 20 %, far below the average for national elections. It may be that voting at all levels of government is not based on rational calculation, but is an emotional activity, and in most city elections, there is little to get emotional over. Local elections tend to be about nonemotional subjects—sewers, roads, garbage, and water systems. Citizens care if the services are provided, but believe ideological differences do not have much to do with how they are provided. As one mayor told me, "There is not a Republican or Democratic way to fill a pothole." Local elections tend to be relatively boring compared to races for national offices, and so they do not stir the emotions necessary to get voters to the polls.

If that is the case, however, what about all the emotion stirred over zoning issues? The 30 people filling the city council chambers over rezoning the two ten- and twenty-acre parcels were certainly emotional and motivated. But, they were only 30 out of 1,800 potential voters. They were loud and angry, but were a tiny minority. I assume that all 30 voted in the next election since some of them ran for seats on the city council. They all lost. Their heat, excitement, and anger were limited to just them, not to voters in general.

We know that voting is a very limited way to express one's values and preferences. But, showing up to city council or planning commission meetings in an organized group can be very effective. Some states, such as Utah, have passed laws requiring councils and commissions to ignore public "clamor" when making land use decisions. That is, a subdivision request that meets the requirements of city ordinances may not be denied simply because a group of citizens shows up to oppose it. But having to vote in front of 30 angry neighbors is difficult, and city council members often try to get around legal mandates by stalling—they can table the proposal for consideration at a future meeting, seek legal clarification, or send the proposal back to city staff for more study. They can also reject the proposal and essentially dare the developer to take them to court.

Throughout *Freedom in Constitutional Contract* Buchanan emphasized that legal rules are necessary to constrain political decisions. I found myself having to remind city council members that they were, in fact, constrained by legal rules. One of the most powerful rules for constraining local elected officials in Utah is that the state legislature removed governmental immunity from a city council or planning commission member who knowingly violated the law when voting—rejecting a legal subdivision, for example. After one vote in which a three/two vote would have rejected a development agreement reached years earlier, I asked the city attorney to explain that the three members could, and in all likelihood would, given the developer's reputation, be sued individually for his losses. After that explanation, one of the three agreed to change his vote so that the developer could move forward. Because they were on the losing side, the other two were able to continue to symbolically oppose the plan even though they could not legally oppose it.

While I was in city politics, I also became one of fifteen members of the board of directors of the Utah League of Cities and Towns. The need for clear constitutional restraints on politicians' choices was reinforced as I watched well-meaning politicians behave badly. I was the lone vote against requesting that the legislature grant cities the authority to tax cell phone owners for simply having a cell phone. When I pointed out that cell phones cause no additional costs to cities and asked by what theory of regulation they should be taxed, the response was, "They represent a huge pile of untaxed cash." I regularly was one of two or three voting against new proposals to increase cities' taxing authority.

Local government, it turns out, is not the site of principle triumphing over interest. It is populated with the people in the Virginia public choice models. There is often language about principle, but there is much more "there oughta be a law" reaction to perceived problems. "There oughta be a law" easily leads to "doing the right thing," which opens wide the city council chamber doors for self-interest, sometimes wrapped in principled language, and other times not. Local, part-time politicians are usually motivated, at least in part, by a sense of civic duty, but that sense is seldom constrained by an ideological yardstick for measuring policy proposals. Without that yardstick, proposals based in moral language and promoted by respected people make it appear that "doing the right thing" is, in fact, doing the right thing. The ineffectiveness of ideological constraints on local government power leads me to conclude that politicians at all levels need to be constrained by something approaching Buchanan's constitutional contract. Without enforced constraints, politicians will pursue all sorts of actions that reduce freedom.

In *The Calculus of Consent*, Buchanan and Tullock suggested examining the bases for collective action by asking, "When will a society composed of free and rational utility-maximizing individuals choose to undertake action collectively rather than privately?" They narrowed the question by asking, "When will an individual member of the group find it advantageous to enter into a "political" relationship with his fellows?" As Buchanan had explained previously in his article, "An Economic Theory of Clubs" (1965), collective action can stop short of political relationships. People can and do organize themselves into networks of self-government to provide private goods and club goods, if not local public goods.

In his essay, "Ethical Rules, Expected Values and Large Numbers" (Chap. 11 of *Freedom in Constitutional Contract*), Buchanan argued that a critical determinant of whether people will cooperate voluntarily is group size—that people will adopt different ethical rules in different-sized groups. He wrote:

> Volunteer fire departments arise in villages, not metropolitan centers. Crime rates increase consistently with city size. Africans behave differently in tribal culture than in industrialized urban settings. There is honor among thieves. The Mafia has its own standards. Time-tested honor systems in universities and colleges collapse when enrollments exceed critical size limits. Litter is more likely to be found on heavily traveled routes than on residential streets (1977, p. 162).

He might have added that citizens of Providence, Utah, act different in neighborhoods than in the larger political arena. I observed many examples of people stopping short of political relationships and organizing less formally to accomplish collective ends. In many cases, the same people who came to city council meetings to control others' actions cooperated with their immediate neighbors to provide goods voluntarily, to invest their time and money to make their neighborhood better.

To understand small group collective action, it may be useful to remember Tullock's analysis of coups and revolutions in *The Social Dilemma*. He suggests looking to the private rewards of collective action and to the need for organization. He expects that both private incentives and organization are necessary for collective action. We might expect the same for local collective action.

My first adult experience with organizing voluntary responses to collective action problems was when my wife and I joined a group of local parents who were interested in creating a superior youth baseball program. The city council allowed us to take over the city youth baseball system. We formed a nonprofit corporation, purchased insurance, joined the Western Boys Baseball Association, and advertised tryouts. We experienced all the problems of youth sports—overly excited parents, getting volunteers to show up to work in the snack stand, coaches giving preferential treatment to their own sons, hurt feelings, etc. We also saw the benefits to our own sons of having a competitive, superior baseball program. As evidence that we paid organizational costs in order for our sons to benefit, consider that all of us who created the organization left it when our sons moved on to higher levels of baseball or other activities.

As his sons grew older, one father wanted a regulation-size baseball field for his sons' teams to play on. He sought permission from the city council to convert another relatively unused softball field, raised $100,000 in private donations, and organized donated labor to create what has been easily the best baseball field in the region for the past 15 years. The only fields that now compete with it are ones in nearby cities funded by public money. Other parents of younger children saw the success of that field and got permission to completely rebuild the youth field. They raised $20,000 in private donations and organized donated labor to create a similar youth field. These two fields are owned and maintained by the city but were created by private initiative and ambition.

Our daughter lives in Providence with her husband and two young boys. When she was diagnosed with thyroid cancer, we saw neighbors organize themselves to assist her and her family. They donated a small chest freezer full of food packed with frozen meals to last through her recovery. Moms offered to tend the children. This example of neighborhood spontaneity happened because someone organized it, made assignments, collected donations, and shepherded the effort. It was spontaneous only in the sense that no one asked government to help.

One obvious feature of the American arid West is irrigation canals. Almost all of the canals were created by private canal companies, and pioneers dug the earliest ones using hand tools and horse-drawn scrapers. The canal companies sold shares of water to their members, and the companies continue to operate the canals today, and shareholders can sell portions or all of their shares. As cropland has been converted to residential subdivisions, people have purchased water shares for watering lawns and gardens. One problem is that the canals run through the subdivisions. Under state law, a canal company is not liable for damages from a leak in the canal or if someone drowns in the canal. In a Providence subdivision, seven families had an open canal run through their backyards. The families decided they wanted to have the canal put in a covered pipe and approached the canal company to see what could be worked out. The canal company agreed to pay a portion of the cost of pipe to replace the canal and the families paid the major share of the cost. The families prorated the cost among themselves based on the number of feet of pipe needed to cross their property and paid from $2,000 to $4,000 each. One family chose not to participate, but the other six families wanted the pipe strongly enough to pay the free-rider share. This collective action game had a small number of players, so the organizational costs were low, and the private benefits to each family were high—high enough to cover the costs of the underground pipe.

Another club good provided by a local organization was a veteran's war memorial. Several World War II veterans asked the city council's permission to build a war memorial in a prominent corner of a city park. They wanted to commission a bronze statue and list the names of any Providence citizens who had served in US wars. There were fewer than ten men in the group, so organizational costs were low, and since one of them donated most of the $50,000 raised for the monument, raising funds was relatively easy. They requested some city support in the form of labor by city employees in preparing the site, but they raised money for the monument and for an endowment they gave the city to provide for some of the ongoing maintenance costs.

Another group was formed to create a monument celebrating the pioneers who founded the city in 1859. This group originally planned to put the monument on private property, but donate the property and monument to the city. They noticed, however, that the World War II veterans were unhappy with city maintenance of the veterans' memorial and changed their minds. They created a nonprofit corporation to own and maintain the monument because they wanted to have ongoing control of the site.

A terminally ill friend from the university moved into Providence, while I was the mayor. He was part of a network of professor friends and did not plan to integrate himself into his new neighborhood. When I visited him that winter, I noticed that his driveway and sidewalks were clear of snow. Knowing that he was unable to do any physical work, I asked who was clearing the snow. He did not know. He could have hired someone, but every time it snowed, someone appeared and cleared the snow away without him knowing it was happening. I asked some people in the neighborhood, and they said the people on his street had organized a snow-clearing group. Some had visited to get to know him and found him to be well taken care of by friends and professional help and that he really was not interested in expanding his circle of friends. The neighbors chose to not intrude in his life but to organize themselves to keep his driveway and sidewalk free of snow, quietly and anonymously. They were another small, neighborhood group for whom organizational costs were low, and the project only lasted for a few months.

A great deal of low-cost spontaneous activity can emerge in cities if city officials will just get out of the way. Cities can integrate citizens into city projects such as building ball fields or parks. When my friends asked if they could create high-quality baseball fields, the city council agreed to let them do it. By contrast, my public works director refused when a neighborhood group asked if they could help lay sod for a new park. He said he would not have the control over volunteers that he would have over employees. I had to explain that we were not just building a neighborhood park; we were building a neighborhood affiliation with the park. If neighbors worked to create the park, they would feel ownership, which would encourage them to keep their eyes on the park to control vandalism and report problems such as malfunctioning sprinklers. He had assumed it was the city's job to provide and manage parks and had not thought of how involving the neighborhood could make his job easier. When I proposed allowing people to shut off traffic on their street while they hold a neighborhood party or allowing people to create basketball courts by placing moveable basketball standards on opposite sides of cul-de-sacs, the public works director objected by citing safety and risk management concerns.

My public works director's concerns are real ones from a risk management perspective. We can no longer staff the snack stand at the baseball fields with volunteers because of government-imposed public health concerns. In fact, meeting legal requirements has caused the city to take over the baseball program that we had created. Allowing kids to play in a cul-de-sac makes the city liable for injuries. Using volunteer labor puts the city at risk for lawsuits if someone gets hurt. The legal system makes it more difficult for cities to get out of the way of people making their neighborhoods their own.

There are surely people who choose to not join in the activities in their neighborhoods, or in sports leagues, or contributing time and money to building monuments. You do not have to donate to a project to pipe an irrigation canal or work in the baseball snack stand if you do not want to; if you do not believe it contributes to your happiness. The virtue I value most about all these associations is that they are voluntary. By contrast, you must pay taxes to support local government activities.

Voluntary associations are just that—voluntary. Government associations are coerced.

Even in local politics, it is easy to recognize the problems of government predicted by Virginia public choice. Government is government, regardless of how close it is to "the people." People use all levels of government for their own ends. Local voters are rationally ignorant, irresponsible, and refrain from political participation. Local politicians go about doing "good" with other people's money by dispensing favors and restricting choices. Elections are about whom can best mobilize emotions. Local good intentions are not disciplined by responsibility in the market sense so often costs exceed benefits.

My experience in local government has increased my appreciation of federalism as a way to discourage government powers being used for personal benefit. I cannot conclude that American federalism works well, given my experience in local government. But it works better than allowing autonomy at the local level. Of course, state and federal rules interfere in negative ways, such as is the case with risk management rules. They also interfere in positive ways. Without state rules restricting land use actions by local government, property rights would be greatly reduced, for example. Requiring open meetings and posted agendas restrict "good old boy" networks from ruling small towns. Those rules also increase the costs of making local government decisions. If you believe, as I do, that governments are more likely to choose bad rules than to choose good rules, increasing decision-making costs may be a good thing.

One of the most valuable lessons I take from my time in local government is that there is a lot of voluntary collective action taking place below the surface of local politics. Applying a Buchanan and Tullock analysis to this form of collective action provides some coherence to what otherwise appears to be happy spontaneity. By examining incentives, decision and organization costs, and time and money costs, an underlying logic appears. People organize locally when there are psychic, monetary, or other payoffs to the organizers. Small groups are organized more easily than large groups. Organizing for short-term projects is easier than for long-term projects. Ethical rules are easier to follow and to enforce in small groups.

Cities and towns like mine do survive and thrive, despite the public choice problems of local politics. One reason for surviving and thriving is surely the organic, spontaneous, informal collective action organized among citizens. Local order may be much less about voting and governing and more about the ongoing actions of people volunteering to help each other through churches, clubs, neighborhoods, sports leagues, or sometimes just by themselves; sharing garden produce; bringing in meals for people they do not even know just because they want to help; and crying for and helping the family with the fatally ill child. I saw all these things during my time in local government, and they made me realize that politics is a feeble substitute for voluntary collective action, which I believe is the core of self-government and liberty. Viewing these actions through a Buchanan and Tullock lens helped me understand the conditions for allowing and encouraging them to emerge and the difficulties of them being sustained through time.

References

Buchanan JM (1965) An economic theory of clubs. Economica (New series) 32(125):1–14

Buchanan JM (1977) Freedom in constitutional contract: perspectives of a political economist. Texas A & M University Press, College Station

Tullock G (1974) The social dilemma: the economics of war and revolution. University Publications, Blacksburg

Index

D.R. Lee (ed.), *Public Choice, Past and Present: The Legacy of James M. Buchanan and Gordon Tullock*, Studies in Public Choice 28, DOI 10.1007/978-1-4614-5909-5,

MIX
Papier aus verantwortungsvollen Quellen
Paper from responsible sources
FSC® C105338

If you have any concerns about our products,
you can contact us on
ProductSafety@springernature.com

In case Publisher is established outside the EU,
the EU authorized representative is:
Springer Nature Customer Service Center GmbH
Europaplatz 3, 69115 Heidelberg, Germany

Printed by Libri Plureos GmbH
in Hamburg, Germany